By the
Work of Their Hands

Studies in
Afro-American Folklife

By the Work of Their Hands

Studies in Afro-American Folklife

by
John Michael Vlach

with a Foreword by
Lawrence W. Levine

University Press of Virginia

Charlottesville and London

The University Press of Virginia
Copyright © 1991 by the Rector and Visitors of the University of Virginia

First Published in 1991 by UMI Research Press, a Bell & Howell Company
First University Press of Virginia printing 1991

Library of Congress Cataloging-in-Publication Data

Vlach, John Michael, 1948–
    By the work of their hands : studies in Afro-American Folklife /
by John Michael Vlach ; with a foreword by Lawrence Levine.
        p.   cm.
    Includes bibliographical references and index.
    ISBN 0-8139-1366-7 (paper)
        1. Afro-American decorative arts.   2. Afro-Americans—Material
culture.   I. Title.
    NK839.3.A35V54   1991a
    745'.089'96073—dc20   91-26003
                                                            CIP

Printed in the United States of America

For my father

Contents

Foreword

Everybody wants to tell us what a Negro is. . . . But if you would tell me who I am, at least take the trouble to discover what I have been.

Ralph Ellison, *Shadow and Act*

Robert Louis Stevenson once described how he and his schoolmates would walk around at dusk in their long coats, each boy appearing to all the world as "a mere pillar of darkness," when in fact each had a hidden lantern shining at his belt. To the older Stevenson this scene of boyhood bliss and deception became a paradigm for the human condition. A good part of reality, Stevenson mused, "runs underground. The observer (poor soul, with his documents!) is all abroad. For to look at the man is but to court deception. . . . To one who has not the secret of the lanterns, the scene upon the links is meaningless. And hence the haunting and truly spectral unreality of realistic books."[1]

For black Americans, African cultural heritage has played the role that the "secret of the lanterns" did in Stevenson's allegory. American scholarship from the Civil War to the mid-twentieth century was dominated by those who had lost the "secret" of African culture and who perceived black Americans as "mere pillars" of cultural darkness—of imperfect acculturation to Euro-American culture—rather than as complex amalgams of African and European cultures. It is hardly surprising, then, that American scholarship for more than a hundred years was characterized by a "haunting and truly spectral unreality" which depicted African-Americans as the one group that had lost its entire indigenous culture and, alone among all of the peoples that constituted the United States, was, in the words of the sociologist E. Franklin Frazier, "not distinguished by culture from the dominant group."[2] "The Negro, when he landed in the United States," Robert Park observed, "left behind him almost everything but his dark complexion and his tropical temperament."[3] "American Negro culture," the Swedish scholar Gunnar Myrdal insisted in his influential work, *An American Dilemma*, "is not something independent of general American culture. It is a distorted development, or a pathological condition, of the general American culture."[4] "The Negro," Nathan Glazer and Daniel Patrick Moynihan agreed, "is only an American and nothing else. He has no culture and values to guard and protect."[5]

Such scholars—and they were characteristic of their respective disciplines—would have done well to listen more seriously to the former slave who told an interviewer from Fisk University, "If you want Negro history, you will have to get [it] from somebody who wore the shoe, and by and by from one to the other you will get a book."[6] John Vlach is one of those scholars who, in the past two decades, have indeed listened to those "who wore the shoe," both during and after the period of slavery, and through such attention have been able to challenge what Vlach calls "the imagined cultural amnesia" of Africans once they arrived in America. In essay after essay, Vlach demonstrates just how much was remembered and just how rich and vibrant was the African tradition that helped to mold African-American culture not only in the performing arts, which have received the most intense scholarly attention, but in the less well-known universe of material culture as well.

In his preface Vlach speaks of "the complexity one finds in black artifacts," which in turn "stems from their inherently complex cultural history." Such complexity of form and origins requires scholarship with the requisite patience and tolerance for complexity: a scholarship not prone to jump to simple or familiar conclusions, not content to remain on the surface or make unreflective connections; a scholarship not unmindful of syncretic developments with other cultures; a scholarship not rooted too deeply in only one disciplinary mode. Vlach has provided precisely that type of patience, tolerance, and reflection and exactly the necessary intercultural approach and interdisciplinary proficiency. He takes us on a journey from the colonial period to the twentieth century, from Texas to Virginia, with more than a few stops in Africa and the Caribbean. He teaches us to appreciate a broad range of material culture from folk art to quilts to baskets to ironwork to gravestones to houses. He introduces us not only to the things people create but to the people who create them and thus helps to familiarize us with what he terms "an unheralded populace that has lived on for years beneath the view of history." He shares with us his ingenuity, his eclectic knowledge, his genuine appreciation for and understanding of the culture and the people who create that culture. He communicates his excitement, his engagement, his wonder. He teaches us by first teaching himself and allowing us to be privy to the process. His approach helps us to perceive not merely the past *or* the present but the past *and* the present—tradition *and* contemporary usage. Vlach demonstrates that if people do not separate the products of their culture and their hands into rigidly distinct categories, then neither should scholars whose approach always must try to reflect "the reality of life as lived and experienced by the people being studied." By concentrating on this reality, Vlach helps to create the beginnings of what he calls an "alternative history" based upon the things people made for themselves.

"Once one encounters the sorts of objects discussed here," Vlach assures us, "the existence of Afro-American material traditions can no longer be denied. Further, once eyes are opened, understanding and appreciation may follow." I can think of no better reason to read this pioneering volume.

LAWRENCE W. LEVINE

Notes

1. Robert Louis Stevenson, *Across the Plains* (London: Chatto and Windus, 1892), 206–28.

2. E. Franklin Frazier, *The Negro in the United States* (revised ed., New York: Macmillan Co., 1957), 680–81.

3. Robert E. Park, "The Conflict and Fusion of Cultures with Special Reference to the Negro," *Journal of Negro History* 4 (1919): 116–18.

4. Gunnar Myrdal, *An American Dilemma* (New York: Harper, 1962), 928–29.

5. Nathan Glazer and Daniel Moynihan, *Beyond the Melting Pot* (Cambridge, Mass.: M.I.T. Press, 1963), 53.

6. Fisk University, *Unwritten History of Slavery: Autobiographical Accounts of Negro Ex-Slaves,* Ophelia Settle Egypt, J. Masuoka, and Charles S. Johnson, eds. (Nashville: 1945, unpublished typescript), 45–46.

Preface

Two decades ago Robert Farris Thompson, pioneering historian of Afro-American art, pondered the reasons why so little had ever been written about African-influenced art in the United States, and he came to the conclusion that "few are likely to study a field believed not to exist." In the intervening two decades, however, remarkable strides have been made not only in the field of Afro-American art but in the broader subject of Afro-American material culture as well. These developments are owed, in part, to the incessant calls to action by scholars like Thompson. Also important was the growing recognition during the late 1960s by historians that the prevalent portrait of black American culture as a "pathological imitation" of the dominant white culture was seriously in error. Because of vigorous attempts to rethink the black experience, a new view emerged, one in which blacks, first as slaves and later as free people, were seen as the creators of a distinctive New World culture. This was a position consistent with the black nationalist movement of the 1960s and one that the great black scholar W. E. B. Du Bois had taken as far back as 1903 in his book *The Souls of Black Folk*. If Blacks could be credited with a culture of their own, it was certainly feasible that they were capable of distinctive material expressions. At last one could assume with confidence that Afro-American artifacts, objects of folk art and craft, did exist. What remained was their discovery and description.

Yet these tasks have proved quite challenging. First of all, in the late twentieth century all Americans have become, for the most part, consumers of rather than makers of their material culture. It is not so easy to locate traditional artisans of any sort these days. While active bearers of traditional culture still exist, painstaking detective work is required to find them and then, of course, they are participants in their own time and circumstances. Their experiences are not necessarily indicative of the earlier periods and conditions about which we have so many important questions. A contemporary Afro-American blacksmith is more of an exemplar of the twentieth century than a representative of the antebellum period even if there may be some continuities with the past in his working techniques or in his repertoire of artifacts.

The creolized or mixed historical background of Afro-American culture complicates even the most rudimentary description of black artifacts. While it is generally assumed that black American culture exhibits a blending of European and African ideas, these two sources were never at equal strength, and consequently the specific combination of cultural influences is often difficult to estimate. It is hard to tell, so long after the fact, exactly how many Afro-American cultural expressions may have developed. Most scholars of material culture recognize that any object has three basic components: form, construction, and use. Usually it is the case that these three features will conform to an overarching cultural code, but with Afro-American objects one can expect these elements to reflect divergent identities. The form of an artifact might be African, its construction Anglo-American, and its use pattern highly personalized. One can imagine other potential combinations such that object or artwork looks Euro-American while it is made according to a Black style. Black quilts provide a good example of this sort of confusion; frequently they look like Anglo-American "crazy" quilts when they are deliberately designed in improvisational off-balance, asymmetrical patterns.

The complexity one finds in black artifacts stems from their inherently complex cultural history, one marked by a continually varying encounter between two different cultural groups both of whom were experiencing constantly shifting social and economic pressures. Even if one is fortunate enough to discover a bona fide example of traditional Afro-American material culture, its evaluation must remain tentative until the full background of the tradition is studied. Such a comprehensive under-standing of Afro-American culture will be achieved only after it is recognized that while the culture of black Americans is rooted in the New World, its antecedents are certainly transoceanic. Black cultural history, at least initially, is a migration saga lasting four centuries and involving over 10,000,000 African people, 400,000 of whom ended up in the United States. This saga involves, as well, numerous people of European origin who created the conditions with which Africans and their Afro-American descendants had to contend. Of course, with the end of chattel slavery in the United States, the story of black culture entails new themes decidedly more American in focus. Certainly we see here the recipe for further complexity in the interpretation of Afro-American material culture; we have objects that are multileveled in content and meaning surrounded by a nar-rative that is multistranded and of overwhelming proportions. These are challenges that, while they are neither unexpected nor insurmountable, help to explain why there has been reluctance among scholars to plunge more deeply into the study of the tangible dimensions of black American history and culture.

It is my intent in this volume to demonstrate how one can meet the challenges encountered in the study of Afro-American artifacts, a subject that has held my attention for the past twenty years and about which I have been writing since 1973. I have brought together nine essays out of more than twenty-five that I have written on Afro-American topics— including two that have never been published. After shaping one of them into a general introduction, I offer three sets of essays covering the following topics: folk arts and crafts, artisans' lives, and black buildings. There is considerable variety in these essays; general surveys are balanced by specific case studies. In geographical coverage this selection focuses on the American South but the articles range from South Carolina to Texas and from Louisiana to Virginia. Where pertinent, discussion of African and Caribbean connections is included as well. The majority of my studies focus on the historical past, primarily on the antebellum nineteenth century, but neither the colonial period nor the twentieth century is overlooked. While the majority of these essays are treatments of artifacts, three of them focus expressly on an essential human aspect of material culture, the artisan's role as a designer and maker. Further, whenever possible I identify the makers and users of artifacts. Collectively these essays outline in strokes both broad and fine the content of Afro-American folklife.

I use the term *folklife* deliberately. Because my methods of study and interpretation are aligned in varying degrees with social history, anthropology, art history, architectural history, decorative arts research, cultural geography, and archaeology, this collection of essays could have been tagged with several labels. But I use the term *folklife,* first, because by training I am a folklorist. But more importantly I use the term because it provides a useful multidisciplinary and synthetic vantage point from which to view cultural data and processes. Don Yoder has defined folklife as the total lifeway of a group of people including their verbal, material, and spiritual forms of expression. As such, folklife serves as an alternative to the anthropologist's concept of "culture"; its advantage being that folklife unites in one idea a group's sense of tradition and their current everyday experience. Under the banner of folklife, history and culture are fused into a single entity; different cultural forms are linked within a single perspective, or single cultural forms are set against the backdrop of their pertinent cultural history. Afro-American folk art and folk architecture, for example, when treated as dimensions of black folklife, are seen not as separate phenomena but as two of the several ways that pervasive cultural attitudes find expression. Seemingly separate genres when viewed from the folklife perspective acquire "blurred" boundaries and thus blend and overlap in the scholar's mind, a condition that accurately mirrors the reality of life as lived and experienced by the people being studied. I have set my essays out under three different headings, but I mean for them all to be understood as equivalent material dimensions of Afro-American folklife.

Historian of American material culture studies Thomas Schlereth has observed that the field has seemingly passed through three phases or, as he calls them, "ages." These include the ages of collection, description, and interpretation. Contemporary students of American material culture are alleged by Schlereth to have entered into the current "age of interpretation" in about 1965 with the current students building upon the record of earlier exploratory and classificatory efforts. This chronology is interesting for it indicates that, just as American material culture researchers were about to claim a new level of maturity and sophistication, the study of Afro-American artifacts was barely entering the collection or discovery phase. Commonly, new areas of academic research, particularly fields in the humanities, concentrate at first on the questions of origin, typology, and chronology. These are matters that must be well understood before more refined interpretation can be attempted; these are the matters that have so far dominated the study of Afro-American material culture. However, given the growing sophistication found generally in the study of American material culture, particularly in the field of social history, it is not unexpected that some of this activity would affect researchers working with Afro-American objects. To cite but one example, Robert Farris Thompson, who was trained first as an art historian, is now well known for his anthropological treatments linking visual and gestural symbolism. It would seem that in the study of the material culture of black Americans the ages of collection, classification, and interpretation have happened all at the same time.

Because Afro-American folklife has yet to attract many scholars, it remains an underdeveloped, and hence a seemingly young, field of study even though at least two generations of scholars have made important contributions. We still need answers to basic questions for almost every aspect of black material culture; we need to know what was made, when, by whom, for whom, and how. McClung Fleming, in an article that serves as a basic primer on how to study an artifact, converts these questions into scholarly objectives. He notes that all artifacts have five basic properties: design, construction, materials, use, and history. Further, he observes that without a secure knowledge of the essential facts needed to describe these properties, a researcher will never be able to move on to effective cultural analysis, evaluation, or even simple identification. Responding to Fleming's recommendations, I have attempted generally in my research to always provide as complete a description as possible. This is, I think, an appropriate mode for this stage of research when facts are relatively few and therefore precious. Moreover, by using mainly an expository technique, the keepers of the tradition are given more of their own voice either directly or through their material creations. The title of this collection, *By the Work of Their Hands,* stresses that intention.

Sometimes my writings have been described by others as "ethnography," a categorization that downplays their interpretative potential. I take no umbrage from that label since I have usually cloaked my theoretical findings behind a thick fabric of cultural and historical detail. Should one need some neat pegs upon which to hang these essays, several are certainly available. Some of the articles illustrate the process anthropologists call *acculturation.* My studies of individual artisans could be seen as investigations of the social roles played by artists, as descriptions of how communities forge bonds of identity on the basis of shared art. My work with built form elaborates upon the little-understood proxemic codes that human beings use to construct spatial symbols. My alliances with anthropology, sociology, communication theory, and other fields could be highlighted to support a claim to theoretical sophistication but to do so might only fill these pages with off-putting jargon and would only be self-serving. In the history of the United States the stories of the politically and economically disenfranchised are rarely told and when they are, it is usually from the perspective of those who hold power. My scholarly efforts are directed at creating an alternative history that uses what are considered unconventional documents—the buildings and things ordinary people made or make for themselves. Those artifacts are generally the best link we have to the creators of black American culture because they left little in writing in the past and they write little about themselves today. Oral data is valuable and indispensable but the artifacts of the past are the actuality of the past. If we can learn to read them, then we can effectively travel back to specific times and places and recapture worlds that were either lost or obscured by willful forgetfulness. Contemporary artifacts are equally important too for they embody and express what people generally cannot put into words—their creative urges and heartfelt emotions.

Impressive sounding theoretical phrases and "-isms" alone will do little to advance the study of Afro-American folklife. What is needed is more research both in the archives and in the field. Innumerable primary documents lie in thousands of courthouse basements all over the South waiting to be read. Thousands of traditional artisans ply their trades daily; a recently published guess about the number of Afro-American quilts put their total at 800,000 (a count that is probably low). There are still black buildings of all sorts—from houses to churches to stores—that have yet to be studied. Even some slave housing still stands. Since these buildings are increasingly found in a dilapidated condition, they must be recorded soon or not at all. The field of Afro-American folklife needs action. If enough scholars respond to this call, theory and interpretation are sure to follow. But first the story of the black Americans needs to be gathered. It is an account often written not with words but with things made by the work of their hands.

Introduction

The Nature and Pattern
of Afro-American Material Culture

The remarkable epic that describes the evolution of Afro-American material culture cannot be recovered by conventional art historical methods alone. The nature of the data requires that attention be focused not only on objects and their makers but on broad issues related to cultural context. Most Afro-American artifacts are not made by a cadre of closely linked artists who derive inspiration from each other. Afro-American folk crafts, for example, cannot be approached in the same way we would seek to understand the artworks produced during the Harlem Renaissance. Because the artifactual traditions of black Americans were practiced over so long a period and in so many different places, an analysis of objects alone might only produce a false pattern. Black artisans maintained their alternative sense of creativity only through working out a complex amalgam of cultural influences. Even when we simplify the cultural history of Afro-America we find that two basic strands, African and European, are interwoven. Out of this interaction a new cultural reality was forged—the black American. In some cases the admixture of sources favors African elements; in other places and periods European features seem to dominate. While the particular combination varies, we are keenly aware that the differences are a matter of degree rather than kind.

Most historical treatments of black art and artifacts consider the unity of Afro-American creation in a linear perspective, but this is far too simple an approach.[1] It is postulated that skill in the crafts, say in carpentry, leads to expertise in cabinet-making, which may then lead to an opportunity to work in architecture, and then later open the door for recognition in the areas of painting and sculpture. It is suggested that Joshua Johnston (1765–1830), for example, was accepted in Baltimore as a black portrait painter because he had been preceded by a generation of expertly adept black craftsmen. The ceramic jars of Dave the Potter are offered as an example, but the bulk of Dave's work was done after 1840 and exclusively in South Carolina. If there is a unity to Afro-American art, it is a cultural unity, and it is displayed most forcefully in specific tradition-bound genres. The customary precedents that inform folk art and craft are not necessarily the same as those that motivate the fine arts.

The crucial source that gives black material culture its special identity is, of course, its African heritage. This heritage, this cultural legacy, has long been the source of scholarly debate as well as social tension. Generally, its presence has been denied, and often the deeper motive behind that denial has been racial exploitation. As Melville J. Herskovits has shown, a people bereft of a history—without a past—has no reliable source for its identity. When Blacks were considered to have lost their heritage, he argued, they were then more easily looked upon as a commodity or as tools. Thus he warned: "A people that denies its past cannot escape being prey to doubt of its value today and of its potential for the future."[2] In the last three decades the awareness of Africa among American Blacks has increased, while at the same time awareness of African influences in their own history has remained some what underdeveloped. This may be due to the widespread influence of sociologist E. Franklin Frazier who, in his masterwork *The Negro Family in the United States,* effectively portrayed black domestic life as the product of white domination.[3] Africa became a heritage denied.

While there may be few elements of African kinship patterns in Afro-American family affairs, the survival of African influences has long been noted in the areas of religion, music, oral literature, and dance. It was Herskovits who first systematically identified the presence of African influences in contemporary black American culture and coined the term *Africanism.* His research was initially rebuked as mere trait chasing, as the assembling of odd facts and idiosyncrasies, but such criticisms were misplaced. An Africanism is not an isolated cultural element but an assertive proof of an alternative history. It is a link to an unwritten past; it is an index of the existence of African influences. Paul Bohannon has written that all elements of a culture are encoded twice, once in reality and once in the mind.[4] A Black folktale with African characteristics is then more than an entertaining story; it is an indication of the continued maintenance of an African mentality. It is because of the continued existence of African ideas in America that Afro-American traditions continue to flourish in the United States.

Africanisms have been more difficult to discover in material expressions than in the performing arts. It has been generally assumed that Africans were divested of material reminders of their homeland and prevented from making objects that would help them recreate some tangible aspect of the life they had lost. Even Herskovits writes:

If, then, the acculturative situation be analyzed in terms of differing opportunities for retention of Africanisms in various aspects of culture, it is apparent that African forms of technology . . . had but a relatively slight chance for survival. Utensils, clothing, and food were supplied the slaves by their masters, and it is but natural that these should have been what was most convenient to procure, least expensive to provide, and other things being equal, most like the types to which the slave owners were accustomed. Thus African draped cloths were replaced by tailored clothing, however ragged, the short-handled broad-bladed hoe gave way to the longer, slimmer-bladed implement of Europe, and such techniques as weaving and ironworking and woodworking were almost entirely lost.[5]

This dreary evaluation would seem to eliminate all hope of ever identifying an Afro-American tradition in material culture. Yet the tradition does exist. First, there are some pure retentions of African items, many of which were unknown when Herskovits wrote his study. Second, because artifacts—like verbal and musical creations—are based on ideas, an African idea may motivate the making of an object which itself is perceived as Anglo-American. Objects that are describably African starkly and directly assert themselves as black creations. Where Afro-American influences are of a stylistic nature, the impact of black traditions is more subtle. Both kinds of objects require study in order to document the entire struggle of black artisans to attain cultural self-determination. What is common to objects that are overtly Afro-American and those that manifest only subtle traces of black influence is the retention of a similar creative philosophy. If we are truly to understand Afro-American material culture, we must understand the intellectual premises upon which its creation is based.

When dealing with tangible aspects of Afro-American culture one unavoidably confronts what W. E. B. Du Bois called "the two-ness of the Negro."[6] By this he meant to describe a kind of complexity that has been an intimate part of the black experience. In terms of cultural history, we also note a certain duality. Black material culture can claim the heritage of a distant past reaching back to Africa and simultaneously a more recent historical source of inspiration—the response to America. Two reservoirs of creativity were available to be tapped by black artisans. Perhaps the same could be said of most craftsmen in the New World, but Afro-American artisans worked within a set of circumstances that were special in the American experience. As slaves they had new patterns of performance imposed upon them; the European world was thrust into their consciousness. The objects they made were, then, a result of dual historical influences, distant past and recent past, and twin cultural influences, African and European.[7] In the "two-ness of the Negro" we find duality doubled.

Anthropologists have given the name *syncretism* to the process by which a group of people renders the chaos of merging cultures into an intelligible pattern. Basically, what happens is that the new culture is comprehended by degrees. Those features of the novel pattern that are most similar to the established cultural ethos are understood and accepted first. After a shared groundwork is established, the more confusing elements of a new culture may be approached. The syncretic process is essentially a technique for preserving one's identity, a method of intelligent and cogent problem-solving under harsh social pressures. For example, Africans in the New World had little problem accepting Catholic saints; they reinterpreted them as the gods of a pantheon. Thus they acquired a Western religion while at the same time preserving their ancestral heritage.

The complexity of Afro-American culture must certainly carry over into the domain of the artifactual. We must then be prepared to evaluate examples of black art and craft on several levels, for each object will likely be the end product of a syncretic process. To properly appreciate these works, the viewer has to appreciate the particular object not only as it is but also in the way that it is reinterpreted. If, for example, modern plastic dolls are placed on a voodoo altar in Mobile, Alabama, we should be prepared to read them as both the product of petrochemical technology and the physical referent of Yemaja, Yoruba goddess of sea water.

Less difficult to understand, but exceedingly less common, are objects of craft and art that are directly retained from the African heritage—a few tools, a few musical instruments, some rare textiles, and examples of graveyard decoration. These items are so much like African works that it is not difficult to identify their source of inspiration. Rather, it is difficult to explain how they have remained so pure in form and content. Many factors must be considered. Among these are the degree of contact between Afro-and Euro-American groups, the length of separation from the African homeland, the degree of acceptance among Euro-Americans of Afro-American customs, and the demographic composition of the Afro-American community. The Sea Islands off the coasts of South Carolina and Georgia, and sections of the piney woods of Mississippi and Alabama, are areas of relative isolation where African-derived custom has been able to flourish without the imposition of white disapproval. In South Carolina, where Blacks outnumbered Whites five to one throughout most of the eighteenth century, the colony looked "more like a Negro country than a country settled by white people."[8] British settlers were generally inept at dealing with their new semi-tropical environment and apparently turned much of the actual conduct of the work over to their enslaved African laborers. In this situation several elements of African agricultural technology were put to use, including tools that are still made today.[9] Thus we see that a complex array of factors did at times promote the retention of African-derived material culture. We must then be aware of other instances in which the factors of geography, history, and population combine in the necessary sequence to give support to Afro-American folklife.

Given the multilevel nature of Afro-American material culture and the complex network of supportive social circumstances in which this material expression seems to thrive, we soon come to realize that black creativity is marked by constant, individuating change. While improvisation is a universal characteristic of imaginative humans, the extensive sense of improvisation commonplace in the Afro-American experience is rather special. In this case spontaneous change represents a cultural norm rather than single, independent inventions. It is an integral part of the process of African art to constantly reshape the old and the familiar into something contemporary and unique, to simultaneously express one's self and reinforce the image of the community. This is particularly true in the verbal arts. Among the Limba of Sierra Leone, action elements that are the basic stock and trade of the taleteller are constantly combined in ways never heard before.[10] Consequently, every time a story is told, it is a novel creation even though it will also share some features with previous works of oral literature. The same principle in verbal artistry holds among the Xhosa of South Africa, whose gifted narrators rework "core clichés" to create "expansible images" that add elaborate linguistic embroidery to simple tales.[11] Among the Ashanti of Ghana there exists a cycle of narratives that feature a spider hero named *Ananse.* The stories are never same, for Ashanti narrators have acquired the skill of cleverly balancing the old and the new. The spider hero remains a central figure of the tradition, but his exploits grow in number and content.[12]

Improvisation is not restricted to the verbal arts, nor is it restricted to one tribe or one area—it is a pan-African reality. African music also demonstrates this inclination toward free-form improvisation. The melodic line in West African music is extremely variable and moves loosely, almost randomly, over a rock-steady bass line.[13] Other instances of an improvisational aesthetic could be pointed out in textiles and decorative arts[14] or architecture.[15]

When we look for African influences in Afro-American material culture, we should be mindful not only of the content of an artifact but the process of its design and creation. In other words, we must develop a sense of style and performance in addition to a competence for judging form and content. Stylistic consistency appears to be a major source of the integrity of ethnic identity in black material culture. In Afro-American oral literature it is not always the content of the story that makes it Afro-American but the way it is performed. The same holds for the Delta bluesman. Singing alone to the accompaniment of a guitar is not a particularly African format, but through inventive phrasing and elaborate melodic and rhythmic embellishment the blues singer produces a song fraught with African texture and feeling. This is also true of Afro-American artisans whose media and forms may be borrowed from Euro-American sources: the end product of their struggles to wrestle media into objects will reflect more of their black heritage than the source of their cultural borrowing.

The adversities that Afro-Americans have historically endured have encouraged them to be resourceful. They, more than other newcomers to this land, had to reinterpret what for many was already commonplace. More than other immigrants they had to seek strategies to retain their rightful cultural heritage. But they, more than others, may have been better equipped for that struggle and the perplexing problems of cultural disequilibrium, because of their cultural legacy of improvisatory skills. Afro-American blacksmith Philip Simmons spoke for many craftsmen when he said to me, "You've got to change to stay alive." Constant modification of the art of living, "the art of culture,"[16] gives a sense of dynamism to the ordinary and the humdrum. In the realm of material culture, dynamic resourcefulness gives rise to a quality of excitement that is impressed on otherwise unremarkable objects, giving them the imprint of ethnic identity.

For black material culture, then, improvisation is the touchstone of creativity. Whether manifested boldly or subtly, it is ever present, transforming the American into the Afro-American. Should we fail to recognize and understand this, we risk the danger of mistaking imagination for error, variation for imprecision.

The material record of Afro-American culture embraces diversity. Some artifacts represent African custom unchanged: coiled grass baskets and some musical instruments are examples of uninterrupted survival. This is in contrast to the making of quilts, where we find the incorporation of African patterns into the tops of Euro-American objects. A highly animated black style has also been maintained in the carving of wooden walking sticks and other implements. Skills of a pragmatic nature are demonstrated in the making of certain small boats found along the eastern seaboard and in the forging of wrought iron gates, balconies, and fences. Architecture has gone largely unconsidered as an area of Afro-American expertise, but many buildings in the South were erected with the labor of black carpenters, masons, and plasterers; more importantly, common house types can embody African designs and spatial philosophies. Black burial grounds remain today the context for the practice of African-derived custom: grave sites carry markers and various types of decoration that clearly represent an Afro-American approach to the other world. There are other forms that might be mentioned but this sample is enough to effectively make the point that Afro-American material culture engages a range of media and social contexts.

Material culture is a tangible expression of human desire and thus it signals a competence that moves within people. Wherever there have been Afro-Americans, there has been Afro-American material culture. The history of black population patterns from 1790 to 1860 (fig. I.1) can thus tell us much about black artifacts.[17] At first the heaviest concentrations of Blacks were found in the tidewater areas of Maryland, Virginia, and North Carolina, and along the coast of South Carolina. These were precisely the areas where one can find distinctive Afro-American traditions in basketry and boatbuilding. The oldest black artifacts that we know of are from this same region. Tidewater Virginia, having one of the largest early concentrations of African slaves, experienced the direct implantation of African-derived culture. It is not too surprising then to find a slave-made drum, an African iron statue, and several mud-walled cabins surviving there as examples of the black influences that were once so pervasive in everyday life in Virginia. This observation applies as well for coastal South Carolina. There the evidence is, however, more utilitarian in nature, consisting of the tools for rice harvesting and nets for fishing.

By 1860, as the frontier of the United States receded before the onslaught of the general westward movement of the American populace, Blacks had moved a considerable distance inland. Black populations were massed solidly through the Tidewater and Piedmont areas of the southeastern United States, from the coast right up to the slopes of the Appalachian mountains. A long arc of black settlement also stretched from South Carolina through central Georgia, Alabama, and Mississippi, almost to Tennessee. Finally, throughout the Mississippi River Valley, from Louisiana on up to northern Kentucky and central Missouri, the dispersement of slaves followed the meandering courses of America's mightiest rivers—the Mississippi, Missouri, and Ohio. Just prior to the Civil War, Blacks ranged over the entire South and were in positions from which they would eventually move further to the North and West. If we look closely at this population pattern we soon observe a connection that ties together all of Afro-America. And it is a connection that confirms speculations regarding the impact of black material culture.

A distinctive quilting form, the string or strip quilt, is found in black communities from Maryland down the eastern seaboard to Georgia and inland from the coast to Mississippi. Within this sweeping curve, from

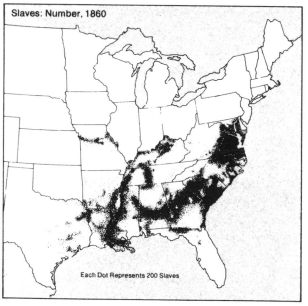

Figure I.1. Distribution of the Slave Population in the
United States in 1790 and in 1860
(After Fogel and Engerman, Time on the
Cross: The Economic Slavery of the Negro
[Boston: Little, Brown & Co., 1974])

the South Carolina Low Country all the way to Louisiana, we also find a black coiled-basketmaking tradition, and from Georgia to Mississippi, there is a complementary dispersion of fife-making artisans. The close match-up between the patterns of migration and settlement and the diffusion of black arts and crafts gives us a key to understanding the similarities in Afro-American wood carvings as far apart as Georgia and Missouri. Not only was there a flow of people from Georgia well into the Midwest, there was a flow of ideas as well. The east to west migration of artistic ideas was complemented by the south to north movement from the Gulf Coast along the Mississippi. The distribution of black population along this route matches the eventual distribution of the shotgun house. It, too, followed the rivers as far north and west as St. Joseph, Missouri, and as far north and east as Cincinnati. Overlaying these two movements is the pattern of distinctive Afro-American grave decoration; the custom is found wherever there are black churches. We might be able some day to argue that this extremely African set of practices entered the United States at several points—Annapolis, Jamestown, Wilmington, Charleston, Savannah, Mobile, New Orleans— and was perpetuated wherever possible as Blacks radiated out from these ports of entry.

Since 1865 black material traditions have either become entrenched in their source areas in the South, usually in out-of-the-way places, or they have followed the movement of black people north to urban centers, where objects like quilts relieve the monotony of city life. Wherever such arts are practiced, contemporary developments depend on a sense of communal history that developed in the South. The directional sense heard in the expression ''down home,'' a phrase commonly used in the black vernacular, is an important indication of the role of the South as a seed bed for black material culture.

Herskovits once spoke of New World African peoples as belonging to ''cultures lying within a given historic stream.''[18] He also charted the African retentions for all Afro-American communities and demonstrated how this stream flowed not only from Africa to the New World but from South America to the northern cities of the United States.[19] While he rated the ''Africanness'' of African-derived art and technology in black communities in the United States from ''somewhat African'' to ''absent,'' it is time to revise his estimates decidedly upward. Afro-American culture surges strongly in the South and is not a mere trickle at the end of the stream.

The significance of Afro-American material culture has only begun to be recognized. Robert Farris Thompson signaled the need for more attention when he wrote: ''Mankind must applaud Afro-American [folk] art in the United States for its sheer existence, a triumph of creative will over the forces of destruction."[20] While it may be too soon to make a summary statement about all of Afro-American material culture, one thing is definite: once one encounters the sorts of objects discussed here, the existence of Afro-American material traditions can no longer be denied. Further, once eyes are opened, understanding and appreciation may follow.

Hugh Honour has written that Europeans who saw America from afar envisioned a world of fantasy, which potentially could nourish an ideal society.[21] Black people, too, had a vision, but it was a vision from within America. Their ideal world was, at first, the one they had left behind rather than a world newly discovered. In the record of their material creations we see how the black view of a preferred way of life shifts by degrees away from Africa and towards America. Old customs and attitudes are not completely given up, but their influence does diminish. In the process of shifting their world view Africans made themselves into a new people, a crucial achievement sensitively recorded in the artifacts they created.

Notes

1. James Porter, "Four Problems in the History of Negro Art," *Journal of Negro History* 27 (1942), 11.

2. Melville J. Herskovits, *The Myth of the Negro Past,* 1941 (reprinted ed., Boston: Beacon Press, 1958), 32.

3. E. Franklin Frazier, *The Negro Family in the United States,* 1939 (reprinted ed., Chicago: University of Chicago Press, 1966), 17.

4. Paul Bohannon, "Rethinking Culture: A Project for Current Anthropologists," *Current Anthropology* 14 (1973), 361–62.

5. Herskovits, *Myth of the Negro Past,* 136–37.

6. W. E. B. Du Bois, *The Souls of Black Folk,* 1903 (reprinted ed., New York: Fawcett, 1961), 17.

7. Indian influences might also be mentioned, for there was some interchange between Blacks and Native Americans. See William S. Willis, "Divide and Rule: Red, White, and Black in the Southeast," *Journal of Negro History* 48 (1963), 157–76. The impact of this contact was slight, however, when compared to the social exchange with Whites. Indeed, it seems that Blacks had more impact on Indians than the Indians had on Blacks.

8. Peter H. Wood, *Black Majority: Negroes in Colonial South Carolina from 1670 through the Stono Rebellion* (New York: W. W. Norton, 1974), 132.

9. Peter H. Wood, " 'It Was a Negro Taught Them': A New Look at Labor in Early South Carolina," *Journal of Asian and African Studies* 9 (1974), 159–79.

10. Ruth H. Finnegan, *Limba Stories and Story-Telling* (London: Oxford University Press, 1967), 64 et passim.

11. Harold Scheub, "The Art of Nongenile Mazithatha Zenai, A Gcaleka Ntsomi Performer," in Richard M. Dorson, ed., *African Folklore* (Garden City, N.Y.: Doubleday, 1972), 115–42.

12. See R. S. Rattray, *Akan-Ashanti Folktales* (London: Oxford University Press, 1930) for examples of spider stories.

13. See Alan Lomax, *Folksong Style and Culture* (Washington, D.C.: American Association for the Advancement of Science, 1968). Compare cantometric profiles for African and European music.

14. See Roy Sieber, *African Textiles and Decorative Arts* (New York: Museum of Modern Art, 1972).

15. John Michael Vlach, "Affecting Architecture of the Yoruba," *African Arts* 10, no. 1 (1976), 48–53.

16. David Bidney, *Theoretical Anthropology* (New York: Shocken Books, 1953), xxxix.

17. See Robert William Fogel and Stanley L. Engerman, *Time on the Cross: The Economics of Negro Slavery* (Boston: Little, Brown, 1974), 44–52.

18. Melville J. Herskovits, "On Some Modes of Ethnographic Comparison," reprinted in Frances S. Herskovits, ed., *The New World Negro: Selected Papers in Afroamerican Studies* (Bloomington: Indiana University Press, 1966), 81.

19. Melville J. Herskovits, "Problem, Method, and Theory in Afroamerican Studies," reprinted in *New World Negro,* 53.

20. Robert Farris Thompson, "African Influence on the Art of the United States," in Armstead L. Robinson, Craig C. Foster, and Donald H. Ogilvie, eds., *Black Studies in the University* (New Haven: Yale University Press, 1969), 172.

21. Hugh Honour, *The European Vision of America* (Cleveland: Cleveland Museum of Art, 1975), 14.

Part One

Folk Arts and Crafts

Introduction to Part One

The three articles gathered here under the heading of "folk arts and crafts" present, first, a broad overview of the topic and then two specifically focused treatments of Afro-American material culture in Virginia and Texas, respectively. The opening essay was essentially commissioned by the Winterthur Museum as part of its much-debated 1976 conference on American folk art. One of the stated purposes of that meeting was to rethink the definition of American folk art and, because Afro-American creativity was then believed to be confined largely to the performing arts, my contribution to the discussion was a survey of Afro-American artifacts expressive of a distinctive cultural perspective. This evidence helped to broaden the conventional thinking about the dearth of black folk art in the United States and challenged the authority of the accepted canon of American folk objects. The article on the domestic material culture of slaves in Virginia was also a commissioned essay, in this case by the Smithsonian Institution's National Museum of American History. In its original "report" format, the essay was used by museum curators to develop an exhibition on the daily life of slaves in the eighteenth century. Consequently, what was needed was a detailed composite inventory of the contents of a representative slave cabin. Folklorists usually collect their primary data from living informants, but in this instance the period under study was so far back in the past that written sources—probate inventories, diaries, letters, travelers' accounts—were the chief source of information. Similarly, in my study of Afro-American craft traditions in nineteenth-century Texas, there was no hope of finding living informants. However, due to the extensive efforts during the 1930s by interview teams employed by the Federal Writers Project, thousands of pages of testimony from the lips of ex-slaves were available to be sifted for details about material culture items. As a consequence of reading closely through this archival material, the bearers of black craft traditions could speak for themselves.

A comprehensive examination of black folk art and craft can be found in John Michael Vlach, *The Afro-American Tradition in Decorative Arts* (Cleveland: Cleveland Museum of Art, 1978). However, readers should also consult more recent works that extend and deepen our knowledge of the subject. Indispensable to the study of Afro-American traditional aesthetics are the works of Robert Farris Thompson, in particular his *Flash of the Spirit: African and Afro-American Art and Philosophy* (New York: Random House, 1983). For an extended treatment of the continuity of Central African custom in the United States see his "The Structure of Recollection: The Kongo New World Visual Tradition" in Robert Farris Thompson and Joseph Cornet, *The Four Moments of the Sun: Kongo Art in Two Worlds* (Washington, D.C.: National Gallery of Art, 1981), 141–210. Also useful as a summation of scholarly work in this field of research is William Ferris's anthology, *Afro-American Folk Art and Crafts* (Boston: G. K. Hall, 1983).

The greatest concentration of new research on Afro-American folk art and crafts has been directed at quilting. Maude Southwell Wahlman has published a number of articles on this genre of textile art. One of her basic essays, "Aesthetic Principles in Afro-American Quilts" (co-authored with John Scully), appears in Ferris's anthology. Some of Mary Anne McDonald's research is presented in her article "Jennie Burnett: Afro-American Quilter," in *Five North Carolina Folk Artists* (Chapel Hill: Ackland Museum, 1986), 29–39. There have been several museum exhibitions devoted exclusively to Afro-American quilts: *Something to Keep You Warm: The Roland Freeman Collection of Black American Quilts from the Mississippi Heartland* (Jackson: Mississippi Department of Archives and History, 1981) curated by Roland Freeman; *Ten Afro-American Quilters* (University, Miss.: Center for the Study of Southern Culture, 1983), curated by Maude Southwell Wahlman and Ella King Torrey; and most recently, *Who'd a Thought It: Improvisation in African-American Quiltmaking* (San Francisco: San Francisco Craft and Folk Art Museum, 1987) curated by Eli Leon. This last mentioned exhibit was accompanied by a lengthy illustrated catalogue containing essays by Leon and Robert Farris Thompson. Several states have undertaken surveys of quilts made or owned by their citizens; the surveys in North and South Carolina, Kentucky, and Michigan are noteworthy for the number of quilts identified as Afro-American.

Other new work on traditional Afro-American material culture includes: Doris Adelaide Derby, "Black Women Basketmakers: A Study of Domestic Economy in Charleston County, South Carolina," Ph.D. dissertation, University of Illinois, 1980; Dale Rosengarten, *Row upon Row: Sea Grass Baskets of the South Carolina Lowcountry* (Columbia, S.C.:

McKissick Museum, 1986); Robert Lloyd Webb, *"Ring the Banjar!" The Banjo in America from Folklore to Factory* (Cambridge, Mass.: MIT Museum, 1984); and John Michael Vlach, "International Encounters at the Crossroads of Clay: European, Asian, and African Influences on Edgefield Pottery," in *Crossroads of Clay* (Columbia, S.C.: McKissick Museum, 1990, 17–40).

1

Arrival and Survival: The Maintenance of an Afro-American Tradition in Folk Art and Craft

It is generally assumed that every ethnic group in our nation of migrants—what has recently been called "A Nation of Nations"—made some contribution to America's material culture.[1] Be it house type, foodway, technological expertise, or mode of costume or decoration, it is thought that somewhere in the artifactual domain the presence of the Old World is recorded in the New. Yet there has been one group that has been excused from the honor roll of material contributors. People of African descent are usually credited with expertise in music, dance, and rhetoric, but their achievements in the arts and crafts, until the late nineteenth and early twentieth centuries, have been ignored. This circumstance is in large part due to the fact that Africans were given a status different from the rest of the groups who populated this land. Europeans, Native Americans, and Asians are acknowledged as bearers of distinct cultures, while Africans, since they were brought unwillingly as slaves, are considered to be culturally bereft. This is, of course, a racist myth and one which was thoroughly debunked by Melville Herskovits.[2]

Contemporary studies in anthropology, sociology, history, and folklore have shown the tenacity of African cultural concepts in the New World and their stability despite conditions of duress. The imagined cultural amnesia that was supposed to have afflicted Africans, once they arrived in America, is a convenient scheme for placing them at the bottom of the social heap, but it is far from being an accurate appraisal of their abilities. If they were stripped of their culture, then whence came their narrative style, their musical ear, their kinetic sense—all of which are demonstrably African?[3] Even where such accomplishments in the performing arts are admitted, other aspects of cultural survival are excluded. Verbal and gestural

This article originally appeared in Ian M. G. Quimby and Scott T. Swank, eds., *Perspectives on American Folk Art* (New York: W. W. Norton, 1980): 177–217. Reprinted by permission.

forms, the argument runs, are held in the mind and therefore can be retained. Artifacts, however, because they require an overt physical manifestation, are thought to be controllable. Even Herskovits argued that "utensils, clothing, and food were supplied the slaves by their masters and it is but natural that these should have been what was most convenient to procure, least expensive to provide, and . . . most like the types to which the slave owners were accustomed."[4] This statement first ignored the fact that artifacts, like songs, tales, and religious beliefs, are based on mental concepts. Recognizing the conceptual dimension of objects allows us to understand that it is possible for an African idea to be lodged in a seemingly European object. Second, historical studies are just bringing to light a new understanding of early plantation life that indicates that slaves often had much to teach their masters about the New World.[5] If we dispense with the negative assumptions that have usually preceded study of the history and culture of American Blacks and declare the African to be a culturally competent immigrant, then there is much to be learned about his contribution to the material culture of the United States.

What follows is an analysis of eight areas of material expression selected from the domains of art and craft. The approach in each case will be to consider the earliest known forms and then to follow subsequent developments chronologically. Since much of the material culture of Blacks in America is shared by Whites, it has been difficult to isolate Afro-American artifacts from similar artifacts made and used by Whites.[6] But this circumstance should not cause us to abandon the search for earlier distinct forms. What seems to happen, again and again, is that African-derived artifacts and skills are cloaked with layers of Euro-American influence. As a consequence, African and Afro-American objects in the end appear Euro-American.

Basketry

The first major agricultural export in colonial South Carolina was rice. In the cultivation of rice African skills proved to be exceedingly valuable to plantation owners. Indeed, the strain of rice grown in the Low Country was allegedly brought from Madagascar in the 1680s.[7] Peter H. Wood provides the following summary of Black agricultural talent:

> Those Africans who are accustomed to growing rice on one side of the Atlantic, and who found themselves raising the same crop on the other side did not markedly alter their annual routine. When New World slaves planted in the Spring by pressing a hole with the heel and covering the seeds with the foot, the motion used was demonstratably similar to that employed in West Africa. In Summer, when Carolina Blacks moved through the rice fields in a row, hoeing in unison to work songs, the pattern of cultivation was

Figure 1.1.   Rice Fanner, South Carolina, ca. 1850
Rush, oak; H. 2″, Diam. 20¾″.
(Charleston Museum. Photo: Martin Linsey)

not one imposed by European owners but rather one learned from West African forebears. And in October when the threshed grain was "fanned" in the wind, the wide winnowing baskets were made by Black hands after an African design.[8]

The last statement is particularly significant. Comparing rice fanners from western and central Africa to those used in South Carolina reveals strong similarities in form, materials, techniques of sewing, and use. In both cases, we find grass and reeds tied into bundles that are then coiled into wide trays (fig. 1.1). The making of the coiled baskets by Blacks was apparently known in South Carolina as early as 1690.[9] The baskets proved useful and are still made today.

In the eighteenth century, it appears that two general categories of coiled basket were known, work baskets made by men from tough reeds and split palmetto butt and "show" baskets made by women and children from light grasses and strips of palmetto leaf. In the nineteenth century, new forms were added to the basket repertoire. Large round baskets with shallow sides were still made, but tall storage baskets, oblong baskets, and

Figure 1.2.   Contemporary Sweetgrass Baskets for Sale at a Roadside
Stand in Mt. Pleasant, South Carolina
Note that the basic tray form of the rice fanner has been
elaborated upon by the addition of handles and a row of
circular loops.
(Photographed in summer 1977 by John Michael Vlach)

baskets with strap handles became more common. By the end of the nineteenth century, Black basket sewers attempted to secure a tourist market
for their work, and by the 1930s roadside stands along Highway 17 in
Mount Pleasant became common. The distinction remains, but the work
basket has all but disappeared.

The forms made to sell at these stands seem generally to have been
whatever would appeal to interested passers-by (fig. 1.2). Yet one can sense
that latent in some of these baskets is the shape of the older baskets. Contemporary basket sewers still remember the oldest traditional forms. Mrs.
Queen Ellis, for example, can still make rice fanners on request. New combinations of material are now used, notably, pine needles, colored threads,
plastic cord, and even beer can tops, but with the lack of available
sweetgrass many basket sewers are now returning to rushes, the material
used by their ancestors. The majority of the baskets offered to tourists in

the Charleston area today seem Victorian in style. Sewing baskets and pocketbooks are made in large measure to appeal to white tastes, but if we look closely at the bottom fourth of such baskets, we notice that this section is identical to an "old-timey" church collection basket. Literally we confront the layering of traditions.

Afro-American basketry was initially practiced exclusively in the coastal regions of South Carolina and Georgia. Today it largely survives in Mount Pleasant, at the northern end of the Sea Islands chain. There is adequate proof, nevertheless, that coiled grass and rush baskets were also made in St. Helena, Hilton Head, and Defuskie, near the Georgia border, and just south of Savannah at Brownville.[10] Later, when Blacks moved inland, they carried their basketmaking tradition with them. Nineteenth-century examples of coiled baskets made by Blacks have been recovered from Alabama, Tennessee, and Louisiana.[11] In western Mississippi, Afro-American basket makers are still making coiled baskets from "pine straw" and palm strips. African basketmaking has thus been spread throughout the Deep South, but it remains most visible at the point of its first arrival, the Low Country of the Carolina coast.

Musical Instruments

Another implement associated with rice cultivation is the wooden mortar. Mortars hallowed out of sections of tree trunk are well known both in Africa and Europe. Yet when we learn that Whites in South Carolina tried to develop "engines" to husk rice, we can then focus on Africa as a source for the mortars made and used in South Carolina.[12] Some of these mortars may have served musical functions. Rice husking songs have been amply documented. Women kept a rhythm for their lyrics with the thump of the pestle. Gregory Day has postulated that some exquisitely curved mortars may have doubled as drums.[13] Grooves on their sides could have held a thong to which a drum head was attached. Such an arrangement would have allowed the head to be quickly removed. Such precautions were found by Herskovits in Surinam where drum ceremonies were carried on with water pans substituted for actual drums.[14] The theme of subterfuge is expected from people whose freedom has been stolen.[15] Thus the rice mortar that served the master by cleaning his rice also served the slave to make his music and maybe to send his messages.

There are constant references to rhythmic concepts in the literature of Afro-American music. Drums would have been the common means of establishing the beat for African songs, but in America alternate strategies were used. Nevertheless, in the 1930s the Georgia Writers Project collected eleven reports of drum making from seven different communities.[16] These were generally plain sections of hollowed logs with pegged heads. While simple instruments such as these cannot be given clear antecedents, pegged log drums can be traced back to Place Congo in New Orleans in 1819.[17]

The earliest known drum, like the earliest known coil baskets, is very clearly African (see p. 65). Placed in the British Museum in 1753, it was, possibly, collected as early as 1690 in Virginia.[18] In shape, decoration, and system of head attachment, it is perfectly Akan. But for the fact that it is made of American cedar and deerskin, this drum would probably be considered African. It is instead a document of the clear persistence of alternative cultural concepts not only for material objects but for musical performance as well. The first generation of Africans had a very definite notion of who they were. Over time their ethnic self-concept became weaker, but it still provided a basis for an alternative culture in America.

The process of change in musical instruments is perhaps most clearly represented by the history of the banjo.[19] Now primarily associated with the so-called old-time bluegrass of white country music, the banjo was first a Black instrument. It is difficult to imagine a Gibson "mastertone" as derived from an African instrument, but the connection becomes clear if we first look to a transitional form—the Appalachian folk banjo. This type of banjo has a wooden frame, a fretless neck, an animal skin head, and gut strings. If we were to change the wooden frame to a calabash or a gourd, we would then have the instrument that is described repeatedly as made and played by slaves. Litt Young, an ex-slave from Mississippi, remembered from his youth in 1860 that "Us have small dances Saturday night and ring plays and banjo and fiddle playin' and knockin' bones. There was fiddles made from gourds and banjos from sheep hides."[20] Even Thomas Jefferson admitted in 1781 that the "banjar" was the instrument "which they [Blacks] brought hither from Africa."[21] While the banjo as we know it is no longer physically similar to its Afro-American antecedent, it should be clear that its origins are not to be found among the southern mountain folk but rather amidst Black plantation communities in the Tidewater areas (fig. 1.3).

There are many chordophones in West Africa that could have provided the earliest source for the New World instrument: *balam, garaya, kora, kasso, pomso,* and *bania.* All have a calabash body, fretless neck, and gut strings. The *bania* has the most similar name to banjo, but we should not discount formative input from similar instruments. It is best to recognize the early banjo in America as part of a class of African instruments. The banjo was an Old World instrument that was later made to play New World songs and transformed in the process.

Despite the fact that the banjo changed radically in shape and racial association, there are some African stringed instruments that are still played

Figure 1.3. Anonymous, *The Old Plantation,* ca. 1800
Watercolor on paper; H. 11¾″, W. 17⅞″.
(Abby Aldrich Rockefeller Folk Art Center)

in the United States that have changed very little. The mouth bow is a good example. Eli Owens of Bogalusa, Louisiana, makes and plays the mouth bow in much the same way today as he learned from his grandfather. Were it not for the substitution of a beer can for a gourd resonator, his instrument could be substituted for one from the rain forests of central Africa.

Ironwork

There have been many Afro-American blacksmiths. Wherever there are records of Black craftsmen, many turn out to be ironworkers of some kind: wheelwrights, farriers, gunsmiths, axe makers, ornamental ironmakers. The work of a forge combined many tasks that often required a group of blacksmiths. Hence, there are a number of cases in which Blacks worked as a team. Bernard Moore of Todd's Warehouse, Virginia, employed seventeen slaves in his ironworks in 1769. In 1770 at Providence Forge, Virginia, ten slaves banged out hoes and axes for local farmers. Conditions such as these provide a context in which alternative traditions in ironwork could be fostered.[22]

An unusual example of wrought iron sculpture was discovered during the excavation of the site of a blacksmith shop and slave quarters in Alexandria, Virginia (fig. 1.4). It is a figure of a man, symmetrically posed, with legs spread apart and arms bent and reaching forward. The trunk retains the square shape of the original iron bar from which the statue was forged. Although the figure presents only a minimal image, it is a powerful work. Its direct frontal presentation together with the rough hammer marks clearly visible on all surfaces combine to suggest the primal essence of human form. The date of origin for this statue has been set at sometime in the late eighteenth century.

The circumstances of discovery suggest that the figure was created by a Black artisan. Stylistic evidence further confirms its Black origins. Malcolm Watkins has called it a "remarkable example of African artistic expression in ironwork."[23] Another commentator refers to this piece as "one of the rare objects which link American Negro Art to Africa."[24] Indeed, comparisons with the wrought iron sculpture of the Bamana immediately set off sparks of recognition. If the forms made by Mande-speaking blacksmiths do not correspond exactly with the iron statue from Virginia, there is no question that the handling of mass and medium is very similar. It is in the gray area of attitude that the strongest resemblances emerge.[25] Since the records of the slave trade for colonial Virginia reveal that one-seventh of all the Africans imported between 1710 and 1769 were from the Senegambian area and thus very likely Mande-speakers, it is not difficult to explain this iron statue's strong affinities to the wrought iron sculpture of the western Sudan.[26] Africans of Mandinka origins are mentioned several times in accounts of runaways from the 1770s.[27] Since this figure was made sometime during the late eighteenth century, its creator was probably either African-born or a first generation slave. His memory of his African heritage was still very strong. Watkins's assessment of this object as African, rather than Afro-American, is appropriate; the statue is a remarkable survival rather than an innovative adaption. The value that was invested in this sculpture is indicated by the fact that it was hidden from common view, buried in the dirt floor of the smith. Apparently, it had to be abandoned, and it only emerged again with the chance excavation of a water line.

Slave blacksmiths also remembered how to make weapons. In 1792 a group of nine hundred rebellious slaves from Virginia armed themselves with three hundred spears made by a blacksmith in their group.[28] Many other rebellions were also provided with weapons made by slave blacksmiths. The records do not reveal whether these weapons were African in design, but speculation in this regard is not out of place.

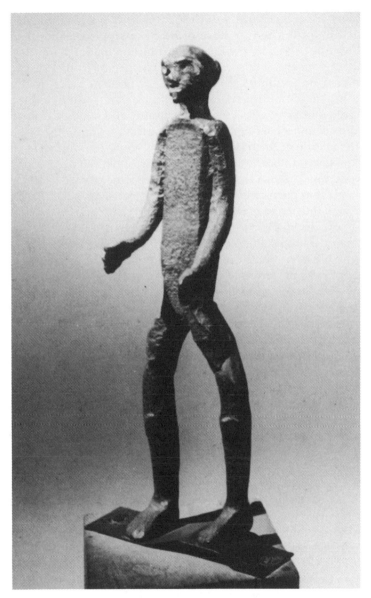

Figure 1.4.   Wrought-iron Figure, Alexandria, Virginia,
Late Eighteenth Century
H. 11″.
*(Collection of Adele Earnest. Photo:
Smithsonian Institution)*

Most Afro-American ironwork was made under the direction of white blacksmiths. In New Orleans, from 1802 onward, records show that Blacks were used in local forges.[29] Since primarily European patterns were executed, we must consider the Black contribution one of manpower rather than design concept. Yet specialists in ornamental ironwork constantly comment on the distinct subtleties of New Orleans grillwork. We may suspect that these minor variations could be due to the reinterpretation of European motifs by Afro-American artisans. The same situation pertains also to the decorative wrought iron of Charleston, South Carolina, except that in the middle of the nineteenth century about one-fourth of the Afro-American blacksmiths were free men. Christopher Werner, a prominent metal worker in Charleston, owned five slaves. One of them, "Uncle Toby" Richardson, is remembered as a "top rank artist in iron."[30] Werner is credited with the design of the famous "Sword Gate" (fig. 1.5), but Richardson, perhaps, should get the credit for making it.

Traditional blacksmithing is still practiced in Charleston by Philip Simmons, who has been a blacksmith for fifty-two years. Having learned from an ex-slave blacksmith whose father was also a blacksmith, Simmons's work represents the culmination of more than 125 years of ironworking experience. Some of Simmons's older works fit well within the Anglo-German design canons for Charleston wrought iron, but in the last fifteen years he has taken the local traditions (for he alone carries on the tradition) into a new era. His ironwork is becoming very sculptural. His most famous gate, the "Snake Gate," is decorated with a very dangerous looking rattlesnake (fig. 1.6). Simmons has said of his creation:

> On the first sight I made the snake—the body. But the eye, I had to make several changes. Like the first, second, third, fourth time I placed the eye in the head of the snake, it look at me. That *was* the snake. . . . The eye was complicated. You put the eye in it and you just see something that look like a dead snake. He look dead. You know that's true. You got to get that eye set that he look live. You look at it now sitting up there in the gate. Now you see it looking after you anywhere you are. Any side you looking on, it's looking dead at you. That's the important thing about the snake—to look alive.[31]

The Afro-American ironworking traditions of Charleston will not end with Philip Simmons. He has trained two men, Silas Sessions and Ronnie Pringle, who work as his helpers but who are, nevertheless, very adept craftsmen in their own right. We may safely project this tradition ahead for another thirty or forty years. Elsewhere in the country there are other Black ironworkers. In Bluefield, West Virginia, W. P. Hamilton carries on the practical tasks of a farrier. There are general smiths in rural towns in Alabama and Mississippi. They tend to the many repair-and-mend jobs of their communities. In those tasks their performance is very much like that

Figure 1.5.   Toby Richardson and Four Unknown Black Artisans, Sword
              Gate, Designed by Christopher Werner, Charleston, S.C.,
              Mid-Nineteenth Century
              Wrought iron.
              (Photo: Martin Linsey)

of any white blacksmith, but these similarities should not obscure the different vision of their ancestors.

Boatbuilding

It is commonly accepted that European settlers learned to make dugout
canoes from Indians. It is not so commonly known that the men who often
maneuvered this shallow water craft were African. A traveler to Maryland

Figure 1.6.   Phillip Simmons, Snake Gate (detail), Charleston, S.C., ca. 1960
(Photo: Martin Linsey)

in 1736 remarked that a log dugout was "a very small and dangerous sort
of canoe, liable to be overturn'd by the least motion of the Sitters in it.
The Negroes manage them dextrously, with a Paddle."[32] Africans were
purchased, it seems, for their boating skills as well as their agricultural
know-how. One Black boatman in Virginia was described in the following manner in 1772: "He calls himself Bonna, and says he came from a
Place of that name in the Ibo Country, in Africa, where he served in the
capacity of a canoe man."[33]

Blacks not only manned the boats of colonial America, they also made
them, particularly log dugouts or boats made of several logs. Numerous
newspaper accounts from South Carolina describe a boat called a pettiauger
that was hewn by slaves from cypress logs and painted bright colors. A
surviving boat from a Santee River plantation is adequate proof of the skill
of Black boatwrights (fig. 1.7). Two massive sections of hewn cypress were
pieced together to form a thirty-foot copy of a naval ship's boat. Multiple
log dugouts made in the Chesapeake area seem to derive from Caribbean
boats known as periaguas. The West Indian craft had a hewn log base with

Figure 1.7.   Plantation barge *Bessie,* White Oak Plantation, Santee River,
S.C., ca. 1855
Cypress; L. 29½'.
(Charleston Museum. Photo: Martin Linsey)

sides raised by hewn planks. This is the same strategy used on the
Chesapeake bay, except that in some cases as many as nine logs were pieced
together. Boats made this way have tentatively been credited to a slave
named Aaron from York County, Virginia, sometime in the last quarter
of the eighteenth century.[34] A three-log canoe was quite large and could
be an effective craft with which to tong and drag for oysters. When fitted
with a mast, sail, and centerboard, it would not even appear to be made
from logs (fig. 1.8). Most log canoes were built in the nineteenth century,
and few of them survive today. The survivors have been fitted with gasoline
inboards and forward cuddies, and only a long look at the hull can detect
the work of the log hewers.

The affiliation of Blacks with the water has not been restricted to boatbuilding. In some of the earliest historical records for South Carolina, Blacks
are recognized as prodigious fishermen. In the West Indies, some plantation slaves were given free access to boats and nets to provide a seafood
supplement to the produce of the farm.[35] Blacks still constitute about one-
half of the crewmen on the skipjacks, the last sail-powered work vessels
in the United States. In the Sea Islands of South Carolina, distinctive cast
nets are used to catch shrimp, and their boats, called "bateaux," are made

Figure 1.8.   Rendering of a Poquoson Log Canoe Dredging for Crabs, ca. 1890
(From a U. S. Fish Commission Report)

in a manner possibly derived from the older log pettiaugers. Black fishermen can be found up and down the Atlantic seaboard. Often their rigs cannot be distinguished from those of white fishermen, but, if we assume that they are only copying the ways of the majority, we miss most of their story. Africans were taken from one coast to another only to find further opportunity to carry on their usual tasks, and their descendants have often followed them to the water.

Pottery

Throughout the South, folk pottery has been produced by numerous family-owned shops. Almost all of these shops were operated by Whites. Only occasionally is a solitary Black potter or potter's helper encountered. No major tradition for Afro-American pottery exists *except* in the Edgefield District of western South Carolina. In an area now encompassed by Edgefield and Aiken counties, between 1815 and 1880 a great number of Blacks were once put to work making pottery. At the present time, about

Figure 1.9.   Dave the Potter, "Great and Noble Jar,"
Miles Mills, S.C., May 13, 1859
Stoneware, ash glaze; H. 29″, Diam. 26″.
(Charleston Museum. Photo: Martin Linsey)

forty slave craftsmen and laborers can be identified. One researcher thinks that eventually more than 150 will be named.[36]

The wares made in South Carolina were mostly utilitarian in function and in form were very similar to Anglo-American pottery types. Yet in the case of Dave the Potter, the only slave to sign and date his works, we have evidence of a deviation from normal practices.[37] First, Dave concentrated on large storage jars. This type of jar is not unusual except that his vessels tended to be monumental in scale. The largest, thought to hold more than forty-four gallons, was made in sections (fig. 1.9). Dave threw it while another slave, Baddler, turned the wheel. Dave also inscribed his pots with rhymed couplets such as "Great and Noble Jar / Hold Sheep, Goat, and Bear," "Dave Belongs to Mr. Miles / Where the oven bakes and the pot biles," or "Pretty little girl on a virge, / volca[n]ic mountain how they burge." Poetry and gigantic size are modest variations of the Anglo-American tradition, but they are clues to the existence of alternative possibilities in design and execution—clues that help to explain a more unusual group of ceramics also discovered in the Edgefield District.

Figure 1.10.   Face Vessel, Edgefield District, S.C., ca. 1860
Stoneware, kaolin, ash glaze; H. 8½".
(Augusta-Richmond County Museum,
Augusta, Ga. Photo: Martin Linsey)

This series of decorative works consists of miniature vessels approximately five inches tall, usually jugs, which are sculpted as human heads (fig. 1.10). The function of these vessels is still unknown. We may postulate a symbolic, rather than utilitarian, purpose because of the care taken in modeling the very small bodies. The most typical examples have porcelainlike kaolin inserted into a stoneware body. This combination of different clay bodies is a unique achievement in world ceramic history, and the resulting contrast in media has been noted by Robert Farris Thompson as a key aesthetic link to African sources of inspiration. He traces the stylized face jugs of South Carolina to central African, particularly Bakongo, origins. He finds "the same pinpoint pupils within white eyes, the same long hooked nose, the same siting of the nose at a point relatively high above the lips, the same open mouth with bared teeth, the same widening of the mouth so that it extends across the width of the jaw."[38]

Figure 1.11.   Face Vessel, Bath, S.C., ca. 1850
Stoneware, ash glaze; H. 8⅜″, Diam. 7⅛″.
(Augusta-Richmond County Museum,
Augusta, Ga. Photo: Martin Linsey)

In the same part of Africa, there is a distinctive type of earthenware vessel called a *m'vungo*. Its distinguishing formal features are a stirrup handle combined with a single canted spout. Some of the larger Edgefield face vessels, particularly those thought to have been made in the early phases of Edgefield pottery production, share these features (fig. 1.11). These pots may be considered African in form if not decoration. Vessels with stirrup handles and canted spouts are still made in the West Indies by Black potters.[39] They are called "monkeys" or "monkey jugs," terms which also occur in South Carolina. Apparently, this type of ceramic vessel entered South Carolina via the Caribbean, but its origins extend across the Atlantic to Africa. Describing the sculpted jugs of Edgefield, E. A. Barber wrote that they were "generally known as monkey jugs not on account of their resemblance to the head of an ape but because porous vessels which were made for holding water and cooling it be evaporation were called by that name.''[40] The earliest face vessels made by Blacks in Edgefield derived their form from the African water carrier, a form familiar to the potters. Later they switched to stoneware clay and produced smaller versions.

While face vessels made in America have usually been traced to European sources, namely British toby jugs and German bellarmines, we should not discount possible African ceramic inspiration. Vessels sculpted into heads have been found in Ghana, Ivory Coast, and Mali. In style they have several features which compare well with Edgefield wares. With respect to the question of genre, the face vessel is as much African as it is European. The synthesis of western ceramic technology and materials (i.e., stoneware clay, glazes, wood-fired kilns, throwing wheels) and African pottery forms and design concepts is a hybrid object; it is neither African nor European. Even if these hybrid vessels are markedly influenced by Western technique, we should not cut short our search for African-inspired motivation in their making.

Textiles

Luiza Combs was born somewhere on the Guinea Coast in 1853 and brought to the United States at the beginning of the Civil War. She must have known little of slavery but nevertheless endured the hardships of the Black experience in the era of Reconstruction. The legacy of her handiwork, which she passed on to her children, is a wool blanket with a stripe pattern. Mrs. Combs raised the sheep to produce the wool. She sheared them and carded the fleece. After spinning the yarn, she dyed it and wove it. Every step of production was under her control; every aesthetic choice was her decision. The mixture of bright red-orange, lavender, blue, and light orange may be recognized as an African color scheme, although much more comparative study of the color preferences of African ethnic groups is needed.[41] The stripe design is common enough in Anglo-American weaving, but it is also an African pattern. Luiza Combs's blanket gives us a hint of the kinds of textiles that might have been made by slaves under the supervision of white owners. Those coverlets, blankets, and fabrics may have been African and American simultaneously.

In other textiles, particularly appliquéd quilts, there are clearer African influences. The most extensively studied Afro-American quilts are those of Harriet Powers of Athens, Georgia (fig. 1.12). At least two of her quilts survive.[42] Made in the late nineteenth century, their content is largely derived from the Bible, although one of them also depicts five scenes of local historical events. A number of features of Mrs. Powers's appliquéd figures are directly comparable to West African appliquéd textiles. Her rendering

Figure 1.12.   Harriet Powers, Bible Quilt, Athens, Ca., ca. 1895–98
Cotton, pieced and appliqued with details, embroidered with
cotton and metallic yarns; H. 69″, W. 105″.
(Museum of Fine Arts, Boston)

of animals—notably fish, pigs, birds, and horned beasts—are comparable
to those made by the Fon people of Dahomey. The same background
motifs—the short-armed cross, rosettes, crescents, and hearts—also occur
on Dahomean cloths.[43] The most impressive correlation is a perceived continuity in style. Human figures, in both Mrs. Powers's quilts and Dahomean
appliquéd cloths, are rendered as bold, iconic statements. Her figures are
stiffly posed and have minimal detail as opposed to the highly representa-
tional expressions found in Anglo-American appliquéd quilting. Mrs.
Powers's primal symbolism has immediate impact. Like most traditional
African art, her quilts have a communicative quality that is direct and
powerful. No other appliquéd quilts made by Black Americans have been
found which are as African in feeling as those of Mrs. Powers. We cannot,
therefore, speak of an Afro-American tradition of appliquéd quilting. It
is clear, however, that the farther back in time we can probe, the closer
are the ties to African inspiration.

   In the genre of pieced quilts, we find that Black quilters often took

Figure 1.13.   Mrs. Floyd McIntosh, Quilt, Pinola, Miss., ca. 1930
Cotton; H. 72″, W. 79″.
(Mississippi State Historical Museum)

over Anglo-American designs, such as the log cabin pattern. There is a distinct preference among Blacks for designs featuring long strips (fig. 1.13). Known as either "string quilts" or "strip quilts," this type of quilt is known in Black communities from Maryland to Georgia to east Texas. The tradition for this form apparently stems from the widespread West African practice of making larger textiles from thin strips woven on horizontal looms. The strips, ranging from four to ten inches in width, were cut into ten-foot lengths and edge-sewn together to create random patterns.[44] Afro-American strip quilts often manifest an improvised notion of design, although not with total disregard for an overall plan. Generally there is a feeling of spirited playfulness with shape and color that, in the Anglo-American canon of quilting principles, would have to be labeled crazy if not a mistake. A quilt from the vicinity of Triune, Tennessee, clearly demonstrates the hybrid nature of some aspects of Afro-American quilting

Figure 1.14.   Quilt, Triune, Tenn., ca. 1910
Cotton; H. 81″, W. 80″.
(Collection of Richard H. and Kathleen L.
Hulan. Photo: Martin Linsey)

design (fig. 1.14). It is composed of assorted quilting blocks, all of which are fairly standard examples of Anglo-American stitchery. The blocks, however, are sewn together in strips without regard to individual pattern. The resulting strips, of different widths, are then edge-sewn together to form the quilt. What we have in the end is Euro-American content structured into what may be an African-derived order.

Another way that an alternative sense of design shows itself in Black quilting is by a simple reinterpretation of standard quilting concepts. Geometric block patterns are the main structural design element in Anglo-American pieced quilts. Usually they are small in size and repeated several times in the composition of the whole quilt. Black quilters break with this notion by rendering the single quilt block as the whole pattern. A single twelve-patch block may constitute the entire design, or one log cabin unit may fill up the quilt where one normally expects to find eighty tiny groups of concentric squares. A new definition of the Euro-American pattern is thus achieved. The final product is definitely related to white design sources, but it is only rendered after those designs have been filtered through a decidedly Black aesthetic. If we understand the difference between design product and design process, we can pinpoint the influences of the American heritage on twentieth-century Black textiles. Without this insight, we risk mistaking imagination for error, variation for imprecision, improvisation for chaos.

Wood Carving

In 1939 an African ritual in Georgia involving sculpted figures was recalled in the following words: "I remember the African men used to all the time make little clay images. Sometimes they like men, sometimes they like animals. Once they put a spear in his hand and walk around him and he was the chief. . . . Sometimes they try to make the image out of wood."[45] This oral fragment records the continuity of African talents for sculpture that are generally presumed to have been lost in the New World. It is evident from this remembrance that sculpture did not disappear from the cultural repertoire of African slaves. Moreover, some sensitivity for wood carving was passed on to subsequent generations of Afro-Americans.

The most common Black sculptural form is the carved walking stick. From the middle of the nineteenth century up to the present there have been Afro-American carvers of decorated canes.[46] A common characteristic of those works is a preference for reptile motifs: snakes, lizards, turtles, and alligators. Other African traits codified by Thompson are monochromy; smooth, luminous surfaces; and mixed media.[47] Within such general stylistic constraints, there is a wide variety of personal expression. Some canes are slender with incised carving, while others, such as those made by Howard Miller of Dixie, Georgia, have figures rendered in full relief. One of the better-known Afro-American carvers is William Rogers of Darien, Georgia. Among the several different types of carving created by him are walking sticks, animal figures, and utilitarian items. In each case the style of carving is bold. Rogers characteristically employed beads to mark the eyes of human and animal figures. His canes would never be mistaken for those of Howard Miller, even though both carvers are from Georgia, they worked in the same period, and they used the alligator motif. The Afro-Georgian carving tradition allowed freedom of expression within a general set of formal criteria.

Black wood carving was not limited to Georgia alone. Recently, Black carvers have been found in Mississippi whose work strongly echoes the

Figure 1.15.   Henry Gudgell, Walking Stick, Livingston County, Mo., ca. 1863
Wood; L. 36¼".
(Yale University Art Gallery)

Georgia canes both in style and content. Leon Rucker, for example, decorates his canes with snakes and lizards (among other motifs) and marks their eyes with brass studs.[48] Another Mississippi carver is Lester Willis, whose repertoire appears to be quite varied. Some of his canes have only the owner's name incised on them, others have quotations from Scripture, and others are topped with carved figures of men with top hats and the like. Willis said of carving: "In 1933 when the panic was on, most everybody in the community was on welfare, you know, and the bucket brigade; but I kept the wolf away from my door with walking sticks and that's the truth."[49] Sculpture for him was a mode of artistic expression and a means of earning a livelihood.

The most spectacular of all the known Afro-American canes is one that was carved in Livingston County in north central Missouri. It was here that Henry Gudgell, born a slave in Kentucky in 1826, made an extensively decorated cane for one John Bryan in 1867.[50] Gudgell was known as a blacksmith, wheelwright, coppersmith, and silversmith, and so it comes as no surprise that he was adept at sculpture as well (fig. 1.15). His walking stick can be separated into two sections by differences in the selection of motifs. The handle section has, first, a five-inch section of serpentine fluting above a smaller section of the same curvilinear decoration bracketed by plain bands. This portion of the cane is followed by two raised rings, a band of raised diamond forms, and two final encircling rings. These geometric motifs, which cover about a fourth of the cane, are followed by a series of naturalistic figures. These are expertly described by Thompson:

At the top appear a lizard and a tortoise, both carved as if seen from above. The figure of a man appears below. He is dressed in shirt, trousers and shoes. His knees are bent and the arms are extended as if the figure were embracing the shaft of the cane. On the opposite side of the cane below the hands of the figure is a bent branch from which sprouts a single veined leaf. The fork of the branch mirrors the blending of the knees of the human figure. The lower register of the cane is embellished with an entwined serpent, an echo of the serpentine coil of the handle.[51]

A cane so African in character seems out of place in Missouri. It would have made more sense for this cane to have been carved in Georgia. Yet when we consider the movement of the tradition for carved walking sticks from Georgia to Mississippi, the source of inspiration for this north Missouri walking stick becomes clear. The Mississippi and Missouri rivers served as a route over which Black culture traits were carried northward and westward from the Deep South. Henry Gudgell's walking stick represents the furthest penetration of the Black cane-carving tradition in the United States.

A very ornate wooden throne has recently been discovered and linked to a Black Presbyterian church in Victoria, Texas. What function this massive chair served is still uncertain, but it is clear that it is a very special item. Carved from one piece of wood, the chair has four legs and a high back with a solid splat, and it stands on a ponderous turtle. Also riding on the back of this amphibian pedestal are a pair of full-maned lions rendered in profile and two bears carved as if seen from above. The legs of the chair have male and female figures incised in then, and the crest rail of the chair back is decorated with two large rose blossoms. On the rear of the splat, carved in high relief, is a small tableau that appears to represent a judge perched on his bench flanked by facing figures. This wonderous assemblage of human, animal, and floral motifs stands three feet tall and is very reminiscent of a mysterious Afro-American throne and altar made by James Hampton of Washington, D.C.[52] Hampton's work was apparently motivated by a particularly idiosyncratic theology; the Victoria throne seems to share the same sense of purpose. If nothing else, we can at least acknowledge a vivid imagination inspired by religious fervor. It would be farfetched to attempt comparisons between this piece and the massive thrones of the Tikar of Cameroon or the highly figured chairs of the Chokwe of Zaire, without knowing more about the aesthetic influences that affected the carver. Until more is known we can only identify this throne as Afro-American by virtue of its use and some of its stylistic elements. Whoever made this chair was saying more about himself than about his community. Such carvings may indicate a departure from tradition, a departure that after two hundred years is to be expected. Nevertheless, it should be abundantly clear that remarks about the absence of Black wood carving are premature.

Figure 1.16.   Black Graveyard, Sea Islands, S.C., 1933
(Library of Congress)

Grave Decoration

A white plantation mistress in 1850 noted that: "Negro graves were always decorated with the last article used by the departed, and broken pitchers and broken bits of colored glass were considered more appropriate than the white shells from the beach nearby. Sometimes they carved rude wooden figures like images of idols, and sometimes a patchwork quilt was laid upon the grave."[53] This decorative practice (perhaps it would be better to say religious practice) survives with great tenacity throughout Afro-America today. Graves of Blacks in South Carolina, for example, are covered with glassware, enameled metal containers, and seashells (fig. 1.16). Pitchers with the bottoms broken out are commonly set atop graves. The range of materials used to ornament gravesites is enormous. The following list is not exhaustive: cups, saucers, bowls, clocks, salt and pepper shakers, oyster shells, toys, bric-a-brac statues, light bulbs, flashlights, gunlocks, bits of plaster, mirrors.[54] Some unwary archaeologists

Figure 1.17.   Rendering of Congo Chieftain's Grave
(From E. J. Glave, "Fetishism in Congo Land," Century
Magazine *41 [1891]: 827)*

who have surveyed Black graveyards report that they appear to contain
nothing more than "late period garbage of no interest."[55] Far from being
garbage, these heaps of objects are offerings or sanctified testimonies; they
are the material messages of the living intended to placate the potential
fury of the deceased.

The precedents for this type of burial decoration are to be found in
African practices. Two cases will illustrate this fact. In 1891, E. J. Glave,
speaking of his travels through Zaire, wrote, "Natives mark the final resting-
places of their friends by ornamenting their graves with crockery, empty
bottles, old cooking pots, etc., etc., all of which are rendered useless by
being cracked or penetrated with holes."[56] His illustration of a Congo
chief's grave would not be out of place in central Alabama (fig. 1.17). The
same funeral custom occurs in Gabon. In 1904, missionary Robert Hamill
Nassau reported that

> Over or near the graves of the rich are built little huts, where are laid the common
> articles used by them in their life—pieces of crockery, knives, sometimes a table, mirrors,
> and other goods obtained in foreign trade. Once, in ascending the Ogwe [River], I ob-

served tied to the branches of a large tree extending over the stream from the top of the bank, a wooden trade-chest, five pitchers and mugs, several fathoms of calico prints. I was informed that the grave of a lately deceased chief was near.[57]

Practices such as these are still being stringently observed today.[58] We must try to understand the Afro-American extension of this tradition within the context of folk belief regarding death and the world of the spirits. Sarah Washington of Eulonia, Georgia, commented, "I don't guess you be bother much by the spirits if you give 'em a good funeral and put the things what belong to 'em on top of the grave." Her husband Ben seconded her opinion: "You puts all the things what they use last like the dishes and the medicine bottle. The spirits need these same as the man. Then the spirit rest and don't wander about."[59] Similar statements have also been collected in Mississippi, where it was reported that the cup and saucer used in the last illness, if placed on the grave, would keep the deceased from coming back.[60] An Alabama resident is recorded as saying, "Unless you bury a person's things with him, he will come back after them."[61] The existence of returning spirits is thus widely acknowledged in Afro-American folk belief. Their ability to return was clear to Jane Lewis of Darien, Georgia: "We take what victuals left and put it in a dish by the chimley and that's for the spirit to have a last good meal. We cover up the dish and there's many a time I hear the spirit lift 'em."[62] More recently, in South Carolina, a Black woman said that, after several sleepless nights following her daughter's funeral, the girl appeared in a dream and told her that she needed her hand lotion. The woman hurriedly placed the item on the grave, thereby putting an end to her insomnia.[63] The demands of the dead lead the living to follow a distinctive mode of grave decoration.

Many contemporary burials are marked with homemade headstones made of concrete. Apparently they are attempts to imitate the tablet forms made by professional stonecutters. Even in the imitation of a popular item, a folk element still emerges. Most concrete markers have a piece of broken glass inset in them with a piece of white paper set behind them. Grave goods are normally white—be they seashell, plaster, light bulb, or ceramic container. The preference for white might be traced to Bakongo belief that their deceased ancestors were white in color; therefore, white was the color of death.[64] Second, most grave decorations are broken to show that a life has ended.[65] Thus, the broken glass and the white color are symbolic elements which could have central significance in the Afro-American folk belief system. These elements are combined with a form well known in American culture as a marker of death. The result is an expression that is ostensibly American but that also allows for the maintenance of African concepts of death.

Figure 1.18.   Cyrus Bowens, Graveyard Sculptures, Sunbury, Ga., ca. 1920
Wood; H. (approx.) 13'.
(Photo: Malcolm and Muriel Bell, 1939)

Wooden markers are also used in Black graveyards. One slab of wood will mark the head, while a notched stake will indicate the foot of the grave. Often the head marker will be cut out in the vague form of a human body, representing the outline of the head, neck, shoulders, and torso. These markers are appropriate icons of lost human life. They give the vague shape of the body but no details. When bleached by the sun, these markers appear almost cadaverous. The most unusual wooden gravemarkers were made by Cyrus Bowens of Sunbury, Georgia, around 1920 (fig. 1.18). Of his masterwork only the center piece remains. Now badly deteriorated, it once was a simple spherical head resting on a pole that had the name Bowens carved in capital letters. It could be considered a three-dimensional version of the more common wooden slab marker. The two flanking pieces were much more elaborate. One apparently represented a snake, while the other assemblage was an impressive vertical construction reaching almost thirteen feet into the air. Another part of this cluster of sculptures was a curving bracket from which was hung a sign bearing the names of the deceased members of the Bowens family. From all of Bowens's pieces, we sense that he considered sweeping curves to be creative forms. It is tempting to recall the dominance of reptile forms in Afro-American wood carving and to view Bowens's work as another instance of the snake motif. Bowens died in 1966 before anyone thought to ask him about his work. It is clear, however, that for Bowens the world of the dead was a world of wonderous forms, perhaps a world of awe.

Conclusion

Having surveyed eight forms of traditional Afro-American art and craft, we can assert that previous assessments have underrated the survival of African material culture in the United States. Even Herskovits saw the technology and art of North American Blacks as lacking any trace of African custom.[66] His negative evaluation was probably due to a lack of historical depth in the materials that he analyzed. The older examples of Black art and craft, those produced by people who were either born in Africa or who must have known African-born slaves, are in every instance much influenced by African practices. In some cases, such as basketry, musical instruments, and grave decoration, the customs survive with great purity despite the addition of new ideas to the traditional repertoire. What seems to happen most often is that an African concept is combined with an Anglo-American one, as in the case of quilting, pottery, boatbuilding, blacksmithing, or cane carving. In these creative forms of expression, the African influences are concentrated in the area of design and decoration, while the materials, the technology, and the concept of genre are seemingly Western. Through a process identified by anthropologists as "syncretism," those elements of two diverse cultures that are most similar are interwoven to create a new entity, a cultural hybrid. The artifact resulting from this process of synthesis will simultaneously be interpreted by both groups in their own terms.

Afro-American walking sticks resemble canes made by white carvers, but they also repeat motifs found in African authority staffs. Black quilts seem "crazy" or sloppy to white observers, while to their makers they are the commonplace "string" or "patchy" designs. Nineteenth-century stoneware face vessels from South Carolina are often labeled grotesque jugs, although, for their Black makers, they may have served as ritualistic objects. Afro-American cemeteries look like junkyards to Whites, while Blacks consider their practices crucial for their spiritual well-being. Hence, we must be on our guard against ethnocentrism in our analysis of Black art and craft. Much of it appears to be tied to Euro-American patterns, and, certainly, Western influences cannot be discounted. Nevertheless, if we fail to understand that there is a Black history behind Black artifacts, we risk missing the essence of Afro-American creativity. The things that look white are largely the result of reinterpretation, not imitation.

Afro-American artifacts fall into two major categories: the retained African artifact (comparatively rare) and the hybrid artifact (very common). The retentions carry us back to a time when Africans first arrived on the shores of America. The hybrid objects tells the tale of survival in a creolized culture. A minority people in the midst of a hostile alien population, they used indirect strategies to maintain their sense of social integrity. They bent or adjusted the concepts of the majority culture to serve their own ends. The role-playing, punning, satire, and subterfuge, historically noted among American Blacks, are indications of a dual mind-set that solved the problem of maintaining a strong sense of self when, socially, their existence was held in low regard.[67] Ralph Ellison has referred to this condition of mind as a "complex double vision, a fluid ambivalent response to men and events, which represents at its finest, a profoundly civilized adjustment to the cost of being human in this modern world."[68] The examples of Afro-American folk art and craft surveyed here are concrete expressions of the Black response to the New World. That response was to build upon their own sense of history and forge a new order in which they might take pride in their accomplishments—although white society often ignores or claims these achievements for itself.

Notes

1. *A Nation of Nations,* exhibition catalogue, ed. Peter C. Marzio (New York: Harper & Row, 1976). The title appears to be derived from Walt Whitman's epithet "a teeming nation of nations."

2. Melville J. Herskovits, *The Myth of the Negro Past* (1941; reprint ed., Boston: Beacon Press, 1958).

3. See Alan Lomax, *Folksong Style and Culture* (Washington, D.C.: American Association for the Advancement of Science, 1968), 92; Joanne Wheeler Kealiinohomoku, "A Comparative Study of Dance as a Constellation of Motor Behaviors among African and United States Negroes" (M.A. thesis, Northwestern University, 1965); Daniel J. Crowley, *I Could Talk Old-Story Good: Creativity in Bahamian Folklore* (Berkeley: University of California Press, 1966), 40–44.

4. Herskovits, *Myth of the Negro Past,* 136–37.

5. Peter H. Wood, " 'It Was a Negro Taught Them': A New Look at Labor in Early South Carolina," *Journal of Asian and African Studies* 9 (1974): 159–79.

6. Henry Glassie, *Pattern in the Material Folk Culture of the Eastern United States* (Philadelphia: University of Pennsylvania Press, 1968), 115.

7. Duncan Clinch Heywood, *Seed from Madagascar* (Chapel Hill: University of North Carolina Press, 1937).

8. Wood, " 'It Was a Negro Taught Them,' " 172.

9. Much of this account of Sea Islands coil basketry is derived from personal communication with Gregory Day, who spent five years researching the careers of black basket sewers in Mount Pleasant. See also Gerald L. Davis, "Afro-American Coil Basketry in Charleston County, South Carolina: Affective Characteristics of an Artistic Craft in Social Context," in *American Folklife,* Don Yoder, ed. (Austin: University of Texas Press, 1976), 151–84.

10. Rossa Belle Cooley, *Homes of the Freed* (1926; reprint ed., New York: Negro Universities Press, 1970), 144; Elsie Clews Parsons, *Folk-Lore of the Sea Islands, South Carolina,* Memoirs of the American Folk-lore Society 10 (1923): 208; *Drums and Shadows: Survival Studies among the Georgia Coastal Negroes,* Georgia Writers Project (Athens: University of Georgia Press, 1940), 52.

11. On display at the Smithsonian Institution, Museum of History and Technology in an exhibit entitled "A Nation of Nations."

12. Peter Wood, *Black Majority: Negroes in Colonial South Carolina from 1670 through the Stono Rebellion* (New York: W. W. Norton, 1974), 61–62.

13. Harold Courlander, *Negro Folk Music: U.S.A.* (New York: Columbia University Press, 1963), 116–17; Day to author, February 1976.

14. Herskovits, *Myth of the Negro Past,* 142.

15. William D. Pierson, "Puttin' Down Old Massa: African Satire in the New World," in *African Folklore in the New World,* Daniel J. Crowley, ed. (Austin: University of Texas Press, 1977), 20–34.

16. *Drums and Shadows,* 52.

17. Benjamin H. B. Latrobe, *Impressions Respecting New Orleans,* Samuel Wilson, Jr., ed. (New York: Columbia University Press, 1951), 51.

18. C. Malcolm Watkins, "A Plantation of Differences—People from Everywhere," in *A Nation of Nations,* 74.

19. For a history of the banjo, see Dena J. Epstein, "The Folk Banjo: A Documentary History," *Ethnomusicology* 20 (1976): 347–71.

20. Norman Yetman, *Life under the "Peculiar Institution": Selections from the Slave Narrative Collection* (New York: Holt, Rinehart, and Winston, 1970), 167.

21. Adrienne Koch and William Peden, eds., *The Life and Selected Writings of Thomas Jefferson* (New York: Modern Library, 1944), 258.

22. Carl Bridenbaugh, *The Colonial Craftsman* (1950; reprint ed., Chicago: University of Chicago Press, 1961), 18.

23. Watkins, "A Plantation of Differences," 77.

24. *Made of Iron* (Houston, Tex.: University of St. Thomas Art Department, 1966), 107.

25. See Robert Goldwater, *Bambara Sculpture from the Western Sudan* (New York: University Publishers, 1960), 52, pl. 88.

26. Philip D. Curtin, *The Atlantic Slave Trade: A Census* (Madison: University of Wisconsin Press, 1969), 157.

27. Gerald W. Mullin, *Flight and Rebellion: Slave Resistance in Eighteenth-Century Virginia* (New York: Oxford University Press, 1972), 44–45, 173.

28. Herbert Aptheker, *American Negro Slave Revolts* (New York: Columbia University Press, 1943), 192–95.

29. Marcus Christian, *Negro Ironworkers of Louisiana, 1718–1900* (Gretna, La.: Pelican Publishing, 1972), 17.

30. Mary Willia Shuey, "Charleston 'Signed' Ironwork," *The Reading Puddle Ball* 4, no. 1 (1935): 5.

31. Interview with Philip Simmons, June 30, 1976.

32. Quoted in M. V. Brewington, *Chesapeake Bay Log Canoes and Bugeyes* (Cambridge, Md.: Cornell Maritime Press, 1963), 4.

33. Quoted in Wood, *Black Majority,* 203.

34. Brewington, *Chesapeake Bay Log Canoes and Bugeyes,* 31 n. 21.

35. Richard Price, "Caribbean Fishing and Fisherman: A Historical Sketch," *American Anthropologist* 68 (1966):1363–83.

36. For a history of Edgefield pottery, see Stephen T. Ferrell and T. M. Ferrell, *Early Decorated Stoneware of the Edgefield District, South Carolina,* exhibition catalogue (Greenville, S.C.: Greenville County Museum of Art, 1976).

37. Robert Farris Thompson, "African Influences on the Art of the United States," *Black Studies in the University,* Armstead L. Robinson, Craig C. Foster, and Donald H. Ogilvie, eds. (New Haven: Yale University Press, 1969), 139–40.

38. Thompson, "African Influences," 145–46.

39. Jerome Handler, "Pottery Making in Rural Barbados," *Southwestern Journal of Anthropology* 19 (1963): 321–22.

40. E. A. Barber, *The Pottery and Porcelain of the United States* (1893; reprint ed., New York: Feingold & Lewis, 1976), 466.

41. Roy Sieber to author, April 1977.

42. For a more complete history of the works of Harriet Powers, see Gladys-Marie Fry, "Harriet Powers: Portrait of a Black Quilter," in *Missing Pieces: Georgia Folk Art, 1770–1976,* exhibition catalogue, Anna Wadsworth, ed. (Atlanta: Georgia Council for the Arts and Humanities, 1976), 16–23.

43. Melville J. Herskovits, *Dahomey: An Ancient West African Kingdom,* 2 vols. (New York: J. J. Augustin, 1938), 1: frontispiece, pls. 7, 15, 33, 34, 39; 2: 328–43, pls. 51, 52, 67, 69, 84, 86–89.

44. Roy Sieber, *African Textile and Decorative Arts* (New York: Museum of Modern Art, 1972), 181, 191–92.

45. *Drums and Shadows,* 106.

46. Thompson, "African Influences," 150–55.

47. Ibid., 163–66.

48. Worth Long, "Leon Rucker: Woodcarver," in *Black People and Their Culture,* Linn Shapiro, ed. (Washington, D.C.: Smithsonian Institution, 1976), 33–34.

49. Quoted from William R. Ferris, Jr., *Made in Mississippi,* 22 min., 16 mm., color film, Center for Southern Folklore, Memphis, Tennessee.

50. Thompson, "African Influences," 133.

51. Ibid., 135.

52. Elinor Lander Horowitz, *Contemporary American Folk Artists* (New York: J. B. Lippincott, 1975), 127–32; Lynda Roscoe, "James Hampton's Throne," in *Naives and Visionaries,* exhibition catalogue (Minneapolis: Walker Art Center, 1974), 13–20.

53. Quoted in John W. Blassingame, *The Slave Community: Plantation Life in the Antebellum South* (New York: Oxford University Press, 1972), 37.

54. H. Carrington Bolton, "Decoration of Negro Graves in South Carolina," *Journal of American Folklore* 4 (1891): 214; Ernest Ingersoll, "Decoration of Negro Graves," *Journal of American Folklore* 5 (1892): 68–69; Henry C. Davis, "Negro Folklore in South Carolina," *Journal of American Folklore* 27 (1914): 248; Lydia Parrish, *Slave Songs of the Georgia Sea Islands* (1942; reprint ed., Hatboro, Pa.: Folklore Associates, 1965), 31; Margaret Davis Cate, *Early Days of Coastal Georgia* (St. Simons Island, Ga.: Fort Frederica Assn., 1955), 207–15.

55. John D. Combes, "Ethnography, Archaeology, and Burial Practices among Coastal South Carolina Blacks," *Conference on Historic Site Archaeology Papers,* vol. 7 (Columbia, S.C.: Institute of Archaeology and Anthropology, 1972), 52.

56. E. J. Glave, "Fetishism in Congo Land," *Century Magazine* 41 (1891): 825.

57. Robert Hamill Nassau, *Fetishism in West Africa* (London: Duckworth, 1904), 232.

58. Andre Raponde-Walker and Roger Sillens, *Rites et croyances des peuples du Gabon* (Paris: Présence Africaine, 1962), 107.

59. *Drums and Shadows,* 136.

60. Newbell Niles Puckett, *The Magic and Folk Beliefs of the Southern Negro* (1926; reprint ed., New York: Dover, 1969), 104.

61. Puckett, *Magic and Folk Beliefs,* 103.

62. *Drums and Shadows,* 147.

63. Combes, "Burial Practices among Coastal South Carolina Blacks," 58.

64. Georges Balandier, *Daily Life in the Kingdom of Kongo from the Sixteenth Century to the Eighteenth Century* (New York: Pantheon Books, 1975), 251–52.

65. *Drums and Shadows,* 130–31.

66. Melville J. Herskovits, "Problem, Method and Theory in Afro-American Studies," in *The New World Negro,* Frances S. Herskovits, ed. (Bloomington: Indiana University Press, 1966), 53.

67. Pierson, "Puttin' Down Old Massa," 20–34; Eugene Genovese, *Roll Jordan Roll: The World the Slaves Made* (New York: Pantheon Books, 1974), 599–612; Blassingame, *The Slave Community,* 132–53.

68. Ralph Ellison, *Shadow and Act* (New York: Vintage, 1972), 131–32.

2

Afro-American Domestic Artifacts in Eighteenth-Century Virginia

Major cultural shifts generally prove difficult to explain since the ideological bases of culture change that lie beneath the observable surface of events can only be grasped through inferential methods. Only rarely has a person experiencing cultural transition been moved to identify and articulate its causes and meanings, and such articulation has frequently been colored by judgment that is unavoidably subjective. There are other kinds of evidence, though, that seem relatively free from the taint of personal bias: the dry, callous, and insensitive statistics of time and place—the bills of sale, the day books, the wills, the registers of births and deaths. These records, originally intended as incidental accompaniments to other events, become "witnesses in spite of themselves."[1] Although coiled passively on the page, statistics can be made to spring forward to give testimony. The artifact, too, is like the silent cipher that companions real experience. Beginning with such contextual elements—things and words and numbers—one can reach backwards from fact to event to cause.

Indeed, this may be the only way to come into contact with Black life in eighteenth-century Virginia. Since no slaves from the period are known to have written about their captivity and servitude, we are forced to reconstruct a narrative out of odd fragments of the slave experience. But dusty records and dusty objects, when studied with care and patience, can help to explain the cultural transformation that changed Africans into Afro-Americans. What follows is an attempt to describe the material aspects of the domestic routine of the eighteenth-century slave in Virginia and to suggest, more broadly, what that experience reveals about Black culture during the period.

While generally referring to Virginia, I will target Sabine Hall, a plantation in Richmond County owned by Landon Carter. Sabine Hall con-

This article originally appeared in *Material Culture* 19 (1987): 3–23. Reprinted by permission of the Pioneer America Society.

sisted of several thousand acres divided into five separate quarters in addition to the "home fields" adjacent to Carter's massive brick mansion. This dwelling, built in 1740, featured a center-passage double-pile plan and a seven-bay Palladian facade decorated with elaborate stonework. Set amid formal gardens, the house was sited on high ground and overlooked a series of terraces leading down to the Rappahanock River some three miles away.[2] While Carter, like his contemporaries, concentrated on raising tobacco, he also devoted portions of his fields to livestock, wheat, barley, corn, and cotton. Carter's extensive diaries, kept from 1752 to 1778, provide significant detail on the conduct of eighteenth-century Tidewater plantation life, including glimpses into the woodlands, fields, barns, and houses where he kept his almost 200 slaves.[3] Data from other plantations situated along the Rappahanock River and in the Northern Neck of Virginia will be used to supplement the portrait derived from Carter's account of Sabine Hall. Information concerning plantation conduct in southern Maryland and the Virginia Piedmont, when relevant, will be used to help determine the regional peculiarities of slave life in the Virginia Tidewater.

Slave Artifacts: An Inventory of Common Objects

The quarters, those tracts of land upon which slave dwellings were located, were filled with various classes of artifacts—tools for working, equipment for maintaining a household, and items of clothing. Of these three classes, clothing was perhaps the most essential to a slave's sense of identity since it was his most permanent and personal possession. Throughout Landon Carter's diaries various passing statements are made concerning the clothing of his slaves. For example, on May 15, 1776, when he distributed cotton cloth so that his slaves might begin to make their summer clothes, he wrote: "My house wenches rec[eived] 4 yards each and 2 yards each waist coat." He also mentioned breeches, shirts, shifts, and petticoats as standard items of slave apparel. Some of the cloth used was purchased from local merchants as the November 15, 1770 entry records: "Lucy [his daughter] goes there to buy the 6 pieces more, 2 pieces of Oznabrig and some coarse thread."[4] But Carter, wanting to make his plantation more independent and profitable, was constantly increasing his own production of cloth. In 1777 he hired a white weaver named Stoughton to produce linen from the flax grown at Sabine Hall. It was then that his right-hand man, a slave named Nassau, informed him that "not one bit of the lint is wasted."[5]

By this time slaves were also using spinning wheels.[6] Previously Carter had set some of his slaves to making cotton cloth although they did not always achieve the production levels he desired. "My spinners," he wrote in 1770, "imagining I was gone yesterday instead of their usual day's work spun but two ounces a piece."[7] The inventory of Carter's estate mentions a special building called the "weaving manufactory" in which were kept two looms, one cotton gin, four flax wheels, five great wheels, five pairs of wood cards and one coarse hackle.[8] Carter is not explicit about the specific articles of dress made with this fiber and equipment, referring only to "men's suits," "women's suits," and "boy's suits." He is, however, definite about slave-made "stockings" of which he observed that 333,000 stitches were required per pair.[9]

Further details about the specifics of slave clothing must be gathered from other sources. While accounts of slave dress are minimal, Joseph Ball, the master of Morattico, a plantation located downriver from Sabine Hall, was very precise concerning slave clothing. In a letter of instruction written in February 1743 to his nephew, Joseph Chinn, he identified types of cloth, criteria for tailoring and local customs for seasonal dress:

> And every one of the workers must have a good suit of Welch plaiding made as it should be, not too scanty nor bobtailed. And each must have two shirts or shifts of the Oznabrig. And each of the children must have a coat of the worser cotton or plaiding of Virginia cloth and have two shirts or shifts of Oznabrig and workers must each of them have summer suits of the brown rolls. And all the workers must have good strong shoes and stockings and they that go after the creatures, or muck in the wet must have two pair of shoes. Bess, Winny, Nan, Hannah, and Frank must have their shifts and linen petticoats and their children linnen cut out, and thread and needles given them, and they must make them themselves, and they must not become too scanty, nor bobtailed. Therefore the folks must have their linen made by somebody that will make it as it should be. An you must get a Taylor to make the woolen cloths strong and well. And all should be done in good time, and not for winter to be half over before they get their winter cloths, summer to be half over before they get their summer cloths, as the common Virginia fashion is.[10]

What the foregoing indicates is that not only did slaves make their own clothing, but that they may have had two sets. That slaves were given light cotton for summer wear and heavier wool or Oznabrig cloth for winter implies that each slave could possibly have had as many as four changes of clothes in all. Considering that a slave cabin had from eight to fifteen occupants, the amount of clothing stored may have required a chest or box to hold it.[11] At the very least, clothing not being worn was likely to be hung on nails driven into the walls or piled in the corners.

The basic costume for slave men consisted of shirt, pants, stockings, and shoes, and for women a long shift and an over blouse. Thomas Anburey, an eighteenth-century visitor to Virginia, described slave clothing as "consisting of a shirt and trousers of coarse, thin, hard, hempen stuff, in the summer, with an addition of a very course woolen jacket, breeches and shoes in winter."[12] No doubt they had also such other apparel items as hats, coats, vests, shawls, kerchiefs, and belts. But these more elaborate items may have been received from masters rather than having been made by the slaves themselves. Joseph Ball noted in a letter accompanying a supply of tools he was shipping from England: "I have also sent some of my old Cloathes for my Negroes and also some baby things for the Negro children." An earlier load of hardware included instructions that Poor Will was to receive the "grey coat" and Mingo to get the "stiff shirt,"[13] indicating that while slaves were generally simply dressed, they were also able to obtain items of finery as hand-me-downs.

The diversity of the slave experience is reflected in dress and other personal items. Field slaves had minimum clothing and furnishings, while slaves employed as house servants were equipped with better quality items. Nassau, Landon Carter's personal servant, owned "a set of raisors which he had purchased" in addition to a large wardrobe which probably included a livery suit and a silver-laced livery hat.[14] Aron Jameson, the favored slave of Joseph Ball, was sent from England to Morattico with "Three Such of Wearing cloths (one New) and two pair of new shoes; and several pair of stockings, a pair of boots, and twelve shirts, eight of which are new . . . three hats, twelve neckcloths, two handkerchiefs,"[15] certain to set him apart from the field slaves he was to join within the year. Until he divested himself of his "surplus" clothing, it is difficult to imagine his complete entry and acceptance into the slave community. His clothing, by quantity alone, would have marked him as different.

Along with clothing, food was an obviously vital slave possession. The slave diet consisted mainly of corn prepared in about four or five ways. Landon Carter's diary has hundreds of entries describing the planting, growing, harvesting, storage, and consumption of corn. Eighteenth-century traveler J. F. D. Smyth characterized the slave regimen as work punctuated by brief respites when some corn product was eaten.

> He [the slave] is called up in the morning at day break, and is seldom allowed time enough to swallow three mouthfuls of homminy, or hoe-cake, but is driven out immediately to the field to hard labor. . . . About noon he eats his dinner and he is seldom allowed an hour for that purpose. His meal consists of homminy and salt, and if his master be a man of humanity, he has a little fat, skimmed milk, rusty bacon, or salt herring to relish his homminy or hoe-cake. . . . They then return to severe labour which continues in the field until dusk. . . . It is late at night before he returns to his second scanty meal.[16]

Half a century earlier William Hugh Grove similarly observed: "[Corn.] Tis the only support of the Negroes, who Roast it in the ear, Bake it for Bread, Boyl it when Hulled, Like our Buttered Wheat, the children and better sort breakfast with it and make farmity. The first they call Homeny, the Latter Mush. To Hull it they Beat it in a Mortar as the Scots do their Barley.''[17] The connection between corn and slave life was thus close and constant.

Focusing on the slave diet also requires focusing on the kinds of implements necessary for preparation, many of which can be precisely listed since they were recorded in the inventories of probated estates. A skewer, spit, or sharpened stick was required to roast an ear of corn. A pot was needed to boil the corn and to make ground or pounded corn meal mush. Corn meal was baked in a covered pot or pan into corn bread. Grove noted that slaves made their own meal, suggesting that a slave kitchen was not complete without a grinding or pounding apparatus. Finally, plates or bowls were needed to serve the various corn dishes, with all members of the household probably taking their portion from a communal container. This, at least, is the recollection of food habits recorded from ex-slaves born in the 1840s and 1850s.[18] A minimal diet required only minimal equipment.

Cups or mugs were required for beverages. One drink commonly consumed was hard liquor, usually rum. Slaves were allowed so much liquor that they frequently turned up sick for work in the morning. Landon Carter repeatedly chastised his slaves for being drunk, particularly his servant Nassau, whose punishment he hoped would strongly impress the others. On February 26, 1770, he wrote: "Began this morning to enforce my resolution of correcting the drunkeness in my family [of slaves] by an example on Nassau."[19] To Carter's dismay his overseers were abetting alcoholism by trading rum for chickens in a custom known as the "night shop."[20] Setting aside the social and health problems that alcohol created for a people often desperate for even mental escape, either bottles or jugs were certainly present in the quarters at Sabine Hall. These containers were large enough to fuel an evening's drink and would have been protected as important items.

Landon Carter's diary is silent on matters regarding food preparation by his slaves. Indeed, there are few contemporary descriptions of eighteenth-century slave cooking. However, much can be determined from the implements recorded in probate inventories. In 1701, Ralph Wormley's plantation, located along the southern shore of the Rappahanock in Middlesex County, was described along with its eight quarters. The enumeration of taxable items at the quarters was:

At Pine Quarter—
    1 iron pot, hook, 2 pestells
At Loghouse Quarter—
    2 iron pots, 1 pr. pot hoods & 1 pestell
    1 grindstone

At Quarter over the Creek—
   3 old iron pots, 3 pr. pot hooks
   2 pestells, 2 grindstones
At Flemings Quarter—
   1 iron pot, 2 small pestells
At Robinsons Quarter—
   1 small feather bed, 1 rugg, 1 pr. blankets
   1 Rugg, 1 iron pot and hookes, 1 do. & c. [iron pot & hooks]
   2 iron pestells
At Quarter called Whitakers—
   1 iron pestell, 1 broken iron pot, 1 iron pot & hookes
At New Quarter—
   1 iron pot, hookes and
   pestell, 1 iron pot & pestell
At Black Walnut Quarter—
   large grindstone,, 1 pr. Quirne Stones[21]

Certainly there were more items at these quarters than those listed. What was regarded as important by assessors was metal and, consequently, they looked mainly into the fireplace. There, in nearly all cases, they found iron pots hanging from metal hooks over the flames (fig. 2.1). Near the hearth was a grindstone and a pestle—probably also made of iron to be used with a wooden mortar or an iron pot. These latter items were used to process corn, the pots to cook it—all that was needed to prepare a major portion of the slave diet. Unfortunately, the inventory of Sabine Hall did not include summaries of quarter items. However, the inventory survey I conducted of twenty-three eighteenth-century plantations in the vicinity of Sabine Hall indicates that iron pots were the most common cooking utensil reported for slave dwellings. There is little doubt that Landon Carter's slaves had these same iron pots, varying in size from one to five gallons. While other vessels—gourds and earthenware pots—were also likely to have been used to prepare and serve meals, inventories and other written accounts make no mention of them. However, since musical instruments used by slaves were fashioned from gourds, it may be surmised that dippers, spoons, cups, and bowls were made from them as well.

Rhys Isaac observed that in addition to corn the slave diet included potatoes, greens, fruit, and chickens raised at quarters, plus those supplies that could be extracted from granaries and storehouses.[22] Although such foods could have been boiled in a large iron pot, in about half of the twenty-three Rappahanock Valley plantations surveyed additional cooking utensils were listed, suggesting a variety in the preparation of slave food. Frying pans and skillets were commonly mentioned, along with stew pans, spits, and racks. The complete absence of andirons from inventories, though, suggests that the pots and pans not suspended over the fire on hooks were propped up over the flames on stones. Other items included

Figure 2.1.   View of the Interior of a Slave Cabin at Thornhill Plantation,
in the Vicinity of Watsonia, Alabama
While this 1934 photograph represents a nineteenth-century
slave interior from a lower southern state, it does convey a
sense of what probate records describe for Virginia a century
earlier. It is of interest to note that Thornhill was built by
Virginian James I. Thornton in 1833. Born in 1800, Thornton
would have been familiar with late eighteenth-century slave
quarters in his home state.
*(Historic American Building Survey photo courtesy of
the Library of Congress)*

pewter dishes and basins, iron pots with legs, pales, piggins, biscuit pans,
wheat sieves, pickle bottles, spoons, and fleshing forks. Although a slave
meal could be readied with only a few implements, there were instances
when a clutter of pots, pans, and accessories could be found on the hearth.

While field slaves made do with rudimentary utensils, house slaves
again appear to have been favored. Aron Jameson was given a "small iron
pot and hooks and rack to hang it on, an Iron Skillet, . . . a small spit, an
old pewter basin." Jameson's master also mentioned that he was to have
"his own Meat to himself in a Little powdering tub to be made on
purpose."[23]

The class of slave furnishings that occupied the major part of space was bedding. Although Landon Carter commented only once on slave bedding, when he requested that a slave afflicted with smallpox be given fresh straw for a bed and a warm blanket,[24] probate inventories from other plantations were more explicit: for example, at George Harday's plantation in Prince George's County in Maryland, the assessor found an "old Bed" with an "Oznabrig tick," two "strip and duffle blankets," one "old rug of Oznabrig" and "sheets and a bed cord."[25] Since the description is so elaborate, the assessor may have been listing the bedding of the overseer. Usually such items for slaves were overlooked altogether or summarized as a "parcel of Negroes old Bedding." Yet some slaves did have finer bedding, considering the context of the eighteenth century. Joseph Ball's favored slave Aron had a "Large Mattress stuffed with flocks and Stiched with tufts, and a bolster filled with feathers, the mattress and Bolster both besides their Ticks having Oznabrig Cases; and Two New Coverlets." Ball continued on to instruct his plantation manager: "I would forthwith after his arrival have one of the worst of my old Bedsteads cut short and fit for his Mattress, and have a Cord and hide to it."[26] Most slaves, however, slept on the floors of their cabins on straw or straw-filled ticks under thin blankets. Smyth wrote of slave bedding: "when he [the slave] sleeps, his comforts are equally miserable and limited; for he lies on a bench, or on the ground, with only a scanty single blanket, and not always that, to serve both as his bed and his covering."[27] Joseph Ball was explicit on the matter of slave blankets: "The coarse cotton . . . was consigned for blankets for my Negroes; there must be four yards and a half to each blanket. That they have not two blankets already that is one tolerable old one and one pretty good one, [they] must have what is wanting to make it up."[28]

Tables, chairs, stools, and benches appear to have been rare in slave dwellings. This is to be expected since even the houses of white yeomen were generally devoid of specialized sitting furniture.[29] A one-room quarter in which Smyth was forced to spend the night with seven others—a white overseer and six slaves—had "no book, no convenience, no furniture, no comfort in the house, unless you call by that name a miserable thin chaff bed, somewhat raised from the floor, in a corner of the room, which alternately served him [the overseer] for his chair, his table and his couch."[30] A similar image was conveyed by French visitor Ferdinand-Marie Bayard after inspecting a Virginia slave cabin:

> I made an inventory of the household goods of a family of slaves. A box-like frame made of boards hardly roughed down, upheld by stakes constituted the nuptial couch. Some wheat straw and corn-stalks, on which was spread a very short-napped woolen blanket that was burned in several places, completed the wretched pallet of the enslaved couple.

Bayard then described other household items: "An old pot, tilted on some pieces of brick, was still white with *Homany*. A few rags soaked in water, were hanging in one of the corners of the fireplace. An old pipe, very short and a knife blade, which were sticking in the wall were the only effects that I found in the dwelling."[31] Bayard's account seems plausible. While slaves had few possessions, they were not as few as Smyth suggests. Since generations of slaves were raised in the quarters, there was necessarily an accumulation of ragged and meager artifacts.

It should also be noted that during the eighteenth century elaborate manifestations of material success were restricted to the rich; the norm for the remainder, both Black and White, was a lean, hard existence. John Fontaine, after spending the night at a German minister's residence in the Valley of Virginia in 1715, recorded that "we found nothing to eat but lived on our small provisions and lay upon good straw. We passed the night very indifferently."[32] The condition of Virginia's yeomen had not appreciably improved some seventy years later when Johann Schoepf moved through Isle of Wight County; he found "only a few wretched cabins," and his final destination proved to be nothing more than "a draughty empty place."[33]

The implements slaves used to perform assigned tasks were often kept in their dwellings. Probate inventories record a wide assortment of tools along with the more frequently listed hoes, axes, and wedges. These three tools were considered the most useful for a "backland" quarter where, in addition to cultivation, slaves were charged with clearing land and transforming fallen trees into posts, rails, and kindling. Other tools connected with wood included froes, handsaws, cross-cut saws, draw knives, chisels, and broad axes. With such equipment slaves produced clapboards, shingles, staves, and other wooden products. Such was the case when Richard Corbin deeded to a slave carpenter named Mack "2 hand saw files, a wimble bit, 2 inch augers, a bough, 2 inch chisels, 2 inch & 1/2 do. [chisels], a drawing knife, X crow stock, a cooper's ax, 2 do. [cooper's] adzes, 1 hammer." Corbin also wrote in a letter to a neighbor: "I now send two carpenters Mack and Abram to Moses Neck to build a good barn, mend up the Quarters, and get as many staves and heading as will be sufficient for next years tob. hhds. [tobacco hosgsheads]."[34]

The tools used at Sabine Hall were listed in the estate inventory: sickles, spades, grubbing hoes, weeding hoes, hilling hoes, scythes, pitchforks, wheat cradles, whip saws, carpenter's tools, and blacksmith's tools.[35] While these tools were kept at a storehouse or in the overseer's quarters, they also turned up at the slave quarters. The 1728 inventory of William Gordon's Middlesex County plantation is instructive since his estate listed at the "Negro Quarter, one seven foot steelcut saw, one old iron pot, one

Figure 2.2.   View of Stephen Steptoe, Jr., in Front of a Log Cabin Built
by Him in 1883
Born in 1785 in Northumberland County, Virginia, Steptoe's
cultural sense was certainly shaped by eighteenth-century
precedents. The house and the material contents visible in this
1893 photograph are consistent with late eighteenth-century
period descriptions.
(Courtesy of the Library of Congress)

new do. [iron pot] 4 gall. each, one pr. iron traces with full harness, two
new collars, cart and wheels."[36] Even though tools and farm equipment
belonged to the master, that the slaves were expected to provide many
of their own provisions suggests that such tools need not be viewed as
instruments of oppression. Consider Philip Fithian's observation during
his Sunday promenade around Nomini Hall when he "saw a number of
Negroes very busy at framing together a small House."[37] The tools these
slaves used on their "day off" were probably seen positively by them as
instruments of survival.

Outwardly, the accumulation of artifacts in slave dwellings suggests
a people exploitatively cared for. Given a change of clothes, a few pots
and pans, a place to lie down and some tools to use, slaves appeared under
control. However, such domination was and is a matter of relative interpretation. The physical context and conduct of chattel slavery in
eighteenth-century Virginia incorporated opportunities for the development of a distinct Black subculture (fig. 2.2). To some degree, this cultural
alternative was promoted by the African heritage fresh in the minds of

those slaves recently imported to Virginia. African ideas and behavioral concepts became part of slave furnishings. This mental baggage encouraged either the reinterpretation of local artifacts or the creation of African objects in new surroundings.

Africa in Virginia

In the first half of the eighteenth century the Black population of Virginia had a decidedly African focus, while in the second half of the century Afro-American qualities emerged in the first generations of Virginia-born slaves.[38] The Afro-Virginian, however, was not a totally new man in that he was at least partially equipped with a distinct ethnic heritage that he did not want to abandon and that his masters were, at times, willing that he retain. As late as 1774 Nicholas Cresswell observed the playing of African-derived musical instruments—like the banjo—in Virginia:

> Sundays being the only days these poor creatures [slaves] have to themselves, they generally meet together and amuse themselves with Dancing to the Banjo. This musical instrument (if it may be so called) is made of a Gourd something in the imitation of a Guitar with only four strings and played with the fingers in the same manner. Some of them sing to it which is very droll music indeed. In their songs they generally related the usage they have received from their Masters and Mistresses in a very satirical style and manner.[39]

The songs, music, dance, and instruments served not only to create a pleasant diversion. Within the confines of the event held on the slaves' personal time, the social order of the plantation was inverted. Masters were secretly lampooned and held up to ridicule.[40] The music, rebellious in character, was an African music played on instruments with African origins. The role of instruments in slave life, however, was compounded by slave musicians also playing for Whites. Turning again to Cresswell's observations: "A great number of young people met together with a Fiddle and Banjo played by two Negros, with Plenty of Toddy, which both Men and Women seem to be very fond of. I believe they have danced and drunk till there are few sober people amongst them."[41]

In addition to stringed instruments made from gourds (fig. 2.3), Afro-Virginians also made percussion instruments, principally drums. Smyth encountered at a dance a "quaqua," which was in his words an instrument "somewhat resembling a drum" played together with a banjo.[42] Astonishingly, a Virginia slave drum with perhaps seventeenth-century origins still survives today in the collection of the British Museum. This instrument (fig. 2.4) is so clearly African in form, construction, and mode of decoration that the ethnicity of its maker can confidently be identified as Akan/Ashanti from the area of West Africa now known as Ghana.[43]

Figure 2.3. Front and Side Views of a Gourd-Bodied Fiddle, ca. Nineteenth
Century, Found in St. Mary's County, Maryland
This fiddle is of the type made and played by slaves on
eighteenth-century Virginia plantations.
*(Courtesy of the National Museum of American History,
Division of Musical Instruments)*

Figure 2.4.   Virginia Slave Drum Made during the Late
Seventeenth or Early Eighteenth Century
American cedar and deerskin head. The
form, size and markings are exactly those
of the Ashanti apentemma drum.
*(Currently housed in the British Museum.
Photo courtesy of the National Museum of
American History)*

Slave music correspondingly took the performer in three directions:
into his past, into his own community, and into the related ceremonies
of planters. Regardless of the ultimate impact of African-derived music,
there can be little question but that there were musical instruments in slave
quarters even though inventories never mentioned them. Perhaps the
assessors so thoroughly understood such instruments to be the property
of Blacks that they did not record them as part of the slave owners'
estates.[44]

The efforts of slaves to resist their enslavement has been well documented, including the elaborately planned rebellions led by Denmark Vesey, Gabriel Prosser, and Nat Turner.[45] But resistance to slavery was an ongoing process for many Blacks. The slaves' alternative sense of identity fostered a need for autonomy. Each day the profound human need for some measure of control over one's destiny was deeply felt, resulting to some extent in the slave's living a double life—one for his master's expectations and one for himself. After dark the field slave's world, in particular, took on a different character: the family unit was reassembled, meals were consumed together, inter-plantation visits were conducted, stories were told, songs were sung, and the future was planned. J. F. D. Smyth on one occasion marveled at the surplus energy slaves had once their assigned tasks were completed:

> Instead of retiring to rest, as might naturally be concluded he [the slave] would be glad to do, he generally sets out from home and walks six or seven miles in the night, be the weather ever so sultry, to a negroe dance, in which he performs with astonishing agility, and the vigourous exertions, keeping time and cadence, most exactly with the music of a banjo . . . until he exhausts himself, and scarcely has time, or strength to return home before the hour he is called forth to toil the next morning.[46]

Slaves obviously cared more for a world of their own making, however temporary, than that created by their masters. With certain African cultural elements and with expressive forms like music and dance, the anger and frustration regarding their captivity was temporarily vented as they took back ownership of self.

Landon Carter's slaves took part in the same pattern of passive resistance seen elsewhere in eighteenth-century Virginia.[47] On May 17, 1776, Carter uncovered a conspiracy long in effect among his seamstresses by which they obtained more clothing than he normally allowed: "I always thought my house wenches made the Virginian cloth given them last two years; but it seems, they have every other year as much cloth as will make them two suits, so they just as all the other Negroes have a suit every year, but the only difference is they keep every other year's suit instead of my store."[48] On another occasion he remarked: "I must declare I saw no care on my whole plantation but everybody did as they pleased, Came, Went, Slept or worked as they would."[49]

The Afro-Virginian, according to Isaac, had his own landscape. The slave, he suggests, moved along his own pathway following a set of marks indicative of "slave opportunism."[50] Those marks were often made with the artifacts discussed here. Isaac sketches the private world of slave life:

> Here would stand a corn house, perhaps,that was from time to time illicitly opened, by the loosening of boards in the gable end, to supplement the rations of hungry families. Those who could provide in this way stood tall in the quarters. . . . Such providers

might trade their loot for the much sought liquor that was so valuable for celebrations. Beyond the storehouses and granaries, but well marked in memory, were the places deep in the woods where the slaves might slaughter and barbeque the semi-wild hogs that bore on their ears and rumps the marks of a master's claim to possession. The scattering of settlement through a wooded countryside that enabled the Anglo-Virginian masters to space their property boundaries widely also allowed the counter activities of the Blacks to maintain an alternative territorial system.[51]

While appearing under the complete control of their masters, slaves surreptitiously took partial control of their own lives by establishing a sense of place, the means by which they could more readily identify their houses, clothing, food, and tools as personal belongings. For those slaves with either a personal experience of Africa or the memory of strong ancestral direction, the slave-made landscape provided the means to recapture a measure of freedom symbolized by the mother continent. A lyric in an exotic tongue, a few beats of percussion, the curved shape of a clay vessel, or the taste of hot pepper may have been enough to transform a land of servitude into the fleeting semblance of home. Such sentiments, when repeated over time, formed the basis for the distinctive Black identity in eighteenth-century Virginia.

Conclusions

Eighteenth-century Virginia presents us with a laboratory in which to observe cultural change. In the broadest sense, the colonial period is the saga of Blacks and Whites discovering ways to understand each other in the midst of stress. Local politics, economics, religion, and class structure all underwent some measure of transformation within the century. And since domestic scenarios could not be immune from such transformations, Black home life was thus significantly different in the 1790s from what it had been, say, in the 1720s. Among Whites a new philosophical order based on mechanical models and rationality was progressively imposed on Virginia society, causing the natural world to be understood as neutral and, hence, submissive to human will.[52] This worldview urged individuals to grasp personal success at every opportunity, creating a society characterized by individuality and extreme diversity. At the same time Black Virginians encountered new diversity because of increased familiarity with Whites. Slaves added newly discovered courses of action to their inherited traditions and values, and the blend of old and new resulted in the formation of a hybrid culture. This was the middle stage in the process of Black acculturation into American life.

Black Virginians had at least three models for their behavior over the course of the eighteenth century: African, Anglo-American, and Afro-

American. None of the three held absolute sway over their cultural disposition because social and demographic conditions were always shifting. To a large extent each model was employed to varying degrees in response to occasion and circumstance. At times it was appropriate to be African and at other times American. The enslaved Black could embrace such diverse acts as playing African musical instruments and speaking English, working the master's crop and tending his own garden. Hence, much of slave life was marked by ambiguity; the meaning of any action was open to varying interpretations.

Whenever a people attempts to synthesize several cultural options, an attendant period of confusion, testing, and adjustment always exists. Slaves continually endured a "betwixt and between" state of mind where one act could have simultaneously different interpretations. Although such a mental state was unsettling, it also provided options for real social power and high self-esteem. Existing between cultural orders set up the circumstances for punning satire, secret jokes, and subterfuge through which slave subservience had one meaning for Whites and quite another for Blacks. This plurality of nuances is what occurs in creolized speech when several levels of significance are conveyed in one utterance. Just as slaves spoke a creolized English so too did they develop a creolized mentality to interpret their social circumstances.[53] The Black perspective that evolved during the eighteenth century was the product of a fluid mental set capable of juggling several alternatives. Ralph Ellison would later call this capability a "complex double vision,"[54] that provided Virginia slaves with the means by which they seemed to capitulate to white demands when in fact they were changing at their own pace, a pace more suitable for the maintenance of a stable social existence.

Many of the findings of this study are speculative and cannot be otherwise. Artifacts of eighteenth-century slaves were literally consumed by processes of culture: metal tools were broken, melted down, and recast into new tools; clothing was worn to tatters; fragile household goods were broken into bits of trash; and wooden houses, given minimal maintenance, collapsed into ruins—no house of a field slave from eighteenth-century Virginia survives. We have, for the most part, only the traveler's accounts, the tax assessor's records, and the slave owner's diaries to aid us. Ideally, we should look to the artifactual record as a way to balance the inherent cultural and personal biases found in written evidence.[55] Analyzed together, the two allow a more trustworthy reconstruction of the slave's point of view.

Toward this end, we are not totally without slave artifacts. Evidence remains in the ground at various plantations awaiting archaeological investigation. To date, such research in Virginia has been targeted at seventeenth-century sites or at nineteenth-century sites located outside the Tidewater, the region most central to the formation of the Afro-Virginian community. It is hoped that the evidence of daily life presented here will encourage excavation of eighteenth-century sites of slave occupancy on Tidewater plantations. Landon Carter's Sabine Hall would seem to offer abundant possibilities based on the rich content of his diaries.

While archaeological research is painstaking and expensive, it remains necessary if we are to get "in touch" with the actuality of the slave experience. Nevertheless, it is ironic that the only means we have to reconstruct the Black experience of eighteenth-century Virginia is through the analysis of fragmented things and fragmented accounts. Thus we will never be able to dispense entirely with conjecture. Only by shrewd use of historical imagination will we be able to recreate a sensible narrative of past life. While the dangers of subjective judgment are evident, only with some measure of subjectivity can we flesh out the skeleton of minimal records and recapture the feeling of ordinary people's history. Theories of thought and behavior then become the glue with which we can patch together the "shards" of experience.

Notes

1. Marc Bloc, quoted in Gerald W. Mullin, *Flight and Rebellion: Slave Resistance in Eighteenth-Century Virginia* (New York: Oxford University Press, 1972), x.

2. Thomas T. Waterman, *The Mansions of Virginia, 1700–1776* (Chapel Hill: University of North Carolina Press, 1946), 130–36.

3. Jack P. Greene, ed., *The Diary of Colonel Landon Carter of Sabine Hall, 1752–1778*, 2 vols. (Charlottesville: University Press of Virginia, 1965).

4. Ibid., 1: 523.

5. Ibid., 2: 1128.

6. Ibid., 2: 1072.

7. Ibid., 1: 362.

8. *Inventory of the Estate of Landon Carter,* 1779. MS at the Alderman Library, University of Virginia, Charlottesville.

9. Greene, *Diary of Colonel Landon Carter,* 1: 242; 2: 1067.

10. Joseph Ball, *Joseph Ball Letterbook,* 1743–1780. MS at the Library of Congress, Washington, D.C.

11. See Mullin, *Flight and Rebellion,* 48; and Rhys Isaac, *The Transformation of Virginia, 1740–1790* (Chapel Hill: University of North Carolina Press, 1982), 306.

12. Thomas Anburey, *Travels through the Interior Parts of America* (London: W. Lane, 1789), 2: 333.

13. Ball, *Letterbook,* September 24, 1753.

14. Mullin, *Flight and Rebellion,* 78; Greene, *Diary of Colonel Landon Carter,* 1: 245.

15. Ball, *Letterbook,* April 23, 1754.

16. *A Tour of the United States of America* (London: G. Robinson, 1784), 44–45.

17. Gregory A. Stiverson and Patrick N. Butler, III, "Virginia in 1732: The Travel Journal of William High Grove," *Virginia Magazine of History and Biography* 85 (1977): 33.

18. George P. Rawick, *The American Slave: A Composite Autobiography* (Westport, Conn.: Greenwood Press, 1972), vol. 5, pt. 3: 71.

19. Greene, *Diary of Colonel Landon Carter,* 1: 363.

20. Ibid., 2: 649.

21. MSS of transcribed room-by-room inventories, Colonial Williamsburg.

22. Isaac, *Transformation of Virginia,* 45.

23. Ball, *Letterbook,* April 23, 1754.

24. Greene, *Diary of Colonel Landon Carter,* 1: 141.

25. *Inventory* GS #2, dated 1772. 257–58. Maryland Hall of Records.

26. Ball, *Letterbook,* April 23, 1754.

27. *Tour of the United States,* 46.

28. *Letterbook,* February 18, 1743.

29. Isaac, *Transformation of Virginia,* 73.

30. *Tour of the United States,* 75.

31. Ferdinand-Marie Bayard, *Travels of a Frenchman in Maryland and Virginia with a Description of Baltimore and Philadelphia,* trans. and ed. by Ben C. McCary (Williamsburg: Privately published, 1950), 13.

32. Edward Porter Alexander, ed., *The Journal of John Fontaine* (Williamsburg: Colonial Williamsburg Foundation, 1972), 88.

33. *Travels in the Confederation (1783–84),* trans. by Alfred J. Morrison (New York: Bergman Publishers, 1968), 33.

34. Richard Corbin, *Corbin Family Papers.* MS at Colonial Williamsburg. January 1, 1759.

35. *Inventory of the Estate of Landon Carter,* Alderman Library.

36. Room-by-room inventories, Colonial Williamsburg.

37. Hunter Dickinson Farish, ed., *Journal of and Letters of Philip Vickers Fithian, 1773–1774: A Plantation Tutor of the Old Dominion* (Williamsburg: Colonial Williamsburg Foundation, 1965), 202.

38. Alan Kulikoff, "The Origins of Afro-American Society in Tidewater Maryland and Virginia, 1700–1790," *William and Mary Quarterly* 35 (1978): 229–30.

39. *The Journal of Nicholas Cresswell, 1774–1777* (Port Washington, N.Y.: Kennikat Press, 1968), 18.

40. William D. Pierson, "Puttin' Down Old Massa: African Satire in the New World," in Daniel J. Crowley, ed., *African Folklore in the New World* (Austin: University of Texas Press, 1972), 20–34.

41. *The Journal of Nicholas Cresswell,* 19.

42. *Tour of the United States,* 46.

43. John Michael Vlach, *The Afro-American Tradition in Decorative Arts* (Cleveland: Cleveland Museum of Art, 1978), 22.

44. That certain items may have been considered slave-owned is hinted at by the outcome of a proposal made in the Virginia House of Burgesses in 1752. The proposal held for the destroying of dogs owned by slaves. Landon Carter, a member of the House, vigorously debated against the bill, and it was defeated and the right of slaves to own dogs upheld. See Greene, *Diary of Colonel Landon Carter,* 1: 72, 75.

45. Herbert Aptheker, *American Negro Slave Revolts* (New York: Columbia University Press, 1943).

46. *Tour of the United States,* 46.

47. Mullin, *Flight and Rebellion,* 60–61.

48. Greene, *Diary of Colonel Landon Carter,* 2: 1043.

49. Ibid., 2: 639.

50. *Transformation of Virginia,* 53.

51. Ibid.

52. Henry Glassie, *Folk Housing in Middle Virginia: A Structural Analysis of Historic Artifacts* (Knoxville: University of Tennessee Press, 1975), 160–75.

53. J. L. Dillard, *Black English: Its History and Usage in the United States* (New York: Vintage, 1973), 87–88.

54. *Shadow and Act* (New York: Vintage, 1972), 131.

55. Robert L. Schuyler, "The Spoken Word, the Written Word, Observed and Preserved Behavior, the Contexts Available to the Archaeologist," in Robert L. Schuyler, ed., *Historical Archaeology: A Guide to Substantive Theoretical Contributions* (Farmingdale, N.Y.: Baywood Publishing, 1978), 269–77.

3

Black Craft Traditions in Texas:
An Interpretation of Nineteenth-Century Skills

The study of Afro-American contributions to Texas history has lagged well behind the consideration of the achievements of other groups. This may, in part, be explained by the existence of a "Texas Myth" that promotes a view of the state as a special region wholly distinct from adjacent areas. Obscured by this perspective is the fact that roughly half of the state has close historical and cultural ties to the Old South (fig. 3.1).[1] Dusty cattle drives and forests of oil derricks stand out today as the prevailing images in the national consciousness and divert attention from the intriguing saga of life on the cutting edge of the southern frontier during the nineteenth century when pioneering and slavery were uniquely combined. As long as Texas is seen only as part of the Southwest or the West, the presence of Blacks will remain largely hidden; but if Texas is understood as part of the South, the existence of a Black population should be more readily acknowledged and, it is hoped, will receive the scholarly attention it deserves.

Only recently has a general history of Blacks in Texas been written, and it is mainly a consensus account pieced together from vastly uneven sources. In its necessary breadth, much of the personal texture of the Black experience is missed altogether. A structured program of inquiry should be launched to recover a more detailed Black Texan history before it is too late—before only vague recollections and tenuous generalizations are all that are left. Research projects devoted to specific communities, personalities, and themes are sorely needed. A socially representative topic like folk crafts, for example, could provide the basis for a study with broad implications.[2] The stereotype that Blacks were capable only of simple tasks requiring brute strength or endurance can be effectively challenged by presenting slaves in their roles as craftspersons. More importantly, to show an ability to make artifacts is to reveal a creative capacity and to restore a full humanity to people who are generally perceived only as menial servants. It is also significant, given the biases of Euro-American culture that

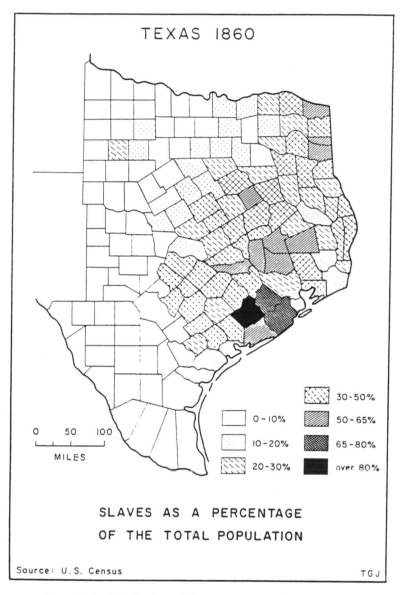

Figure 3.1. Distribution of Slaves in Texas, 1860
This map indicates the relative strength of
southern identity in the state during the
nineteenth century.
*(Courtesy of Terry G. Jordan and the Association
of American Geographers)*

favor material achievement over other forms of expressive behavior, that Blacks be shown as competent craftspersons. It should also be remembered that crafted items were not always the unique handmade objects that fill our contemporary boutique shelves. In nineteenth-century Texas the informal system of family-based teaching then prevalent in rural contexts gave individuals many practical abilities. This system of folk wisdom enabled them to produce valuable goods and implements that were useful in both their homes and their fields, regardless of whether they were White or Black. A study of crafts is not then a mere exercise in classification and description; craft skills constitute the basis from which the traditional material culture of a community is generated. A consideration of these daily skills can show how people take control of their circumstances as best they can. Hand-crafted objects, while plain, are not without significance. They are the tangible evidence of history and, if analyzed with care and sensitivity, these artifacts can reveal self-satisfying accomplishments that, in the Black experience, can be recognized as heroic achievements of the human spirit.

The survey presented here is intended to establish the range of production, service, and domestic craft activities in which Black Texans were engaged during the nineteenth century and to determine what kinds of artifacts might be most relevant to the study of Black Texans. Distinctive traits of those crafts that might be treated as aspects of a Black ethnic legacy will also be noted. Most important, however, is the sense of the active role played by Black people in the settlement and development of Texas that emerges from this survey. It is my hope that Blacks may ultimately be accorded the status of pioneers, even if they were made to wear chains.

From the study of one plantation in Brazoria County, Abigail Curlee concluded that those slaves were used only as field hands or house servants because the account books and ledgers showed that White carpenters and coopers were brought in to provide special services.[3] From such evidence, Alwyn Barr has generalized that "few [slaves] acquired the skills of any particular craft."[4] This kind of historiography should not go unchecked, since interviews conducted with ex-slaves living in Texas in 1938 by members of the Federal Writers Project in almost every instance tell of some kind of skill or artistic ability.[5] Even though the Writers Project narratives have been assailed as flawed with respect to factual accuracy, the contrasting points of view registered in the narratives and academic accounts illustrate the dangers involved in writing history without considering the viewpoints of its participants.[6] Cultural history is necessarily a popular history, and consequently requires the sifting of diverse personal accounts in the search for broader patterns of thought and action. The folk viewpoint contained in the ex-slave narratives and other local accounts provides the much-needed correction to the previous negative or non-existing assessments of Black material culture in Texas. Even granting that ex-slaves' fading memories or seething emotions may have distorted their recollections, their descriptions of the craft activities associated with the commonplace chores of their daily routines are not so prone to error since these matters are tied to events that they generally regarded as unexceptional and about which they had no axe to grind.

Using the accumulation of ordinary daily events to write history may often prove cumbersome and tedious, but the level of authenticity achieved by including more participants in a narrative than just those who left behind documentary evidence certainly validates the effort required. Works like Eugene D. Genovese's *Roll, Jordan, Roll,* Peter H. Wood's *Black Majority,* and Lawrence W. Levine's *Black Culture and Black Consciousness*— all award-winning books—make extensive use of either the ex-slave narratives or evidence of a similar type that is both specific and personal in nature.[7] The historical accounts provided in these cases are rendered from the bottom up rather than the top down, and when Black people are the target of one's efforts, admittance is granted to a new historical terrain that Genovese has called "the world the slaves made." Entrance into the realm of Black Texans is possible through several means, but ex-slave narratives offer an avenue that has not been utilized to its full potential. This is unfortunate because the body of testimony collected from former slaves in Texas was one of the most extensive ever compiled, amounting to more than five thousand pages of typescript. Much could be culled from this raw material; what follows here is a systematic survey of ex-slave comments relevant only to traditional craft activities. Perhaps other matters such as religion, family life, race relations, and the like will be surveyed in the future.

Foremost among the crafts mentioned in the ex-slave narratives are those involved with textiles. That there would be this particular focus seems logical, even obvious, if we consider a plantation as a "machine" for producing cotton fiber. Some of that fiber was consumed right on the plantation rather than being sent north or abroad to be made into cloth. Slave women worked as spinners and weavers as well as workers in the fields (fig. 3.2). Phoebe Henderson, who spent many of her slave days in Panola County, recalled: "After they brought us to Texas in 1859 I worked in the field many a day, plowing and hoeing, but the children didn't do much work 'cept carry water. . . . I worked in the house too. I spinned seven curts [lengths of thread] a day and every night we run two looms, making large curts for plow lines."[8] Anna Miller from the Palo Pinto hill country had a similar recollection: "My work 'twas helping with chores and pick up the brush where my pappy was clearing the land. When I gets bigger,

Figure 3.2.   Photo of an Unknown Black Woman Operating a Spinning
              Wheel, Nineteenth Century
              Note the rolls of fiber in the bucket at her feet and the cards on
              the chair used to prepare the rolls for spinning.
              (Courtesy of the Archives Division, Texas State Library)

I'se plowed, hoed, and done all the going to the mill. I'se helps card, spin, and cuts the thread. We'uns makes all the cloth for to makes the clothes, but we don't get 'em. . . . The weaving was the night work, after working all day in the field." [9]

The textile crafts were evidently a central feature of the slaves' daily routine. Fiber preparation, spinning, and weaving were such familiar chores that many Black women, as a matter of course, learned the special skills required. In most pioneer communities in the United States, settlers had to be self-sufficient enough to provide all the necessary materials for their food, shelter, and clothing. The work of Texas slaves with textiles was not then exceptional. Yet it is important to make this point because slaves are not generally acknowledged as makers of cloth, although their affiliation with "King Cotton" is never disputed. Betty Powers's statement shows just how much the textile crafts were woven into her life. As a child she was often roused from her slumbers in the middle of the night by the sound of the loom: "Pappy makes shoes and mammy weaves, and you could hear the bump, bump of that loom at night, when she done work in the field all day." [10] The heritage of spinning and weaving under such conditions is not easily forgotten.

In some cases the slave weaver's abilities were so appreciated that she was allowed to become a specialist. Near Dayton, where ex-slave Laura Cornish was born, her mother was held back from the fields: "Mama was the seamstress and don't do nothing but weave cloth on the spinning wheel and make clothes." [11] At Double Bayou a plantation mistress had several women who in certain seasons were set exclusively to weaving. Jacob Branch recalled that: "Old Lady 'Liza, she have three women to spin when she get ready [to] make the clothes for everybody. They spin and weave and make all us clothes." [12] Another account from Travis County shows an even higher concentration of attention on textiles as John Sneed remembered: "There's one long house where they spinned and weaved the cloth. There sixteen spinning wheels and eight looms in that house. . . . Most all the clothes what the slaves and the White folks have was made in that house." [13] On one Fayette County plantation a separate building was also set aside for textile manufacture: "There was spinning and weaving cabins, long with a chimney in each end. Us women spins all the thread and weaves cloth for everybody, the White folks too." Thus Silvia King testifies to the importance of this slave craft. [14] Slave-made cloth was not always crude material fit only for slave use; rather it was on occasion of high enough quality to be used in the "Big House." John B. Webster recorded in his plantation ledger on January 1, 1859, that his slave Patsey was "spinning *fine* thread." [15] In one case a slave weaver in Bosque County was awarded a prize for her work. [16]

Slaves learned to work with wool on those plantations that had sheep. Near Goliad, James Lott attempted to raise both sheep and cotton with mixed success, according to Martha Patton: "We made cotton and wool both, yes'm, we made both. We raised cotton. The sheep was so poor they would die. We would go through the woods and find the dead sheep and pick the wool off of them. Then we would wash the wool and spin it into thread and weave it into cloth to make wool clothes."[17] This animal fiber, while it could be worked in much the same manner as cotton, required a few different steps in preparation. Annie Row from Nacogdoches County asserted that a special resolve was needed: "My first work was teasing wool. I bets you don't know what teasing wool am. It am picking the burrs and trash and such out of the wool for to get it ready for carding."[18] Once carded, the fibers could be made into thread for weaving or yarn for knitting. The ability to work with different raw materials underscores the slave weaver's competence in textile crafts.

Our appreciation of that competence can be increased by understanding further the expertise that slaves displayed in decorating cloth with various dyes. The natural color of cotton or wool cloth was a dull white. This cloth often was either bleached to become a bright white or soaked in a dye pot.[19] Indigo was commonly used to produce a shade of blue. Ellen Polk, who lived in Gonzalez County, recalled the use of barks and herbs to make dyes: "The women would go in the woods and take the bark from the tree and parsley from the ground and mix them with copperas and put it all in a big iron pot and boil it. They would strain the water off and dye the cloth. The color was brown."[20] Others specified that live oak bark, mesquite bark, and pecan leaves were used to provide a dark brown dye.[21] Once slaves learned to produce dyes they could give their threads different colors, which in turn could be used to enhance their weaving. Fannie Yarbrough of Kaufman County bragged: "I learned all about spinning and weaving when I was little and by the time I was ten I'd make pretty striped cloth."[22] Evidently she used at least two different colors of thread in either the warp or weft of her loom.

In addition to weaving, some slave women learned to knit, and thus produced stockings as well as bolts of cloth.[23] As seamstresses working with the textiles they had produced, Black women sewed the garments required by their families, fellow slaves, and occasionally their masters' families. When speaking of the way his Smith County owner set out the tasks for slaves, Andrew Goodman mentioned the clothing that the women produced: "He [the master] never did put the niggers out in bad weather. He gave us something to do, in out of the weather, like clothes. In summer we [children] wore long shirts split up the sides, made out of lowerings—that's the same as cotton sacks was made out of. In winter we had good jeans and knitted sweaters and knitted socks."[24] A slave woman from Jasper is remembered as weaving coats for the winter.[25] At Goliad, Martha Patton remembered the making of blankets that were dyed a "pretty" dark brown.[26]

Another textile-associated craft practiced by Texas Blacks was quilting. A quilt combined the product of their weaving, their sewing ability, and their sense of color with a notion of design. The ex-slave narratives do not reveal what specific patterns were employed, but they do suggest that the quilt was an important artifact invested with social as well as aesthetic meaning. Elvira Boles, who left her crying baby behind every day to cut timber and split rails, was happy to return home at night to make what she calls "pretty quilts."[27] No doubt the quilts symbolized family, security, and home for her as well as something beautiful. The pattern may have been very personal in meaning if not form. In circumstances when the piecing of scraps to form the quilt top was done by a group, the pattern was more likely to represent a communal aesthetic, and thus reflect traditional rather than personal creativity. Julia Banks, an ex-slave from San Antonio, observed that quilting bees were a primary form of celebration that provided an odd moment's relief from the drudgery of bondage:

> I used to hear my grandmother tell about the good times they used to have. They would go from one plantation to another and have quiltings and corn huskings. And they would dance. . . . They used to go six or seven miles afoot to corn huskings and quiltings. And those off the other plantation would come over and join in the work. And they would nearly always have a good dinner. Sometimes some of the owners would give them a hog or something nice to eat, but some of them didn't.[28]

The festival atmosphere that developed on such occasions made the quilting bee a memorable event, marked as it was by music, dancing, feasting, and renewing or making friendships. No doubt, the quilts produced were also memorable, and in form they probably embodied patterns determined not just by one quilter or one plantation, but by the larger Black community. Some of the quilts made by Black quilters from other areas of the South are quite distinct from those made by White women both in design and color selection.[29] Black Texan quilts of recent vintage share many traits of form, design, and color use with the distinct Afro-American quilting tradition, and hence quilts may have been a central means of ethnic self-preservation even in the midst of slavery.[30] This implication is to some degree supported by the testimony of Tom Mills, who told of a quilting bee that occurred in the days "after freedom." The bee remained an occasion for extensive feasting, and continued to be an important communal affair, even drawing men into what was mainly a women's art form. Mills noted: "They would have me there, threading needles for them."[31]

Quilting remains today a very prominent craft among Blacks in Texas.[32] Given the earlier importance of this domestic activity, it is no surprise that it should still be significant. It is, however, essential that we recognize that while much of what black quilters did and continue to do is closely related to notions of genre and technique that have their origins in Euro-American history, some Blacks can look within their own history for a sense of origin. Some may look back like Irella Walker to the plantation era when "Us have beds the men make and take wore out clothes and britches and piece them and stuff with cotton for quilts."[33] Contemporary black quilting in Texas can be tied to a long tradition in the textile crafts. Today's quilters had ancestors who carded, spun, dyed, wove, sewed, and knitted as well as making quilted bed covers. Now only the salvage dimension of textile work survives; but in saving scraps, they may also save memories and thus recapture a history of technical competence with cloth.

While black women have a legacy of needles and threads from which they can take pride, black men can look back over a history of woodworking. Most Texan slave owners, like plantation masters elsewhere, had to clear their lands of oak, pine, and cedar, and consequently their slaves were set to work felling trees, splitting logs into rails, sawing planks and boards, and riving out shingles. Beyond this general rough work, those men who showed superior ability in handling wood were allowed to become carpenters. These slaves served their plantation in many ways, making containers and furniture, building houses, and repairing equipment.[34] Anything made of wood fell under their care and maintenance. Carey Davenport recalled that his father had been an accomplished woodworker in Walker County: "My father was a carpenter and old master let him have lumber and he make he own furniture out of dressed lumber and make a box to put clothes in. . . . And he used to make spinning wheels and parts for looms."[35] Given the importance of textiles on plantations, it is understandable why carpenters would work on spinning wheels and looms. It is important to recognize that by serving the machinery of the cloth makers, the carpenter was drawn into that broad communal process. He was not then just an isolated specialist, even though he had special talent. Consider the case of Jordan Goree who, as a slave, built many dwellings and gin houses in and around Huntsville. He is even credited with carving the threaded spiral shafts of several gin presses (fig. 3.3).[36] This precision work earned respect for Goree, but his expertise also facilitated the labor of many other men and women who were charged with the harvesting and processing of cotton. The plantation carpenter became a more central figure even as his skill made him more and more outstanding.

The slave carpenter worked for his fellow slaves as well as for his

Figure 3.3.   Detail of an Engraving Depicting Blacks in a Texas Cotton Field
The structure in the upper right section is a cotton press of the
sort which slave carpenters are said to have built and maintained. Note also the baskets in the foreground used to harvest
the cotton.
(From On a Mustang through Texas *by Alex E. Sweet and
J. Amory Knox [London, 1905])*

owner. Millie Ann Smith recalled that she had a good bed "like our White
folks" that had been built by her grandfather: "My grandpa made all the
beds for the White folks and us niggers too. Massa didn't want anything
shoddy around him, he say not even his nigger quarters."[37]

Further proof of slave skills is seen in various works recorded by the
Index of American Design. This record of craft skills depicts several pieces
of furniture allegedly made by Black Texan cabinetmakers. These include
a four-poster bed made from White oak in a late Empire style, a walnut
writing desk, several chairs, and a chest of drawers (figs. 3.4–5). The date
of manufacture for these items runs from 1820 to 1879, covering the entire period of slavery and well past emancipation. In addition, this furniture comes from north, east, and central Texas. While the number of
pieces constitutes a very small sample, we can at least recognize that
wherever and whenever Black cabinetmakers could be trained, they were
given the opportunity to make fine furniture. The appreciation of their

Figure 3.4.   Rendering of a Slave-Made Desk from the
Red River Valley
*(From the Index of American Design,
National Gallery of Art, Washington, D.C.)*

talents is best seen in the fact that the above-mentioned items are still treasured by their owners as valuable heirlooms.[38]

James J. Gathings, who came to Hill County in 1852, made extensive use of slave labor in several financially profitable industries including a furniture-making operation as well as a sawmill, brickyard, tannery, and flour mill. If one can judge from the annual output of the sawmill, which was estimated in the 1860 tax rolls to be worth $12,000, it might be suggested that the quantity of tables, chairs, and cabinets produced was also substantial. As yet none of this furniture has been identified, but it is apparent that Black carpenters had a greater influence on what was available in the way of local furnishings in the country than has previously been thought.[39]

Figure 3.5. Rendering of a Slave-Made Rocking Chair
from the Sam Houston Home
*(From the Index of American Design,
National Gallery of Art, Washington, D.C.)*

If a slave owner was not so concerned about his slaves, they often took the initiative to provide their own furnishings. Beds were built into the walls of their cabins with two poles inserted into two adjacent walls forming a corner at a post set into the floor. This frame, strung with ropes to support a straw-filled tick, was called a "Georgia hoss."[40] While this roughly constructed type of bed is not the kind of object that would attract much attention as a statement of skill, it was a distinct material marker of the social, and possibly ethnic, difference between Blacks and Whites. According to John Sneed: "The bedsteads make of pieces of split logs fasten with wooden pegs and rope criss-cross. The matress make of shucks tear into strips with maybe a little cotton or prairie hay. You could go out on the prairie most any time and get enough to make the bed and dry it before it put in the tick. The White folks have bought beds haul by ox teams from Austin and feather beds.''[41]

The theme of separation voiced here is also a statement of self-sufficiency and is seen elsewhere in Black woodworking, particularly in carving. According to Yach Stringfellow, Blacks in Brenham were quite handy with a knife: "In the long winter days the men sat round the fire and whittle wood and make butter paddles and troughs for the pigs and such and ax handles and hoe handles and box traps and figure-four traps. They make combs to get the wool clean for spinning.''[42] The same image is conveyed by Silvia King for Fayette County: "The boys and old men whittles traps and wooden spoons and needles to make seine nets and checkers and sleds.''[43] These woodworking skills certainly continued well past the slave era. William Mathews, who came to Texas from Louisiana after emancipation, earned a living with his carving ability up until the 1920s: "Then I make trays and mix bowls. I go out and cut down big poplar and bust off the big block and sit astraddle [on it], and hollow it out big as I wants it, and make the bread tray.''[44] This was not just whittling, but a type of carving requiring deft handling of axe and adze, skills first learned when slaves were sent to clear the fields of trees or maybe remembered from African ancestors who also carved wooden implements.

All across the Deep South, Blacks made mortars for refining either rice or corn. The earliest descriptions of slave-made mortars come from late seventeenth-century South Carolina.[45] Other examples of later vintage have turned up in Mississippi and Louisiana. The mortar made by slaves on Robert Clark's Washington County plantation is another expression of this traditional item. The hollowed log form used for a mortar could also be modified to make other kinds of containers. Wash tubs were also hollowed out of log stumps. The clothes placed in them were beat with poles shaped very much like the pestles used to grind corn.[46]

The cooper or barrelmaker's trade required a high level of joinery skill as the staves were shaped and fit snugly together to form a water-tight container. Apparently some slaves possessed these abilities, since they are remembered as making wooden buckets. In one case from Bosque County, the buckets were made from oak, and in another instance in Bastrop County, cedar was used.[47]

Henry Probasco, born on Andrew McGowen's Walker County plantation, recalled his father's work as plow maker in some detail:

> In the days I'se a boy even the plows was made on the place. The blacksmith did the iron work and wood work am done by pappy, and the plows am mostly wood. Just the point and the shear am iron. My grand pap made mould boards out of wood. No

sir twarnt no steel mould boards then. I'se watch grand pap take the hard wood block and with the ax and the drawshave and the plane and saw and rule, him cut and fit the mould board to the turning plow. The mould board last about one year.[48]

Given the vast number of artifacts that black craftsmen were able to provide, their record of woodworking cannot be minimized except at the cost of accuracy. The many examples of furniture, tools, implements, and containers cited here suggest that there is a proud heritage that contemporary black carpenters in Texas might rightfully claim. The possibility also arises that the material that has previously been labeled "plantation woodwork" can now be properly credited as Afro-American, and thus another portion of black history can be rescued from anonymity.

Almost entirely overlooked as statements of skill because of their plain and simple appearance are the domestic quarters built by slave carpenters. The "quarters" are thought of as rough shacks crudely fashioned with the poorest sense of design imaginable. These minimal box-like structures, while small, should not, however, be taken as a signal of minimal ability, nor should rough log surfaces be interpreted as a sign of technical deficiency. When White pioneers entered the forests, felled trees, and built log cabins, their effort has been interpreted as heroic, as man's subjugation of the wilderness. Black pioneers, even though they were held as slaves, should be credited with an equally important achievement. White and Black Texans built the same kinds of cabins with the same techniques and the same materials.

The importance of black building skills was certainly clear to slave owners who used the labor of their slaves to construct the "big house" as well as the quarters. A. M. Moore recalled of his Harrison County plantation: "They [the white folks] lived in a big log house but you wouldn't know it was log house unless you went up in the attic where it wasn't ceiled. The slaves helped master build the house. The quarters looked like a little town, with houses all in lines."[49] Harriet Barret similarly observed a continuity in the architecture of Whites and Blacks: "Us have log quarters with stick posts for bed and deerskin stretch over it. . . . They [White people] live in big log house, four rooms in it and the great hall both ways through it."[50] It was also noted in Orange and Waller Counties that quarters and plantation houses were both built from logs, except that the slave owners' houses were usually two stories high.[51] Blacks and Whites in Texas were linked by a shared experience in domestic architecture. The slave and the slave owner both lived in houses designed by joining single log pen units together to form larger structures. The big house on the hill was often a log house not very different from those of Blacks grouped together in slave row.[52] The owners, however, usually had more log pens in their dwellings. If slaves had one-room houses, the master lived in at least a

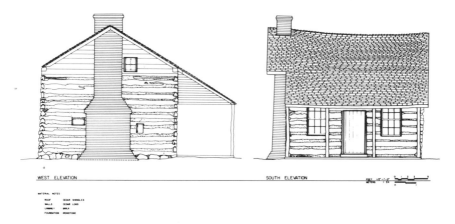

WEST ELEVATION

SOUTH ELEVATION

MATERIAL NOTES

ROOF   CEDAR SHINGLES
WALLS   CEDAR LOGS
CHIMNEY   BRICK
FOUNDATION IRONSTONE

Figure 3.6.   Side and Frontal Views of a Well-Made Log Slave Cabin on
the Cavitt Farm in Robertson County, Texas
*(From the Historic American Building Survey, Library
of Congress)*

two-room cabin; if slaves were housed in double-pen units, their owner
had a four-room dwelling. The size difference helped to maintain the social
hierarchy of the plantations. Yet it is important to note that single-and
double-pen cabins were typical Anglo-American folk houses throughout
the South.[53] Beyond a plantation's boundaries a small house carried no
racial distinction. The slave's cabin, as an artifact, was identical to that
of any struggling farmer, and consequently can be seen as the most basic
element in a general system of architectural design; it is the minimal unit
from which all other house types are generated (fig. 3.6). Plantation
mythology, with its pretentious images of wealth and grandeur, is deflated
by the fact that the master's house was, in many cases, nothing more than
an impressive arrangement of slave-quarter dwelling units.

The ex-slave narratives provide descriptions of several types of structures. The most minimal were temporary shelters of split logs like those
built by Toby Jones of Madisonville: "We cut some trees and split them
open and stood them on end with the tops together for our house."[54] On
the plantation of one Dr. Duvall of Bastrop County, "the slaves all lived
in log cabins back of the big house. They was one-room, two-rooms, and
three-room cabins, depending on the size of the family."[55] Most commonly
mentioned, however, is the two-room cabin in which one room served
as a kitchen and general purpose room, while the other room was used
for sleeping.[56] This type of cabin could be enlarged by the addition of a

lean-to shed across the back, in which case the cooking chores were shifted to the rear and the other rooms were used solely as bedrooms.[57]

After slavery Blacks moved into bigger houses when economic resources permitted it. Thomas Cole, who bought ninety acres of Cass County farm land after the Civil War, recalled: "We got enough land cleared for the small crop, about thirty acres, and builds the barn and sheds ourselves . . . and I built a four-room house of planks from our timber."[58] This house was the usual slave house doubled. Another house built by Blacks after emancipation, the dogtrot, was also a doubling of an early slave house form. In this case, two single pens were built with an open breezeway between them.[59]

In some cases the living accommodations of slaves were remembered as adequate. Jacob Branch, for example, noted: "Us quarters be good, snug little house with flue and oven,"[60] and Harriet Collins recalled that her dwelling was whitewashed and had a paling fence set around it.[61] In Walker County, while the quarters were "not mansion, they am log cabins with dirt floors, but good enough."[62] Yet we should not overlook the exploitation of the slavery system and the fact that plantation housing was at times grossly inadequate. Adeline Cunningham remembered that on her Lavaca County plantation two families were forced to live in one single room, and Betty Powers, in like manner, recounted that fourteen persons had occupied her single-pen cabin.[63] One of the most serious complaints concerning the discomfort of the quarters comes from Annie Row: "All us colored folks lived in the colored quarters. The cabins was built with logs and they have no floor. They have bunks for to sleep on and the fireplace. In the summer time most the colored folks sleeps outside and we'uns had to fight mosquitoes in the night and flies in the day. They was flies and then some more flies, with all their relations in them cabins."[64]

While the slave carpenter seems to have worked mainly with logs as an extension of his roles as clearer of fields and splitter of rails, he also built in frame.[65] One double-pen house documented in Travis County had one room made of logs and the other fashioned from planks.[66] When the carpenter was also a cabinetmaker, the finishing touches were accomplished with care. Mandy Morrow noted that "Grandpappy am the carpenter and cause of that us quarters fixed fine and has regular windows and handmade chairs and a real wood floor."[67] Although masonry buildings were far from common before the middle of the nineteenth century in Texas, there was one instance from Double Bayou where slaves' quarters were made from bricks.[68] In this case there was a brickyard near to the plantation so that it was economically feasible for the owner to have his slave quarters built in so substantial a manner. But what is most significant is that this example suggests that some slave builders had experience with brick and mortar, as well as wood. Where stone was preferred by the plantation owner as a building material, slaves worked with stone. The Friday Mountain home of Thomas Johnson, built in 1852 near Austin, is an impressive limestone mansion built by Black laborers.[69] It would seem then that the Black builder was very adaptable and capable of working in any material. In West Texas, Mazique Sanco, who went into carpentry after service in the Tenth Cavalry at Fort Concho, recalled that most of his houses were either adobe or pecan pole buildings.[70] Down in Medina County, Monroe Brackins remembered his quarters as a "little old picket house with a grass roof over it out of the sage grass."[71] Near Halletsville roofs were thatched with corn shucks and grass.[72]

Despite the variety of materials used in the construction of Black dwellings, there is a definite focus on the use of logs. The kinds of trees near the plantation determined the size and character of the timber, and hence the technique selected for construction. Skinny pine trees yielded round poles that were usually saddle-notched at the ends.[73] White oaks were hewn into rectangular planks and fit together with an elaborate keying technique: V-notching, half-dovetailing, or full-dovetailing.[74] Ellen Polk provided the most extensive account of Afro-American log construction when she described a process for producing logs in a semi-lunate or half-round section, a pattern strongly associated with eastern Texas:

> The house was log cabins. The men slaves built them. They goes into the woods and chops down the big trees and then they make 'em square. Did they have tools? Sure, they had a ax and a hatchet. They split the trees in two and that makes the side of the house and the round side is outside. How they make them logs tight? Just with mud. Then they puts the boards over the mud so it can't fall out. When they makes the boards they splits the end of the log and puts the hatchet in the place and it makes a nice, smooth board.[75]

It is more than apparent that the log culture complex of Texas derives a portion of its content from Blacks. Indeed, many of those features regarded as indicative of Lowland South log construction may derive from the plantation context. Terry G. Jordan has recently observed that the East Texas log cabin complex is the oldest and longest-lived log building tradition in the state, beginning about 1815 and remaining active until the 1930s.[76] This may be a material testimony of the tenacity of traditional carpentry among black Texans since what Jordan labels as the Lower South region in Texas is even now dominated by a Black population.[77]

Basketry, while often perceived now as an ephemeral activity, was in nineteenth-century Texas an essential craft. The produce harvested in the fields had to be carried by hand to the barn, gin house, corn crib, or at least to a wagon (see fig. 3.3). A basket fashioned from strips of split oak proved to be not only light in weight, but extremely durable. An added bonus was that the required raw material was often readily attainable in the wood lots adjacent to the fields. In two accounts from the ex-slave narratives, basketmaking is described in a positive manner, suggesting that through this craft some of the anguish of slavery was mitigated. Mary Edwards noted: "I helped make the baskets for the cotton. The men get White oak wood and we lets it stay in the water for the night and next morning and it soft and us split it in strips for making of the baskets. Everybody try to see who could make the best basket."[78] In Smith County, Robert Goodman traded with his slave craftsmen almost as if they were free people. Andrew Goodman recalled that his former master was a generous man: "In spare time we'd make cornshuck horse collars and all kinds of baskets and Marse bought them off us. What he couldn't use, he sold for us. We'd take post oak and split it thin with drawing knives and let it get tough in the sun and then weave it into cotton baskets and fish baskets and little fancy baskets. The men spent they money [from baskets] on whiskey."[79] The contest atmosphere of the first description and the sense of personal gain in the second confirm the importance that the craft had for black Texans. Here was a plantation activity that could be made to serve them as well as their masters. We can only imagine what a "little fancy basket" might be; but certainly when compared to a cotton basket designed for field use, it can be considered as an aesthetic statement, as artistry in the midst of utility.

There may also have been a sense of communal spirit that was expressed. James F. Perry's day books for Peach Point Plantation reveal that in 1848 gangs of men were sent out to gather "basket timber."[80] They may have returned to make baskets in a group as occurred on other plantations, or perhaps they just piled the wood outside a basketmaker's cabin. If the latter was the case, it is not unlikely that the man who felled the oak tree saw the basket as the finished product of a process that he had initiated. That basket was in part still his achievement.

The technology used in Texas to make split oak baskets and chair bottoms is encountered throughout the United States. While black makers of split oak baskets can be found all across the South, the forms and techniques used are decidedly Euro-American in nature.[81] Such baskets, when found in black communities, then reflect an acquired plantation heritage. Distinctive baskets with African origins have nevertheless been made in the South since about 1690. These are coiled forms employing wrapped bundles of grass, reeds, or pine needles. The forms and techniques employed in this basketry tradition were implanted in the Carolina low country in the late seventeenth century and then spread westward with the growth of the United States. Various coiled basket forms made by Blacks have been found in South Carolina, Georgia, Florida, Mississippi, and Louisiana.[82] The cultural region definable by this kind of basketry can be expanded to Texas. Near Newton on the Rimes plantation, Abram Sells made coiled forms: "Us have hats make out of pine straw, long leaf pine straw, tied together in little bunches and platted round and round till it make a kind of hat. That pine straw great stuff in them days and us use it in lots of ways."[83] While Sells only describes the making of hats, we may speculate that other forms were probably made, too. In Mississippi, Blacks still make pine straw trays and bread baskets with the coiling technique.[84] These sorts of forms may be what Sells meant by "lots of other ways."

It is important to note that the tradition for coiled hats can be traced back to South Carolina, and even back to Africa.[85] These hats in Newton may be an element of African culture, as well as an item known widely in the Black South. Should these wide geographic connections prove impossible to verify, we at least can show that there was a pattern of continuous use of natural fibers in the making of artifacts from childhood through adulthood among Texas Blacks. Coiling grasses was first experimented with during play activities. Josie Brown of Victoria County recalled that before she was old enough to work in the fields, "Us pull the long leaf grass and plait it."[86] The forms made in this way were used with rag dolls and play houses. They could have been small mats or baskets or hats. Later grass products would have a practical use. Abram Sells recalled that plow lines could be fashioned from bear grass, which furnished a very tough rope. With this kind of background with natural materials, coiled basket forms must be seen as a local Black tradition, if not a national one.

Leatherwork was a common craft on Texas plantations. Along with the blacksmith and the carpenter, one slave was usually allowed to develop the special skills and knowledge required for preparing cow hides. The slave tanner not only made leather, but turned it into harnesses and horse collars. Martha Patton's husband was such a person:

> My man, he worked in the tan yard. He fixed the hides to make all the shoes we had, and they made harness and saddles for the government, for the soldiers. To make lime to take the hair off the hides, they would burn limestone rocks. Then they would hew out troughs and soak the hides in lime water till all the hair come off. Then they would take "ooze" made from red oak bark and rub the hides till they were soft and dry.[87]

Frequently mentioned in the ex-slave narratives is the shoemaker; sometimes he was a specialist who only made shoes, in other instances he was also a harnessmaker and blacksmith.[88] Slave shoes were a very special type of foot gear with wooden soles, leather uppers, and sometimes brass toes. These shoes proved to be quite durable, as Henry Probasco observed: "Them last more than twice the time as store shoes, Gosh for mighty! We can't wear them out."[89] One slave cobbler left the hair on the hide, which he turned inside to help keep the wearer's feet warm.[90] Larnce Holt recalled that his father made shoes for both the Whites and Blacks on his Tyler County plantation and remembered that the leather was either left red or dyed black with soot.[91] In one anecdote, Irella Walker provides the details of shoe care, along with testimony regarding the work of the slave shoemaker.

> In summer us go barefoot, but there are shoemakers what make shoes for winter. When a beef killed, the hide kept and cleaned and put in the tanning trough. When the leather ready, the shoes make in the little shoe shop, and when them shoes get dry they hard as a rock. Daddy make us rub tallow or fried grease meat or any other kind grease into that hard shoe leather, and it make them soft, but when the dew and sun get on them they's hard again. [Some] Times the coyotes steal them greased shoes and make off with them. That actually happen a lot of times.[92]

The blacksmith was the pivotal craftsman of his community; all the other skills in some manner depended on his efforts.[93] The woodworkers could not do anything unless the smith made or at least sharpened their tools. The cook depended on the andirons that facilitated the efficient burning of the logs in the hearth. All the tasks of a plantation could be halted if the horses needed shoes, a wagon wheel needed a rim, the plow needed mending. The ironworking needs of any nineteenth-century community were great, and consequently the status of the blacksmith was quite high. Imagine then the importance of that slave who had any skill at the forge and anvil. His valuable service may have even given him a level of compensation for his bondage. In one case such skills proved to be an avenue to freedom, as Sarah Allen testified: "My husband was a teacher. He never was a slave. His father bought freedom through a blacksmith shop some way."[94]

While the recollections of slave blacksmiths in Texas are generally brief, revealing very little of the specific details of their work, the smith is one of the most frequently mentioned Black craftsmen.[95] The most extensive statement of the slave blacksmith's competence is to be found in the testimony of James G. Woorling, the son of a Rains County plantation owner:

> Uncle Dave was an exceptional Negro. He was a natural mechanic, but he could do carpenter work, blacksmithing, shoemaking and many other things equally well. He was a good manager, frugal and industrious, and it is doubtful if he paid out $50.00 in a year's time for food, clothing, and other necessities during the seven years that he lived on the seventy-five acres on our plantation [after emancipation].

He never bought a horse collar, but made them himself, shaping them to prevent galling and packing them with corn husks. He made the hames from oak timber and made the metal accessories.[96]

Uncle Dave's resourcefulness was apparently typical of blacksmiths. Since they were already providing the goods and services essential to other crafts, they also acquired some ability in such diverse specialities as carpentry and leatherwork.[97]

The blacksmith's leadership in the crafts gave him the elevated status that accompanied financial success and made him a likely leader in the social realm of the slave community. This was certainly the case in San Antonio, where Julia Banks recalled: "The way my stepfather got his learning was a colored blacksmith would teach school at night and us children taught our mother. . . . That old blacksmith was the onlyist man that knew how to read and write in slavery time that I knew of."[98] While a literate slave might be exceptional, the fact that he directed his ability toward his community is understandable since the blacksmith served in so many crucial ways.[99]

Some Blacks picked up the ironwork trade after slavery and thus perpetuated the central role that Black men had earlier played in the Texas economy. The experience of Sylvester Wickliffe shows that blanket statements claiming a lack of initiative among emancipated Blacks are mistaken:

After freedom I decide to learn a trade. I apprentice myself to the blacksmith trade for clothes and board. I learn all I can in three year and quit and open a shop on Bayou Torti. . . . I charge $2.00 for to shoe a horse all the way round. Then I beat plows, build two-wheel buggy and hack. I made sweep stocks and Garret and Cottman plow. That after the time of the wood mould board. I make mine with metal.

I come to Texas in 1890, to Liberty and been right round there and Ames for forty-seven year. I start me a gin and blacksmith shop when I first come.[100]

The tradition of service in the era of the plantation was thus transformed into a tradition of independence and industry which drew many men to the forge.

A survey of black artisans published by W. E. B. Du Bois showed that in 1890 there were 537 Blacks employed as blacksmiths and wheelwrights in Texas.[101] One respondent to Du Bois's questionnaire commented at length on the success of black ironworkers. He had observed seven Afro-American blacksmiths who owned shops in Houston with each shop employing from three to five black workmen. He noted further: "Ours being an agricultural state, blacksmiths are in greater demand than perhaps any other tradesmen. You will find a Negro blacksmith in nearly every town and at every country cross-road."[102] It was no wonder then that by 1910 there were still 526 black wheelwrights and blacksmiths in Texas.[103] The value and worth of black ironworkers under slavery was also recognized after the Civil War. Their role retained its significance, and hence their status remained high well into the twentieth century.

The important role of music in Afro-American culture is well known. Yet that music is perceived largely as a vocal expression because the instruments that most often accompany black lyrics were often borrowed from European traditions. Nevertheless, there are some common instruments in the United States that have African origins. The banjo is the most notable example, but there are other percussive instruments like drums, rattles, and gongs, as well as flutes and whistles, that can be closely compared with African prototypes.[104] All across the South slaves played music in the few hours that they were allowed to pursue their own pleasures. In these periods, musical instruments were improvised from any materials at hand. Texas plantations were no exception to this custom. Wash Wilson of Robertson County provides an extensive account of how slaves made their own instruments, of an improvised tradition to match the more ancient one retained from Africa.

> There wasn't no music instruments. Us takes pieces of sheep's rib or cow's jaw or piece [of] iron, with a old kettle, or hollow gourd and some horse hairs to make a drum. Sometimes they'd get a piece of tree trunk and hollow it out and stretch a goat's or sheep's skin over it for the drum. They'd be one to four feet high and a foot up to six feet across. In general two niggers play with the fingers or sticks on this drum. Never saw so many in Texas, but they made some. They'd take the buffalo horn and scrape it out to make the flute. That sure be heared a long ways off. Then they'd take a mule's jawbone and rattle the stick across its teeth. They'd take a barrel and stretch an ox's hide across one end and a man set astride the barrel and beat on that hide with he hands, and he feet, and if he get to feeling the music in he bones, he'd beat on that barrel with he head. Another man beat on wooden side with sticks.[105]

This remarkable inventory of drums, rattles, scrapes, rasps, bones, and flutes shows the versatility of Black Texan instrument makers. The description of drumming is particularly significant since the mutual playing by two men matches up against polyrhythmic approaches to drumming found not only throughout Black music in the United States, but in the West Indies and West and Central Africa.[106] Thus even if the drums made in Texas were not absolutely African in form, the manner in which they were played was.

Reports of musical instruments are given repeatedly in the ex-slave narratives. Harre Quarls of Madison County claimed to have made a fiddle out of a gourd.[107] Similar instruments are also cited in Rusk County.[108] Banjos are mentioned by Blacks from Harrison, Tarrant, Orange, Robertson,

Red River, and Kaufman Counties.[109] Some of these may also have been made from a gourd with a skin stretched over it to form the banjo's head, as was common elsewhere in the South. The quill whistle, a wind instrument well-known among southern Blacks, was also made in Caldwell County. Bill Homer gave the following description: "We plays the quill make from willow stick when the sap am up. You takes the stick and pounds the bark loose and slips it off, then slit the wood in one end and down one side puts holes in the bark and put it back on the stick."[110] The making of musical instruments was of little importance to slave owners, but was of inestimable value to the slaves. The music provided a great deal of enjoyment and gave rise to song, dance, and frolic. In short, music provided relief from the oppression of slave life. Consider the spirit that must have pervaded the following event described by Fred Brown of Kaufman County: "We is allowed to have parties and the dance. . . . They dance the promenade and the jig. Sometimes they have the jigging contest and two niggers puts a glass of water on their heads and then see who can dance the longest without spilling any water. Then we has log rolling. There was two teams about three to a team, and they see which can roll the log the fastest."[111] By making musical instruments Black Texans partially recovered their right to happiness. Craft skill together with musical talent combined to present a sly resistance to the system of slavery.

Conclusions

This brief survey of Black crafts raises several questions about the nature of the Afro-American tradition in material folk culture in Texas. One wonders if it is a distinctly Black tradition or could be more properly labeled as Southern. If there are two intertwined cultural patterns, can we clarify the level of contribution from each ethnic source? Are there any Africanisms in Texas? To what extent have local circumstances and individual personalities shaped the craft performances of black Texans? Are these old skills still meaningful today? These are difficult questions, but at least some partial answers can be given.

The ex-slave narratives provide one key to understanding the meaning of Black displays of material competence. The narratives mention the origins of but a small fraction of the 182,566 slaves counted in 1860;[112] the state-wide distribution of this sample does give it some explanatory power. Statistics derived from the narratives suggest that most Blacks, some 65%, come to Texas from outside the state. Of this portion, most came from the Deep South region (68%), considerably fewer from the Upland South and Chesapeake Tidewater slave holding areas (29%), and a mere 3% from Africa and the West Indies. While there had been Black people in Texas as early as 1528, there were only five known slaves in Texas in 1819.[113] The rapid increase over the next forty years can only be accounted for through massive importation of slaves. With slave states along Texas's eastern border, the origins of many black Texans are self-evident. Indeed the ex-slave narrative statistics suggest that 24% came from Louisiana, Texas's nearest neighbor. American immigrants from various states flooded into Texas territory after 1820, bringing with them their property, which often included slaves.[114] There were only a small number of slaves imported directly from Africa or via Cuba through the port of Galveston, and this trade was closed down after 1836 when a declaration of the Texas Republic made it illegal to import African slaves.[115] There was, no doubt, some smuggling of Africans along the Gulf Coast, but this source of labor was never as trustworthy as purchases from other slave states. The overland routes thus carried an especially active trade after the Texas revolution.[116] Most of the Black people in nineteenth-century Texas were at least one generation (often more) removed from Africa. They had attained considerable exposure to White-dominated society even before entering the state, and any distinctive cultural traits that they might have possessed were necessarily already filtered by decades of southern life. The record of folk crafts in Texas reveals a continued integration of Blacks into White society, albeit at the bottom tier. They were used to provide the same goods and services that White workers would have provided. We would not then expect to find in Texas the same level of African cultural survival found in Tidewater Virginia, the Carolina Low Country, or New Orleans, which were the main beachheads for the arrival of African people in the United States.[117]

Yet there are a modest number of African features in the cultural wherewithal of black Texans. We have already noted the musical instruments, coiled basket forms, carved implements, and thatched roofs that can be assigned African analogues.[118] To this list can be added dippers fashioned from gourds.[119] Those few Blacks born in Africa continued to see themselves as African, and are very clear about their alternative ethnic identity. Silvia King of Fayette County began her narrative: "I know I was borned in Morocco, in Africa."[120] Others descended from Africans were also given a strong sense of their distinctive heritage. Thomas Johns recalled that his father was the son of a "chief of the Kiochi tribe," a people who today might be known as the Chokwe of Zaire and Angola, a group well within the range of the slaver's nets.[121] Johns noted further that his father's teeth were filed, a mark of a specific ethnic identity still found today among the Chokwe. William Davis knew that his father was from the Congo (now Zaire), and remembered that he retained a pride and dignity that was highlighted by "scars on the right side he head and cheek, what he say am tribe marks.''[122] Toby Jones, who came to Texas from South Carolina after emancipation, recalled that during free time on the plantation ''everybody would talk about when they lived in Africa and done what they wanted.''[123] Clearly then there was a healthy memory culture of Africa among Texan Blacks, even though most of them had never been there. In those conversations described by Toby Jones, traditions of custom, belief, song, dance, narrative, and craft were passed to succeeding generations. This is how unquestionably African folktales turn up in the slave narratives and even in the current repertoire of black Texans.[124] Curing practices related to African herbalism were also taught in this way.[125] Perhaps the most overt alternative behavior among some black Texans to be retained from their African forebears was the practice of carrying burdens on their heads. This was observed by Frederick Law Olmsted in Austin in 1856, and recalled by Larnce Holt of Tyler County: ''My mammy have four boys, call Eb and Ander and Tobe. My brother Eb he tote so many buckets of water to the hands in the field he wear all the hair off the top he head.''[126] Taking all these traits together we quickly realize that some attributes of African culture were surprisingly vital in Texas, at least through the plantation era. Diverse African elements gave a flavor to the experiences of black Texans that ensured that their culture would not be totally subjugated by the repressive designs of their owners. While Blacks in Texas were, for the most part, caught up in a southern way of life, they still managed to perpetuate elements of their African heritage.

There were certain skills that Blacks acquired from White people. Some of the tools and tasks they encountered in Texas or elsewhere in the South did not exist in Africa, even if textile arts, woodworking, and blacksmithing were well known there. Men had to be taught to cobble shoes, build swing plows and wagons, and notch logs, to cite a few skills learned in the United States. Empire-style bedsteads and dressers had to be learned from pattern books printed in East Coast style centers. Women had to be taught the intricacies of treadle looms and spinning wheels. Fannie Brown probably spoke for many when she said, ''My missy learned me to spin and weave.''[127] Of the fifty-seven types of artifacts mentioned in this survey, only twelve can be considered African-derived. All these items, when considered as indices of cultural contact, illustrate that Blacks assimilated many White elements into their material culture. A larger share of the Black craft tradition is then the outcome of diligence in learning new ways and means—new content to blend with and eventually displace the lessons taught by Black ancestors. By the middle of the nineteenth century the blending process, often referred to as syncretism,[128] had to a great extent made black Texans competent to participate actively in the economic life of the state, even if they were excluded from its social life. This dichotomy of social options caused Blacks to turn their skills inward; they tended then mainly to serve the ends of the black community. In short, as they became enclaved, traditions that were Euro-American in origin became Afro-American in character.

The twin heritage of Africa and America served a fierce spirit of Black independence that was demonstrated in slave insurrections,[129] repeated escapes, and hopeful spirituals. One might add to this list the displays of self-sufficiency seen in the examples of folk craft presented in the ex-slave narratives. I have noted here the making of clothes, furniture, shelters, tools, containers, shoes, and musical instruments. Abram Sells of Newton County bragged that slaves made everything: "Us even make our own plow line out of cotton and if us run short of cotton sometime made them out of bear grass and we make buttons for us clothes out of little round pieces of gourds and cover them with cloth."[130] If Sells's people are representative, black Texans were thoroughly competent at making a living on the nineteenth-century frontier and were well-prepared by their plantation experiences for freedom and the responsibility of living their own lives, particularly in agricultural settings. Even though owned as human property, slaves often took care of their own material needs as well as those of their masters. Abigail Holbrook was thus wrong to surmise that black Texans were ill-prepared for freedom on the basis of their poor employment record after emancipation in 1865.[131] They did not take low-paying, unskilled jobs because they lacked an ability to do any better. We have seen repeated examples of industry, initiative, creativity, and cleverness among Black crafts people. Most slaves, coming as they did from rural backgrounds, had acquired the practical skills needed to wrest a living from the land. They were ready for freedom but social and economic conditions denied them the opportunity to find either adequate land holdings or profitable employment.[132] Thus the material tradition of Blacks in the service and production crafts became largely a heritage denied rather than a legacy celebrated.

Despite the frustrations which black Texan artisans encountered in the nineteenth century, some Blacks continue to utilize similar traditional skills in home and farm contexts today. Confidence rooted in a spirit of self-sufficiency does not soon wither, for not only do these surviving crafts serve pragmatic ends, but they rekindle images of endurance, stamina, and hope. Silvia King, an African slave cook in Fayette County, was able to turn the tables on her captors by making art as she did her chores. She made "all kinds of pretty figures" in the sand she sprinkled on the floor before she swept it out the door.[133] She transformed mundane drudgery into a creative performance as she endured her bondage. The craft tradition continues to function in a similar way, giving those artisans who are still active some measure of control over their daily lives, in addition to the satisfaction of creativity.

Notes

1. Terry G. Jordan, "The Imprint of the Upper and Lower South on Mid-Nineteenth Century Texas," *Annals of the Association of American Geographers* 57 (1967). Reprinted in David Ward, ed., *Geographic Perspectives in America's Past: Readings on the Historical Geography of the United States* (New York: Oxford University Press, 1979), 210–16, see esp. fig. 1.

2. John Michael Vlach, *The Afro-American Tradition in Decorative Arts* (Cleveland: Cleveland Museum of Art, 1978), explores the interaction of Afro-American art and culture. See also Robert Farris Thompson, "African Influence on the Art of the United States," in Armstead L. Robinson, et al., eds., *Black Studies in the University* (New Haven: Yale University Press, 1969), 128–77. For a more broadly construed defense of the value of studying history through artifacts, see Leland Ferguson, ed., *Historical Archaeology and the Importance of Material Things* (Society for Historical Archaeology, Special Publication Series, No. 2, 1977), and Thomas J. Schlereth, *Artifacts and the American Past* (Nashville: American Association for State and Local History, 1981).

3. "The History of a Texas Slave Plantation," *Southwestern Historical Quarterly* 26 (1922): 108.

4. Alwyn Barr, *Black Texans* (Austin: Jenkins Publishing, 1973), 19.

5. There are several anthologies that provide excerpts from the Works Projects Administration Writers Project interviews conducted with ex-slaves. The most complete compilation is George P. Rawick, *The American Slave: A Composite Autobiography* (Westport, Conn.: Greenwood Press, 1972). Volumes 4 and 5 of this collection reprint all the Texas ex-slave narratives and will hereafter be referred to as *Texas Narratives*. The original interviews were often written up in a feeble attempt to imitate black English. I have, for the sake of clarity, used standard spellings, but retained the original syntax for the quotes presented in this article.

6. C. Vann Woodward, "History from Slave Sources: A Review Article," *American Historical Review* 79 (1974): 475.

7. Eugene D. Genovese, *Roll, Jordan, Roll: The World the Slaves Made* (New York: Vintage, 1972); Peter H. Wood, *Black Majority: Negroes in South Carolina from 1670 through the Stono Rebellion* (New York: W. W. Norton, 1974); and Lawrence W. Levine, *Black Culture and Black Consciousness: Afro-American Folk Thought from Slavery to Freedom* (New York: Oxford University Press, 1977).

8. *Texas Narratives* 4, pt. 2, 135.

9. Ibid. 5, pt. 3, 82.

10. Ibid. 5, pt. 3, 191.

11. Ibid. 4, pt. 1, 257; see also *William Bollaert's Texas,* edited by Eugene Hollon and Ruth Lapham Butler (Norman: University of Oklahoma Press, 1956), 273.

12. *Texas Narratives* 4, pt. 1, 138.

13. Ibid. 5, pt. 4, 47.

14. Ibid. 4, pt. 2, 292.

15. Max S. Lale and Randolph B. Campbell, "The Plantation Journal of John B. Webster, February 17, 1858 –November 5, 1859," *Southwestern Historical Quarterly* 84 (1980): 71. Emphasis added.

16. *Texas Narratives* 5, pt. 3, 253.

17. Ibid. 5, pt. 3, 174.

18. Ibid. 5, pt. 3, 259.

19. Ibid. 4, pt. 2, 292.

20. Ibid. 5, pt. 3, 188.

21. Ibid. 5, pt. 3, 173.

22. Ibid. 5, pt. 4, 225.

23. Ibid. 4, pt. 1, 174.

24. Ibid. 4, pt. 2, 75.

25. Ibid. 5, pt. 3, 114.

26. Ibid. 5, pt. 3, 173.

27. Ibid. 4, pt. 1, 107.

28. Ibid. 4, pt. 1, 97.

29. Vlach, *The Afro-American Tradition in Decorative Arts,* 44–75; also see Maude Wahlman and John Scully, "Design Principles in Afro-American Quilts," in William Ferris, ed., *Afro-American Folk Art and Crafts* (Boston: G. K. Hall, 1983), 79–97.

30. Marilyn Jorgensen, "Matilda Brown: Black Quilter." Seminar paper presented at the University of Texas at Austin, November 1980.

31. *Texas Narratives* 5, pt. 3, 98.

32. Melvin Wade, *Texas Site Report,* in *Final Report to the National Endowment for the Arts, Folk Arts Program,* submitted by Bruce Nickerson, 1979, 20–31, 51–56.

33. *Texas Narratives* 5, pt. 4, 124.

34. Lale and Campbell, "Plantation Journal of John B. Webster," 52. One industrious slave carpenter named Lev was credited with building a wheelbarrow on March 9, 1858.

35. *Texas Narratives* 4, pt. 1, 283.

36. Abigail Curlee Holbrook, "A Glimpse of Life on Ante-Bellum Slave Plantations in Texas," *Southwestern Historical Quarterly* 76 (1972): 380.

37. *Texas Narratives* 5, pt. 4, 42.

38. Ruth Morgan, "The Crafts of Early Texas," *The Southwest Review* 30 (1945): 155–66; James Porter, *Modern Negro Art,* 1943 (reprinted ed., New York: Arno Press, 1960), 202; Erwin O. Christensen, *The Index of American Design* (New York: Macmillan, 1959), 132.

39. Jack M. Jackson, "The Antebellum Plantation in Texas: Myth and the Variation of Reality." Seminar paper presented at the University of Texas at Austin, April 1981.

40. *Texas Narratives* 4, pt. 2, 119.

41. Ibid. 5, pt. 4, 47.

42. Ibid. 5, pt. 4, 69.

43. Ibid. 4, pt. 2, 292.

44. Ibid. 5, pt. 3, 71.

45. Vlach, *The Afro-American Tradition in Decorative Arts,* 8–9, 21.

46. *Texas Narratives* 5, pt. 3, 254.

47. Ibid. 5, pt. 3, 254; 5, pt. 4, 124.

48. Ibid. 5, pt. 3, 205.

49. Ibid. 5, pt. 3, 118.

50. Ibid. 4, pt. 1, 49.

51. Ibid. 4, pt. 1, 18; Rosa Groce Bertleth, "Jared Ellison Groce," *Southwestern Historical Quarterly* 20 (1917): 360.

52. Ibid. 5, pt. 3, 75.

53. Henry Glassie, *Pattern in the Material Folk Culture of the Eastern United States* (Philadelphia: University of Pennsylvania Press, 1968), 101–6; Henry Glassie, "Types of the Southern Mountain Cabin," in Jan Harold Brunvand, *The Study of American Folklore: An Introduction* (New York: W. W. Norton, 1968), 338–70.

54. *Texas Narratives* 4, pt. 2, 251.

55. Ibid. 4, pt. 2, 182.

56. Ibid. 4, pt. 1, 55.

57. Ibid. 5, pt. 3, 253.

58. Ibid. 4, pt. 1, 234.

59. Terry G. Jordan, *Texas Log Buildings: A Folk Architecture* (Austin: University of Texas Press, 1978), 119.

60. *Texas Narratives* 4, pt. 1, 138.

61. Ibid. 4, pt. 1, 243.

62. Ibid. 5, pt. 3, 206.

63. Ibid. 4, pt. 1, 266; 5, pt. 3, 190.

64. Ibid. 5, pt. 3, 258.

65. Ibid. 4, pt. 1, 45.

66. Ibid. 4, pt. 2, 143.

67. Ibid. 5, pt. 3, 139.

68. Ibid. 5, pt. 3, 72.

69. Willie Kemp, "Bear Creek and Friday Mountain," *Frontier Times* (December–February, 1970), 34–35.

70. *Texas Narratives* 5, pt. 4, 2.

71. Ibid. 4, pt. 1, 124.

72. Ibid. 4, pt. 1, 267.

73. Ibid. 5, pt. 3, 197.

74. Ibid. 5, pt. 4, 33; see also Jordan, *Texas Log Buildings,* 49–81.

75. *Texas Narratives* 5, pt. 3, 189.

76. Jordan, *Texas Log Buildings,* 183.

77. Donald W. Meinig, *Imperial Texas: An Interpretive Essay in Cultural Geography* (Austin: University of Texas Press, 1969), 49, 87.

78. *Texas Narratives* 4, pt. 2, 15.

79. Ibid. 4, pt. 2, 76.

80. Abigail Curlee, "A Study of Texas Slave Plantations, 1822 to 1865," Ph.D. Dissertation, University of Texas at Austin, 1932, 116; see also Lale and Randolph, "Plantation Journal of John B. Webster," 65, 76, which demonstrates communal basketmaking on an annual basis in August 1858 and 1859.

81. See Allen H. Eaton, *Handicrafts of the Southern Highlands,* 1937 (reprinted ed., New York: Dover, 1973), 166–78.

82. Gregory Day, *South Carolina Low Country Baskets* (brochure) (Charleston: The Communication Center, 1977); Vlach, *The Afro-American Tradition in Decorative Arts,* 7–14; Thompson, "African Influence on the Art of the United States," 146.

83. *Texas Narratives* 5, pt. 4, 13.

84. Patti Carr Black, ed., *Made by Hand: Mississippi Folk Art* (Jackson, Miss.: State Historical Museum, 1980), 100–101.

85. Vlach, *The Afro-American Tradition in Decorative Arts,* 18–19; compare with photos taken by George Washington Egerton in 1893–95 in Zaire. Photos on file in the Texas Memorial Museum.

86. *Texas Narratives* 4, pt. 1, 164.

87. Ibid. 5, pt. 3, 174.

88. Ibid. 4, pt. 1, 156.

89. Ibid. 4, pt. 2, 44.

90. Ibid. 5, pt. 3, 205.

91. Ibid. 4, pt. 2, 151.

92. Ibid. 5, pt. 4, 123.

93. John Michael Vlach, "The Craftsman and the Communal Image: Philip Simmons, Charleston Blacksmith," *Family Heritage* 2 (1979): 14.

94. *Texas Narratives* 4, pt. 1, 13.

95. Frederick Law Olmsted, *Journey through Texas; or a Saddle Trip on the Southwestern Frontier* (New York: Dix Edwards, 1857), 508; Harold Schoen, "The Free Negro in

the Republic of Texas," *Southwestern Historical Quarterly* 39 (1936): 295; Jeff Hamilton and Lenoir Hunt, *"My Master"* (Dallas: Manfred Van Not, 1940), 14; Barr, *Black Texans,* 4, 59; "W. Steinert's View of Texas in 1849," Gilbert J. Jordan, ed., *Southwestern Historical Quarterly* 81 (1977): 65.

96. *Texas Narratives* 5, pt. 4, 216.

97. Ibid. 4, pt. 1, 156–57.

98. Ibid. 4, pt. 1, 96–97.

99. For a parallel instance of a blacksmith leading his community see John Michael Vlach, *Charleston Blacksmith: The Work of Philip Simmons* (Athens: University of Georgia Press, 1981).

100. *Texas Narratives* 5, pt. 4, 158–59.

101. W. E. B. Du Bois, *The Negro Artisan*, Atlanta University Publication No. 7 (Atlanta: Atlanta University Press, 1902).

102. Ibid., 98–99.

103. W. E. B. Du Bois and Augustus Granville Dill, eds., *The Negro American Artisan,* Atlanta University Publication No. 17 (Atlanta: Atlanta University Press, 1912).

104. Deana J. Epstein, "The Folk Banjo: A Documentary History," *Ethnomusicology* 20 (1976): 347–71; Harold Courlander, *Negro Folk Music: U.S.A.* (New York: Columbia University Press, 1963), 204–20.

105. *Texas Narratives* 5, pt. 4, 198.

106. Harold Courlander, Notes to *African and Afro-American Drums* (Folkways Records Album No. FE 4502 4D, 1962), 3, band 17 documents two men simultaneously playing one drum in Haiti; see also Alan P. Merriam, "African Music," in William R. Bascom and Melville J. Herskovits, eds., *Continuity and Change in African Cultures* (Chicago: University of Chicago Press, 1959), 58.

107. *Texas Narratives* 5, pt. 3, 223.

108. Ibid. 4, pt. 2, 6.

109. Ibid. 4, pt. 1, 286, 109, 114; 5, pt. 4, 237; 4, pt. 2, 234; pt. 1, 158.

110. Ibid. 4, pt. 2, 155.

111. Ibid. 4, pt. 1, 158.

112. Ronnie C. Tyler, Introduction to *The Slave Narratives of Texas,* ed. by Ronnie C. Tyler and Lawrence R. Murphy (Austin: The Encino Press, 1974), xxi.

113. Barr, *Black Texans,* 1.

114. Olmsted, *Journey through Texas,* 88.

115. Fred Robbins, "The Origin and Development of the African Slave Trade in Galveston Texas and Surrounding Areas," *East Texas Historical Journal* 9 (1971): 159.

116. Tyler, *The Slave Narratives of Texas,* xxv.

117. Peter H. Wood, *Black Majority,* 131–66.

118. Vlach, *The Afro-American Tradition in Decorative Arts,* passim.

119. *Texas Narratives* 5, pt. 4, 124.

120. Ibid. 4, pt. 2, 290.

121. Ibid. 4, pt. 2, 201; George Peter Murdock, *Africa: Its People and Their Culture History* (New York: McGraw-Hill, 1959), 293.

122. *Texas Narratives* 4, pt. 2, 290.

123. Ibid. 4, pt. 2, 250.

124. A text of an animal tale known widely in Africa, "Relative Helpers in Race" (A-T 1074), is presented in *Texas Narratives* 5, pt. 3, 204. A more recently told tale of African origin is "The Talking Skull," collected in Waco, Texas by Martha Eamons, *Deep Like Rivers: Stories of My Negro Friends* (Austin: Encino Press, 1969), 32–34; see also Richard M. Dorson, *American Negro Folktales* (Greenwich, Conn.: Fawcett, 1967), 147–48; for an extensive study of this tale in Africa and the New World, see William R. Bascom, "African Folktales in America: I. The Talking Skull Refuses to Talk," *Research in African Literatures* 8 (1977): 266–91, esp. 285–86.

125. *Texas Narratives* 4, pt. 1, 243.

126. Ibid. 4, pt. 2, 151.

127. Ibid. 4, pt. 1, 154.

128. Melville J. Herskovits, *The Myth of the Negro Past,* 1941 (reprinted ed., Boston: Beacon Press, 1958), xxii–xxiii.

129. Wendell G. Addington, "Slave Insurrections in Texas," *Journal of Negro History* 35 (1950): 408–34.

130. *Texas Narratives* 5, pt. 4, 13.

131. Holbrook, "A Glimpse of Life on Ante-Bellum Slave Plantations," 383.

132. Winston Lee Kinsey, "Negro Labor in Texas, 1865–1876," M.A. Thesis, Baylor University, 1965; Bruce Aldren Glasrud, "Black Texans, 1900–1930: A History," Ph.D. Dissertation, Texas Technological College, 1969.

133. *Texas Narratives* 4, pt. 2, 293.

Part Two

Artisans' Lives

Introduction to Part Two

Because the relatively new field of American material culture research is essentially "artifact-driven," scholarly attention is focused more on things, at least initially, than on people. Consequently much more is written about objects than their makers. It should not be surprising then that there are few studies of Afro-American artisans. In my own work I have tried to correct this imbalance both to bring deserved attention to talented bearers of black American traditions and to encourage the use of biographical methods in the study of American artifacts. In the articles reprinted in this section, two detail the careers of individuals, while in the third I identify techniques for the investigation of building tradesmen.

The essay on William Edmondson originally was commissioned by the Tennessee State Museum as part of that institution's efforts to present a comprehensive survey of the noteworthy career of the black stonecarver from Nashville. Edmondson made his mark in American art history in 1937 when he became the first black artist to have a one-person exhibit at the Museum of Modern Art. His rather exotic statues were seen by the New York avant-garde as the works of an unaffected "primitive," as expressions of raw, natural instinct. My task was to determine to what extent his works might be tied to a black folk tradition, and thus I was to seek out the extent to which his sculpture was customary rather than visionary. His folk roots were found not in his celebrated statues, but in the tombstones he carved for the members of his local community. Charting the history of his career made apparent that he moved from the simple to the complex, from craft to art, and from expression aligned with folk custom to sculpture inclined toward fine art.

In Philip Simmons, a blacksmith from Charleston, South Carolina, I encountered a recognized and venerable tradition in full bloom. Simmons had inherited his trade from a long line of blacksmiths that reached back as far as the late eighteenth century. His repertoire and working techniques had precedents that were equally ancient. At first I concentrated on simply describing how Simmons did his work. However, I quickly came to know the power of the man's personality and my attention shifted to his creative process and aesthetic sensibility. Simmons's work as a blacksmith bridged the realms of practicality and decoration; he was constantly asked to make fences and gates that not only worked well but also looked good. Simmons was then both a folk artist and a folk craftsman, and I was able to document these two phases of his trade.

The final essay in this section provides a regional overview of black participation in the building trades in the South primarily during the antebellum period. Originally presented as a speech at a conference on the material culture of black history, I again had an assigned task: to identify specific methods by which the history of slave craftsmen might be recovered. Concentrating on the building trades as an illustrative example, I found that no new techniques were needed. All that was required to write a history of black craftsmen was the sincere belief that it was possible to do so. Further, I suggested that three modes of evidence should be used to develop the narrative of black builders: written documents, oral testimony, and buildings and building sites. The combination of written words, spoken words, and objects provides important cross-checks that prevent one from straying too far into faulty speculation.

For more on William Edmondson see Edmund L. Fuller, *Visions in Stone: The Sculpture of William Edmondson* (Pittsburgh: University of Pittsburgh Press, 1973). Philip Simmons's career is detailed in John Michael Vlach, *Charleston Blacksmith: The Work of Philip Simmons* (Athens: University of Georgia Press, 1981). The contribution of Blacks to the antebellum building trades is examined in several books and articles: Leonard Stavisky, "The Origins of Negro Craftsmanship in Colonial America," *Journal of Negro History* 32 (1947): 417–29; James E. Newton and Ronald L. Lewis, eds., *The Other Slaves: Mechanics, Artisans, and Craftsmen* (Boston: G. K. Hall, 1978); Peter H. Wood, "Whetting, Setting, and Laying Timbers: Black Builders in the Early South," *Southern Exposure* 8 (Spring 1980): 3–8; Catherine W. Bishir, "Black Builders in Antebellum North Carolina," *The North Carolina Historical Review* 49 (1984): 423–61.

Given the lack of research on the subject of black artisans, the earliest studies are still very valuable: W. E. B. Du Bois's *The Negro Artisan* (Atlanta: Atlanta University Press, 1902), and the survey conducted ten years later by Du Bois and Augustus Granville Dill entitled *The Negro American Artisan* (Atlanta: Atlanta University Press, 1912), contain much useful information. The direction of future studies is perhaps signaled by as-yet unpublished dissertations: see, in particular, Whittington Bernard Johnson, "Negro Laboring Classes in Early America, 1750–1820," Ph.D. dissertation, University of Georgia, 1970; and Mary Allison Carll-White, "The Role of the Black Artisan in the Building Trades and the Decorative Arts in South Carolina's Charleston District, 1760–1800," Ph.D. dissertation, University of Tennessee, 1982.

4

From Gravestone to Miracle: Traditional Perspective and the Work of William Edmondson

William Edmondson's career as an artist was, like that of most creative persons, an odyssey of personal discovery (fig. 4.1). Beginning as a maker of simple grave markers, he would eventually attempt a vast array of sculptural commissions. These later works, such as his version of Adam and Eve (fig. 4.2) or his portrayals of heavyweight boxer Jack Johnson and Eleanor Roosevelt, are regarded as his most accomplished achievements, and they serve as the primary basis for his reputation as an important American folk artist. Yet these statues, because of their distinctiveness and their individuality, are just exactly the works that are most atypical and the least traditional of Edmondson's sculptures. An artwork is traditional if it has features of form and content that are usual, ordinary, regular, patterned, conventional, predictable, customary, commonplace. In short, folk art is a familiar art, tightly woven into the fabric of everyday existence that expresses artists' connections to their communities.[1] No work of Edmondson's was more accepted by his community than his gravestones, and consequently it is in these objects that we find the most legitimate basis for analyzing his connections to Afro-American folk culture. Indeed, once we understand what was involved in the design and creation of gravestones, we then have an important key that can open the way to a better understanding of the significance of traditional influences on his other artworks.

For black Americans the cemetery has long had special significance. Beyond its association with the fear and awe of death, which all humans share, the graveyard was, in the past, one of the few places in America where an overt black identity could be asserted and maintained. In some cases the opportunity for group expression took a political direction when

This article originally appeared in *William Edmondson* (Nashville: Tennessee Arts Commission, 1981), pp. 19–29. Reprinted by permission.

Figure 4.1. Louise Dahl-Wolfe, Portrait of William Edmondson, 1937
*(Courtesy of Cheekwood Botanical Gardens and Fine
Arts Center)*

the gathering of slaves at a funeral led to plans for escape or rebellion.
Eugene D. Genovese has noted that, "the slave-holder's regime tried to
supervise slave funerals and feared their providing the occasion for insur-
rectionary plots. In 1687 authorities in the Northern Neck of Virginia
banned public funerals for slaves because they had become convinced of
their role in hatching a dangerous conspiracy. In 1772 the corporation
of New York City required that slave funerals be held during daylight hours
and that maximum attendance be held to twelve."[2] In other instances the
funeral service was held in a distinct manner in which customs inspired
by memories of Africa were perpetuated and preserved. Consider the 1850
reminiscence of Mrs. Telfair Hodgson, the mistress of a coastal Georgia
plantation, who wrote: "Negro graves were always decorated, and broken

Figure 4.2.   ''Eve''
Limestone, 32″ x 11″ x 7″. This statue may
have been inspired by oriental sculptures in
the possession of Sidney Hirsch, a Nashville
intellectual who frequently conversed with
Edmondson and commissioned several pieces
from him.
(Courtesy of Cheekwood Botanical Gardens
and Fine Arts Center)

pitchers and broken bits of colored glass were considered more appropriate than the white shells from the beach nearby. Sometimes they carved rude wooden figures like images of idols, and sometimes a patchwork quilt was laid upon the grave.''[3] When such practices were allowed, graveyards became a vital resource for the maintenance of black identity. The artifacts set on the tops of graves were offerings to the soul or spirit of the deceased that symbolized a family's connection to their departed kin. Placed with the proper attitude, these objects could placate the potential fury of a hostile spirit.[4] The domain of the dead was filled with ever-present visual reminders of a distinctive system of magico-religious belief. For those who understood and believed, the graveyard then reaffirmed their sense of ethnicity as well as satisfying their personal need to communicate with their deceased family members. Often forced to accommodate to the demands of the white majority culture during their lives, these Blacks found in death a means of asserting their own worldview. In the black cemetery it was finally their order that was followed.[5]

When we understand that there is a complex system of belief and identity located in black graveyards, we can see that Edmondson's work as a maker of tombstones was not really as simple as it previously has seemed. The complexity of Afro-American funerary customs lends a level of complexity to his stone markers. While the stones themselves were often only modest tablets with just the name of the deceased and his or her dates of birth and death inscribed upon it, the purposes for which they were intended and the motivations of those who requested that the stones be carved were quite elaborate.

By the time that Edmondson began to carve gravestones in the early 1930s, black funerary customs had understandably assimilated some elements of the Anglo-American way of death. Early twentieth-century black burials are commonly marked with tablet-shaped headstones (a borrowed image from white culture) along with other Afro-American elements of ornamentation (personal items, shells, glassware, ceramic containers, etc.) (see p. 43). The addition of a ''foreign'' symbol to the black mortuary tradition does not, however, indicate a lessening of the fervor for the obligation to revere the deceased, only the acquisition of a new means to honor that obligation. The tombstone became, in a sense, a grave offering conveying care and concern equivalent to a personal item even though it did not possess the same degree of intimacy. It is important to consider then how a gravestone functions, not just how it looks. These markers had a meaningful place in a social system. Edmondson's gravestones were, for his clients, a significant item in an important set of funeral rituals that included a wake, church services, burial observances, and even a sermon preached some months after internment in addition to the marking and decorating of the grave.[6]

By ordering a grave marker the members of Edmondson's community simultaneously confirmed their religious beliefs and their kinship ties. The importance of these moral and social matters consequently placed Edmondson in a critical position from which he provided an equally critical service. The strong bonds that his clients felt for their deceased family members fostered a parallel bond of service between them and the stone carver because of their need for a grave marker. Edmondson was to a great extent the means by which many Blacks in Nashville observed their traditional customs. While the request for a tombstone could be construed solely as a monetary negotiation, the significance of death and funerals in Afro-American culture converted that request into a religious matter. Edmondson's gravestones cannot then be considered apart from the shared beliefs of Nashville's black community. They are not just his expression, but an ethnic statement created out of the context of well-known Afro-American rites that insure the necessary respect for the dead.

The fact that gravestones function in a social system is an important proof that these items have a traditional basis. Resulting not only from an individual's skill but also from collectively maintained attitudes, the gravestone represents communal sentiments; that is, it is a physical statement of the interactions among community members and between the carver and his clients. The manner in which Edmondson acquired some of his raw material is indicative of his intimate and personal connections with his co racial community. When the black quarry workers employed at the Ezell Mill and Stone Company quarry in Newsom Station, Tennessee, came to town with their deliveries of building materials, they would steer past Edmondson's house on 14th Avenue to drop off the odd-sized stones that the contractor thought unusable. These men were no doubt intrigued with Edmondson's creative efforts and supported him by augmenting his supplies of limestone. The quarrymen's goodwill was later underscored when one of their crew was killed in an accident and Edmondson was asked to make a monument for their slain colleague.[7] The social interaction that preceded this commission made the request for a marker an almost natural act. Growing out of intimate face-to-face knowledge (maybe even out of mutual affection), this gravestone is a confirmation of the kind of social interaction upon which tradition thrives.

American folk artists in the twentieth century are hardly ever completely traditional, for no person is now immune to the welter of influences available from mass media or a highly mobile population. Henry Glassie has described the contemporary folk art context as a situation in which "the student of American culture will be dealing with a single society dominated by a governmentally and economically endorsed popular culture within which each individual will have available two possibilities for cultural deviation: one progressively oriented, the other conservatively oriented; the latter may be the subject of folkloristic study.''[8] Edmondson's works, when measured by the standard of cultural conservatism, fall into a range of categorical slots. Some pieces, like his gravestones, are close to the center of a stable folk tradition in terms of form, content, and use. His figures of animals would be located closer to the fringes of tradition for Afro-American folk sculpture, since stone is a medium rarely used by black folk carvers, and because his choice of content in these sculptures is mainly personal in origin.[9] Edmondson's sculptures of humans were, except for general aspects of style, extensively marked by his personal imagination. These last works stem from his private, unshared vision and hence are his works, not his community's. The stone carvings of William Edmondson reflect the complexity of contemporary American society and especially the plurality of options available to an artist; at times he followed the path of familiar tradition, on occasion he would abandon the traditional for the novel and unprecedented.

If not all of Edmondson's work was destined to have a place in the social realm of tradition, most of his sculpture does at least seem to be unified in a formal system tied to a tradition of technique. Throughout his career he never abandoned the making of gravestones. Within four years of his own death in 1951 he was still making grave markers. These stones then constitute a base upon which his career was built. He had turned to stone carving after thirty years of labor at the Nashville, Chattanooga, and St. Louis Railroad shops and at the Women's Hospital.[10] During his final twenty years, he supported himself mainly as a maker of tombstones and he used his traditional occupation as a source of precedent for more adventuresome forms. The minimal, blocky style that characterizes his most accomplished statues can be traced, in part, to the simple block and tablet forms of his grave markers. Thus even Edmondson's nontraditional creations have some traditional attributes, such as symmetry and frontality, even though their intended purpose as works of commissioned art had little connection to his black community. His entire corpus of sculpture possesses a formal consistency because all his pieces were influenced by the way in which he embarked on his role as a stone carver. He began as a traditional craftsman/artisan, but later he would occasionally move away from the strictures of the gravestone tradition. While he explored his environment, both social and personal, to gather inspirations for novel sculptures, he would never reject the familiar formulas acquired during his initial discovery of gravestone design and carving technique.

Edmondson is well-known for the conversations he claimed to have with God. Declaring that he only turned to stonecarving because of divine instruction, his recollection of that moment is quite revealing since the first form he was commanded to make was a gravestone. Edmondson remembered: "I was out in the driveway with some old pieces of stone when I heard a voice telling me to pick up my tools and start to work on a tombstone. I looked up in the sky and right there in the noon day light He hung a tombstone out for me to make."[11] To judge from his first gravestones, God must have shown Edmondson a tablet form. These tablets were sometimes dressed with rusticated edges, or perhaps a portion of the face of the stone would bear a raised triangle with a roughened surface. In addition to simple blocks or stones with rounded shoulders, Edmondson eventually expanded his repertoire to include pointy Gothic shapes, pentangles, spade or tear-drop shapes, blocks topped with circles, and stones with rounded tops and slightly undercut sides that resemble squatty mushrooms. While this variety might be ascribed to Edmondson's visions, it is important to recognize that this range of improvision with geometric shapes has been noted in Afro-American folk grave markers from South Carolina to Texas. When wooden markers are used, the head of a grave often has a circle set over a rectangular slab while at the foot there is a stake topped with an elongated diamond or a V-shaped notch.[12] Even in the few instances where carved stones were common, the same minimal round head icon is found; a set of sandstone monuments from Panola County, Texas, being a noteworthy example.[13] A close analogue to this widespread Afro-American form is the stone that Edmondson made for Mrs. Lou Cockrell, in Nashville's Mt. Ararat Cemetery, in 1942. Another intriguing comparison between Edmondson's work and that of other black gravestone markers arises from the mutual use of a shape that resembles a pentangle; again black cemeteries in Texas contain similar forms.[14] However close Edmondson was to his "Heavenly Daddy," he apparently also knew something about commonplace black funerary images.

If the "simple" geometric patterns employed by Edmondson can be accepted as evidence of his attachment to folk culture, his markers that are topped by sculpture seem to derive from popular culture. In the late nineteenth century American cemeteries were ornamented with elaborate mortuary sculpture. Victorian imagery included noble portraits, allegorical mourning figures, and all manner of animals, cherubs, and decorative devices.[15] These forms found their way into Edmondson's environment and provided him with new options for his creative muse. He had no doubt seen some of this elaborate mortuary sculpture in the Mount Olivet cemetery (which was very close to where many of his clients were buried) and added similar figures to his own stones. He occasionally did minimal portraits but mainly he carved doves and lambs, the conventional Christian symbols of purity and salvation (figs. 4.3–4).[16] The lamb was an extremely popular image of early twentieth-century grave markers, and tombstones with lamb symbols could be purchased from the Sears, Roebuck

Figure 4.3.   Detail of Dove Mounted on a Tombstone
(Photo by Louise Dahl-Wolfe, 1937.
Courtesy of Cheekwood Botanical Gardens
and Fine Arts Center)

and Co. catalog for as little as ten dollars. This trendy fashion in a gravestone decoration placed flocks of fleecy grave ornaments in Edmondson's sight line. Whether he went to the rustically landscaped white cemetery or the scraped field adjacent to a black country church, he was likely to find a reclining lamb fixed to the top of a gravestone. It is not surprising that he adopted this particular image; rather, it is important to remember that this kind of imagery came from outside his community and from beyond the boundaries of his ethnic tradition. His grave markers with sculptures represent, then, an early exploration of novel forms, a first step along the pathway of personal discovery. He did not move erratically towards something unique, but carefully borrowed a sanctioned form from an alternate and easily available cultural source. This evident caution in the selection of imagery might be further interpreted as an indication that his choice of popular imagery was, in fact, influenced by folk conservatism.

Because Edmondson worked with relatively small pieces of stone (stones small enough for him to heft by himself), any creative impulses

Figure 4.4. Tombstone for Bernice Williams with a
Lamb Carved into Its Top
Limestone, 17″ x 12″ x 6″.
(Courtesy of Dr. and Mrs. V. S. LeQuire)

to make a large sculpture required that he join several stones together. This
he accomplished by stacking one stone on top of another, usually without
cement mortar. A typical gravestone had a base with a slot in it into which
a rectangular block, bearing the critical written information, was set. On
top of this tablet rested at least one capping slab (sometimes two slabs were
used), which in turn supported the sculpted ornament. Animals were commonly set into slots in the capping slab or set up with their own integral
pedestal. The range of ornaments used to complete these multiple-unit
gravestones reveals the range of inputs on his carving. Simple geometric

forms like a double circle or a crescent reflect the minimal forms akin to those commonly encountered in traditional black burials. Doves, angels, and preachers suggest the influence of turn-of-the-century sentimentality in funerary iconography. The Victorian mode is also sensed in his use of shield and scroll emblems and in his creation of a pulpit-shaped marker from three carefully shaped stones.[17] The cultural borrowing in which Edmondson engaged brought him eventually to a point where he would utilize forms that were quite uncommon in his own tradition, such as the crucifix or the plain cross. Usually indicative of Catholicism, these two forms are rarely found in the southeastern United States, which has long been the stronghold of fundamentalist Protestantism.[18] Hence Edmondson was on occasion doubly removed from his own tradition when he selected images that not only came from a different social class but from a different religion. In the multiple-unit type of stone, Edmondson was apparently more given to experiment. Perhaps because each of these objects was in part very traditional—the tablet section continued to function as a conventional grave marker—he felt the freedom to try his hand at new images. The tablet was both figuratively and literally the base for his improvisation. The cultural "hybrid" that resulted from this process reflects the betwixt-and-between state of mind of an artist venturing into new territory. Much of Edmondson's sculpture is his and his alone, but his personal accomplishments in art were still tied to his traditional background, even if loosely.

As mentioned earlier, there is an apparent stylistic link between Edmondson's gravestones and his statues. The statues are barely released from the original block. One senses that the top edge of the chunk of stone coincides with the top of the head, the side of the rock with the shoulder, and so forth. Edmondson said of his approach that he carved "stingily," clearly identifying the minimal nature of his style of working.[19] One can see the gradual departure from this approach over the course of his career, but he never left it completely. There is an evident sequence that marks his progress toward free-standing sculpture in the round. The series begins with gravestones that are topped with what appear to be portrait busts. These sculptures consist of rudimentary depictions of faces set within a cloudlike background of roughened stone. This backdrop in some instances could represent an ethereal nimbus or in other cases be an elaborate bushy coiffure. At any rate the depiction of the person is minimal and the qualities of a quarried stone block, of a simple tablet, still dominate the artwork. The figure of Eleanor Roosevelt (fig. 4.5), when compared to these gravestone portraits, appears to be a full-length version of the funerary form: the standing figure is surrounded by an "envelope" of stone. While this statue could represent Mrs. Roosevelt wearing a heavy overcoat (and

Figure 4.5.   "Eleanor Roosevelt"
Limestone, 20" x 13" x 7".
(Courtesy of Mr. and Mrs. Myron King)

Edmondson is thought to have seen her in a wintertime motorcade that passed two blocks from his house),[20] the formal continuity between this piece and his gravestone carvings should not be discounted. From the neck up the statue of Mrs. Roosevelt could pass for a tombstone portrait. The same formal similarity is also found in some of Edmondson's angels. After acknowledging that he may have had a specific aesthetic impact in mind by surrounding these figures in a blanket of stone, we must also recognize that his choice of shape and surface also allowed him to maintain aspects of a form and texture with which he was very familiar. Edmondson apparently found a way to enlarge his repertoire without totally giving up the mode of the tombstone. The blend that he achieved between sculpture and gravestone carving is most easily recognized in his so-called "Girl with Cape" (fig. 4.6), in which a standing figure is clearly encased within the block of a tablet. Indeed Edmondson's standing figures average seven inches in depth, a thickness equivalent to his gravestones.

Edmondson's attachment to and reliance on gravestones as the generative basis for more elaborate sculptures is sensed in his method as well as his choice of forms. When carving grave markers he would prepare a supply of more-or-less standardized tablets and finish them with the required capping stones and inscriptions as the need arose. He approached the carving of large animals in a similar manner, blocking out the major angles for the head, torso, and legs, and then setting these "blanks" aside until he was ready to add the lively details of a particular "varmint" or a "critter." Ironically a visitor to his yard was taken by one of these unfinished forms and purchased it as it was. A bemused Edmondson responded that he could have made something nice from the stone if the caller would have been patient.[21] An important implication here is that, in his view, the craft involved in the preparation of the slab opened up the possibility for sculptural virtuosity. While he gave credit to Jesus for "planting the seed of carving" within him, it is evident that his experience in making tombstones prepared him to make other kinds of sculpture.[22]

Edmondson's gravestones had a sacred connotation, but much of his collected sculpture seems inspired by secular associations, particularly the portrayals of Jezebel, the "School Teacher" (fig. 4.7) and the "Ladies Sitting on the Porch." In these works and many others, Edmondson moved away from the realm of the dead into the contexts of daily life. These sculptures were intended to embellish domestic spaces where they were appreciated as attractive forms rather than as statements of social and moral bonds like the gravestones. The garden pieces done by Edmondson have a decorative purpose too, but in form they are clearly derived from his grave markers. His birdbaths (fig. 4.8) are stacked forms very much like the multiple-unit tombstones consisting of a base stone, a vertical element (usually a stand-

Figure 4.6. "Girl with Cape"
Limestone, 15″ x 7″ x 7″.
(Courtesy of Mrs. Elizabeth Starr)

ing figure), and a bowl section that overhangs the central section. Like the tombstones these sections are fitted into each other and held in place only by the weight of the stones; no mortar was used. The resemblances in form and technique of assembly are further underscored by the occasional use of bird figures as decoration for both genres. Some of the birdbaths were topped off with the same doves used as tombstone finials. Stylistic continuities can also be observed between the caryatid figures that support the bathing bowls and the portrait figures that surmount some gravestone

Figure 4.7.   "The School Teacher"
Limestone, 15″ x 6″ x 8″.
*(Courtesy of Cheekwood Botanical Gardens
and Fine Arts Center)*

Figure 4.8.   Birdbath
(Photo by Louise Dahl-Wolfe, 1937.
Courtesy of Cheekwood Botanical Gardens
and Fine Arts Center)

tablets. It would thus appear that Edmondson relied on his gravestone designs even when he developed fanciful compositions that were intended solely as yard art.

This shift in genres was evidently not a disruptive one since the artifacts, in both cases, were so similar. Consider two of Edmondson's decorative pieces that were topped by stone spheres. In these two instances he used a diamond-shaped tablet for a central section and balanced the stone ball on its tip. These assemblages recall the deliberate manipulation of geometric elements found in the most traditional of Afro-American grave markers. This formal link is strengthened even more when we examine one of these ornamental pieces in which the stone sphere rests on a slab cut in a diamond form that lays horizontally atop the diamond-shaped tablet. The horizontal slab in this instance was used to achieve exactly the same decorative affect found in a gravestone that Edmondson made for Samuel Haley.[23] The major difference here is that the diamond-shaped carving stone on the grave marker supports a dove instead of a stone ball.

Hence we see that once again Edmondson's experience as a carver of traditional gravestones prepared him to make nontraditional items. Tradition was for him a fund of primary concepts upon which he could draw for both communal and personal purposes. And because it was there within him and within his community, his work has a general continuity of form and design even when a piece was intended for a context and purpose beyond the boundaries of his co-ethnic community. Even in those instances when he borrowed elements of form or content from popular or elite sources, his traditional approach to stone carving was still manifested.

Tradition for Edmondson meant more than gravestones; it also, as William H. Wiggins, Jr., has shown, meant religion.[24] Edmondson's whole life was strongly marked by divine intervention, and indeed he claimed once not to know that his carving had any artistic merit: "I is just doing the Lord's work. I didn't know I was no artist till them folks told me I was."[25] He had the ambition to become a preacher but was reticent about speaking in public. This hesitancy he rationalized, it seems, by plunging more fervently into his world of stone, declaring: "He takes my mind off it [preaching] and tells me I got work to do."[26] The extent of his feeling for his stone carving is revealed by the comment of Martha Campbell, his supervisor when he was supported by the Tennessee WPA art project, who noted that he was always at work and that "he was definitely a driven man."[27] Edmondson's religious feelings found extensive expression in his carving. This is perhaps self-evident from his selections of angels, crucifixions, preachers, doves, lambs, Adam and Eve, and Mary and Martha as subjects. However, since he credited all of his knowledge of stone carving to God, every piece that he made had the quality of a testimony, and can be seen as a stony analogue to the vocal witnessing to God's power and majesty often encountered in black church services. While all of his work was "holy," the more elaborate and complicated pieces were "miracles" representing a pinnacle of Edmondson's sculptural achievement. Religion then is unquestionably a pervasive theme in his work and should be regarded as an important influence on Edmondson's self-perception as well as being an important means for him to connect himself to his community.

We have seen here, however, that as artifacts Edmondson's sculptures are also the products of historical, ethnic, and social precedents. Edmondson took cues from the traditional and popular art forms in his cultural environment and later used them for more personal ends. Nevertheless, even when he was at his most idiosyncratic, his works still belonged to a formal system of design that was well within the grip of antecedents basic to his traditional occupation. Repeatedly inspired by visions from God, Edmondson manipulated the rules and content of gravestone carving to eventually produce "miracles." Tradition, a human construct that ensures the stability and sanity of human experience, was bent ultimately to the service of God. Yet all the while that God was being served, Edmondson also managed to put his mark on Afro-American funerary sculpture, leaving behind a legacy in stone that must be understood as belonging to his community as well as to him.

Notes

1. John Michael Vlach, "American Folk Art: Questions and Quandaries," *Winterthur Portfolio* 15 (1980):346.

2. Eugene D. Genovese, *Roll, Jordan, Roll: The World the Slaves Made* (New York: Vintage Books, 1972), 194.

3. Susan II. Torian, "Ante-Bellum and War Memories of Mrs. Telfair Hodgson," *Georgia Historical Quarterly* 27 (1943):35.

4. See Newbell Niles Puckett, *The Magic and Folk Belief of the Southern Negro,* 1926 (rpt. New York: Dover Publications, 1969), 101–7.

5. John Michael Vlach, *The Afro-American Tradition in Decorative Arts* (Cleveland: Cleveland Museum of Art, 1978), 147.

6. For a description of a black funeral see Hortense Powdermaker, *After Freedom: A Cultural Study of the Deep South* (New York: Viking Press, 1939), 249–52.

7. Louise LeQuire, personal communication, March 1981.

8. Henry Glassie, *Pattern in the Material Folk Culture of the Eastern United States* (Philadelphia: University of Pennsylvania Press, 1968), 4.

9. For another example of a black stone carver, see Elizabeth Mosby Adler, " 'It Takes a Smart Guy to Take a Look at a Rock and Do Things like That': George 'Baby' Scott (1865–1945), a Carver and His Repertoire," *Mid-South Folklore* 3 (1975):47–60.

10. Edmund L. Fuller, *Visions in Stone: The Sculpture of William Edmondson* (Pittsburgh: University of Pittsburgh Press, 1973), 27, n. 4.

11. Quoted in *Will Edmondson's Mirkels* (exhibition catalog) (Nashville: Tennessee Fine Arts Center at Cheekwood, 1964), n.p.

12. Personal fieldwork in South Carolina and Georgia, June 1976. See also Donald G. Jeane, "The Traditional Upland South Cemetery," *Landscape* 18 (1969): 39.

13. See Terry G. Jordan, *Traditional Texas Graveyards* (Austin: University of Texas Press, 1982), 47. Similar stones were also used in southern Illinois; see Larry W. Price, "Some Results and Implications of a Cemetery Study," *The Professional Geographer* 18 (1966):204.

14. Terry G. Jordan, "Forest Folk, Prairie Folk: Rural Religious Cultures in North Texas," *Southwestern Historical Quarterly* 80 (1976): 161. It should be noted that geometric forms are also known in the traditions for white gravestones as well. Form alone is not always perfect proof of ethnicity.

15. Edmund V. Gillon, Jr., *Victorian Cemetery Art* (New York: Dover Publications, 1972).

16. George Ferguson, *Signs and Symbols in Christian Art* (New York: Oxford University Press, 1954), 10–11, 19.

17. For the contours of the chronology of American gravestone art, see Richard V. Francaviglia, "The Cemetery as an Evolving Cultural Landscape," *Annals of the Association of American Geographers* 61 (1971):501–9. For an illustration of Edmondson's pulpit stone see Georgeann Fletcher, ed.,*William Edmondson: A Retrospective* (Nashville: Tennessee State Arts Commission, 1981), 24.

18. Wilbur Zelinsky, *The Cultural Geography of the United States* (Englewood Cliffs, N.J.: Prentice Hall, 1973), 97.

19. Fuller, *Visions in Stone,* 16.

20. Louise LeQuire, personal communication, March 1981.

21. Ibid.

22. Fuller, *Visions in Stone,* 3.

23. Ibid., 13.

24. See Wiggins' essay in *William Edmondson: A Retrospective,* 31–41.

25. Fuller, *Visions in Stone,* 22.

26. John Thompson, "Negro Stone Cutter Here Says Gift from Lord: Work Praises," *Tennessean* (Feb. 9, 1941):A-11.

27. Letter from Martha Campbell to Jym Knight, June 26, 1980.

5

Philip Simmons: Afro-American Blacksmith

It was a different day for Philip Simmons. He didn't know it at first; he couldn't. But nevertheless it was on that day that he faced the world as a master blacksmith. The "old man," Peter Simmons (no relation), felt the full burden of his ninety-eight years one day in 1954 and went back to the house. He died a few days later. Philip, the "apprentice boy" and journeyman to Peter, was on his own. The old man had worked to the end.

Philip Simmons's family moved from Wando, South Carolina, to Charleston in 1920. Four years later, at the age of twelve, Philip began to learn the smith's trade. Simmons recalls that after the first four years he had learned to do most things: "By then I was a pretty good mechanic." Peter taught by experience. Philip was first given errands to run and charged with keeping the shop in order. As he became familiar with the craft he was given more ambitious tasks. Always an order was given first and directions only when failure was imminent. Once when young Philip had worn himself out swinging an eight-pound sledge hammer, the master stopped him; his few words of advice: "You just lift the hammer, boy. It'll carry itself down." The lesson was never forgotten. As Philip's skill continued to develop and improve he gradually inherited more of Peter Simmons's work load. By the time the older man reached his last decade, the student was probably more adept than the teacher. Yet it was only when Peter was through with work and life that Philip really became the master.

As Philip Simmons matured from an awkward apprentice to a confident and sure-handed craftsman, the blacksmith business was undergoing a serious decline. Peter Simmons had managed to keep a full slate of jobs, but only barely. There wasn't much demand for a smith, but he had a good reputation and got his share of work. He was chiefly a service craftsman.

This article originally appeared in *Black People and Their Culture* (Washington, D.C.: Smithsonian Institution, 1976), pp. 35–57. Reprinted by permission of the Smithsonian Institution Press.

He repaired buggies, wagon wheels, and plows. Mostly he made tools: caulking irons for plumbers, harpoons and shark hooks for fishermen, chisels for carpenters, stoking irons for colliers, trowels for masons. He also took on farrier work and consequently made horseshoes. He rarely did anything ornamental.[1] He was a craftsman in iron, making and repairing ordinary wrought iron items. Philip was trained to do the same. But all the while he was learning the trade, the role of the blacksmith was being usurped by machines in factories. Times were changing. People no longer used horses and buggies; there were no wagon wheels to make or mend; tools were purchased out of catalogs; ships were fueled with oil. What does a man trained to work metal do when there is no further need for this skill? The answer for Philip Simmons was clear: "You have to change to get along."

So Simmons made a change. He learned to use an electric arc welder and an oxygen-acetylene torch. He had no formal training. He just decided that he needed to do it and so it was done. If there were no buggies to outfit, he would work on trucks and cars instead. He made bumpers and leaf springs, flatbed frames and pipe racks, brackets and hood latches. If a crucial part was hard to find, Simmons could make it from scratch. He also did work on houses, repairing or replacing iron stair railings, balconies, window grills, and fences. He explains that the old work and the new follow the same principle: "A circle is a circle, and an angle is an angle." When asked how he learned to do decorative ironwork, he replied: "I can mash out a leaf same as a horseshoe." In fact, Simmons is very skillful with ornamental wrought iron and has a local reputation in Charleston. His services are continually sought out by restoration contractors to make elaborate gates and other decorations. His "snake" gate at the Gadsden House (on East Bay Street) (see p. 30) and his porch rail and window grills at "Eagle Nest" (43 Meeting Street) are two of his best works (fig. 5.1). Some earlier works from the days when he used hot rivets rather than a welding machine can be found on Stoll's Alley (fig. 5.2).[2]

Thus the tradition of blacksmithing has been carried forward and transformed into the art of ornamental ironwork. Simmons however continues to think of himself as a blacksmith. Ornamental ironwork falls within smithing because "in the old days the blacksmith made the fancy pieces for the ornamental ironworker." Regardless of the semantic distinction between blacksmithing and ironworking, Simmons took up a doomed trade and has made it pay by adapting to changing economic conditions and circumstances.

The significance of Philip Simmons's achievement can only be fully recognized when studied in relationship to the past. Those connections go back beyond Peter Simmons to Guy Simmons (Peter's father) who was also a blacksmith. Philip says he "traces Guy back almost 200 years." This

Figure 5.1. Detail of Window Grill at "Eagle Nest"
(All photographs and drawings by the author)

is certainly an exaggeration, yet the last two hundred years of Afro-American blacksmithing would help place the current situation in proper perspective. The history of Negro ironwork will throw Simmons's own works into sharp relief so that they may be appreciated as part of a long tradition as well as examples of individual talent.

Afro-American Blacksmithing

It should not be surprising to find that Afro-Americans have been very adept at blacksmithing. The smelting of iron and the forging of wrought iron implements and sculpture are widely known throughout Africa.[3] One of the strongest links between African and Afro-American art is in fact a wrought iron figure found on the site of slave quarters in Virginia. It is twelve inches tall, fairly symmetrical in stance, with a small head, outreaching arms, and legs spread apart (see p. 27). It is strikingly similar to some Bambara examples of wrought iron sculpture.[4] Not all ironwork made by black Americans can be given African antecedents but in many cases the slaves trained to shoe horses might have had previous knowledge of metal work.

In the antebellum South it was common practice for slaves to be trained in all the crafts.[5] In 1783 a German physician travelling through the United States wrote that: "There was hardly any craft which has not

Figure 5.2.   Gate at No. 9 Stoll's Alley

been learned and is not carried on by negroes."[6] According to Carl Briden-baugh the plantation economy prohibited the development of a class of craftsmen among Whites and hence in the Carolinas the overwhelming majority of artisans were Negroes.[7] He suggests that a good number of Blacks were involved in the iron-making business:

> Slave labor was well fitted for the heavy work, simple operations, and intense heat at a furnace or a forge. . . . At his forge . . . Bernard Moore had a trained group of Negro workers which he advertised to dispose by lottery in 1769: Billy, aged twenty-two, is an "exceeding trusty good forgeman as well at the finery as under the hammer, and understands putting up his fire"; Mungo, twenty-four, is a good hammer man; Sam, twenty-six, is a good chafering hand; Abraham, twenty-six, a reliable forge carpenter; while Bob, twenty-seven, thoroughly understands the duties of a master collier. The roster of this forge included seventeen skilled slave artisans and is typical of the com-paratively small iron works of the [Chesapeake] area.[8]

Negro blacksmiths were frequently found on plantations where they were masters of all sorts of ironwork. W. E. B. Du Bois wrote of them:

> The Negro blacksmith held almost absolute sway in this line, which included the many branches of forgery and other trades which are now classified under different heads from that of the regular blacksmith. The blacksmith in the days of slavery was expected to make any and everything wrought of iron. He was to all intents and purposes the "machine blacksmith," "horseshoer," "carriage and wagon ironer and trimmer," and often whittled and ironed the hames, the plowstocks and the "singletree" for the farmers and a hundred other things too numerous to mention.[9]

In Charleston Blacks were found at work in all common and specialized crafts. The situation was such that white journeymen could not find employment, Masters often set up shops for skilled slaves and netted a large share of their profits. White craftsmen could not compete with the low rates that slaves charged for their work. As early as 1751 the Charles Town Assembly passed legislation prohibiting any citizen from keeping more than two slaves "to work for Hire, as Porters, Labourers, Fishermen, or Handi-craftsmen." Four years later, slaves were further restricted from working by themselves in shops set up by their masters. They could continue to work, however, if the master employed one White for every two slaves.[10] These were the kind of conditions under which Christopher Werner, a famous German ironworker in Charleston from 1828 to 1878, came to employ three Whites and five Blacks.[11] One of his slaves, "Uncle Toby" Richardson, is described as a "top rank artist in iron." He was so skilled at executing the designs laid out for him that the gates and fences iden-tified as Werner's should be credited to Richardson as well.[12] An industrial census of Charleston in 1848 showed that there were eighty-nine blacksmiths in that area: forty-five were White, forty were slaves, and four were free Blacks.[13] A census of "Free Colored People" in 1856 lists six wheelwrights and six blacksmiths.[14] The circumstances of free black craftsmen in South Carolina before the Civil War might be illustrated by the example of blacksmith Ralph Burnet. In 1850 he owned thirty acres of land, a horse, three milk cows, two cattle, and twelve swine. His agricultural production amounted to 100 bushels of Indian corn, twenty bushels of oats, and two 400-pound bales of cotton.[15] The supplementary income from his farm when added to his gains from smithing probably allowed him to live comfortably.

The fact that there was a fair number of black blacksmiths in South Carolina, whose work was good yet relatively inexpensive, encouraged a pattern of white patronage. Indeed if legislation was needed to curb the rise of black craftsmen, they must have received the larger share of the trade. The years of plantation economics and cheap slave labor established a pattern of dependence on black craftsmen that could not be easily changed. In 1889 Philip A. Bruce commented:

> The negroes who now attend to the mechanical needs of different plantations are men who have established themselves near a country store or at the crossing of two public roads, or wherever there is a site that is convenient to travellers or to the people of large communities. Their shops are generally primitive shanties and supplied only with old fashioned tools and the appliances of their trade. Smithies are the most frequently observed. The principle customers of the blacksmiths are the planters in their vicinity whose horses and mules they shoe or the iron of whose wagon bodies and wheels they mend, but they are also patronized by the strange teamsters who pass along the public roads or stop to rest at the country stores.[16]

It is apparent then that the antebellum popularity of black blacksmiths did not change much after emancipation. Although the foregoing description is critical in tone with respect to the physical appearance of blacksmith shops, it does indicate that a vigorous trade was carried on. Thus, status that Blacks gained as craftsmen under slavery did not vanish with the arrival of freedom.

A survey in 1890 revealed that there were 11,156 black blacksmiths and wheelwrights in the United States, of whom 882 worked in South Carolina.[17] A second census of black craftsmen showed that by 1900 the total number of blacksmiths and wheelwrights had fallen to 10,352 and that in South Carolina the total had fallen to 803.[18] At that time a Charleston farrier said: "There is a good feeling existing between white and colored workers. Conditions are growing better for the Negro skilled laborers because all avenues are open to them. The Negro is the controlling workman in Charleston along all trades."[19] At the time when this optimistic claim was made the fate of all traditional crafts in the United States was rapidly worsening. Charleston perhaps did not feel the crunch so soon. Today Charleston has only two blacksmiths; both are Blacks. Three other ironworkers located near Charleston, who are still active, are also Blacks. The decline in numbers of blacksmiths has been alarmingly swift but the persistence of traditions shows itself even now. Five ironworkers may seem insignificant when compared to the eight hundred who were active only seven decades ago. However, given the history of Afro-American blacksmithing, which featured black craftsmen in a prominent position, it is expected that some vestiges would still remain.

Hence we come to see Philip Simmons as one of the last of Charleston's black blacksmiths. But the story of Afro-American ironwork will not end soon. Simmons is well-known as a maker of gates and fences. The Charleston community is thoroughly enamoured of the lost days of plantation culture, and it delights in holding up to the world a series of icons of the genteel past in the form of elaborate mansions, formal gardens, and wrought iron decorations. It is the celebration of a kind of romantic regionalism, the "spirit of the Low Country," that will insure the continuation of local ironwork. Organizations like the Historic Charleston Foundation, private citizens who restore old homes, and architects who want their buildings outfitted with appropriate Charleston motifs are all finding that there is no way to replace the wrought iron ornaments of the eighteenth and nineteenth centuries other than by having them made to order. Simmons's talents are then in high demand and his work load is ever increasing. He remarked once that he had read a magazine article about the "last" blacksmith in America. Simmons said, "I didn't think about it until much later, but I'm a blacksmith and I'm still working. I never think of blacksmithing as ending." Furthermore he has two young men as partners, Silas Sessions and Ronnie Pringle. Both have worked with Simmons since they were in high school. There is also a high school student who receives vocational training credits while working as an apprentice. Thus the tradition of blacksmithing will continue, although in a somewhat modified form. Silas and Ronnie will weld more and more with electric machines rather than the old forge and anvil technique. They may do more car body work than tool-making. But they know the old ways, and when the community calls upon them to fashion an artifact of a past age, they will be able to reach into their own traditions and bring it forth.

The Community and the Shop

Philip Simmons lives and works on the east side of Charleston, one of several black neighborhoods in the city. It is bordered on its eastern edge by the harbor and split in two by an elevated freeway. The most common building here is a two-story frame "l" house (called "single houses" in Charleston) with its gable facing the street. Houses are packed tightly together and sit close to the sidewalk. Some buildings are in need of work, but most are well-kept and many have been recently painted. There is constant movement on the streets whether it is early in the morning or late at night—kids at play, men and women coming from and going to work, old and young men jostling each other on the corner, folks running up to the corner store for a soda or over to the tavern for a beer. The focus of much activity is C. A. Brown High School, a two-block complex of red brick buildings and asphalt playgrounds. Here local basketball championships occur hourly.

Across the street from the school, a narrow driveway leads to a small gray building (fig. 5.3). This house at 30½ Blake Street is the home of Philip Simmons. The yard is filled with a brick driveway that winds around to the side of the house and back to the blacksmith shop. A few bushes make valiant attempts to grow in a flower bed without much success. A scraggy brown dog guards the yard. "Brownie" doesn't discriminate; he barks at everyone. Flat metal stock of various sizes is stored alongside the drive. The shop, roughly square in shape, is a metal frame covered with galvanized metal siding (fig. 5.4). It has a shed roof, sloping front to rear. To the right of the shop is a storage yard for scrap parts such as old gates, sections of fence, grates, and metal frames. Up against the wall of the shop an area is set up for assembling fence sections. On the left side of the shop factory-made bars in twenty-foot lengths are arranged in a covered rack.

The shop interior is kept neat and organized (fig. 5.5). Junior, the apprentice, is charged with sweeping up, putting tools away, and keeping the metal stock covered and in order. Tools are hung around the walls in their appropriate places. Chisels and punches go over the work table and vise. Tongs are hung above the forge, and bending templates are kept along the back wall. Paint is kept on a shelf while electric tools, drill bits, spare parts for oxygen-acetylene torches, and assorted small items are stored in a tall cabinet.

The items that take up floor space are also placed near the walls. The forge is located in the rear right-hand corner with the anvil close to it. There are tables on both sides of the shop. The one near the forge is used for metal work, usually to bend scrolls, while the other is used for storage. There is a vise mounted on a small platform and a large crate that serves as a support for a bench grinder near the front right-hand corner. The left half of the shop is usually empty during the day but at night a low trailer, loaded with an electric welding machine and a cutting torch, is parked there. Although the shop has two nine-foot wide doors that can be swung open, only the left-hand door is used and it is never closed. There are two

A. 32 Blake St.
B. dog house and supply shed
C. Simmons's house, 30½ Blake St.
D. storage area for flat stock
E. storage area for finished pieces
F. storage rack for bars
G. blacksmith shop
H. lay-out area for fence sections
I. storage area for scrap iron

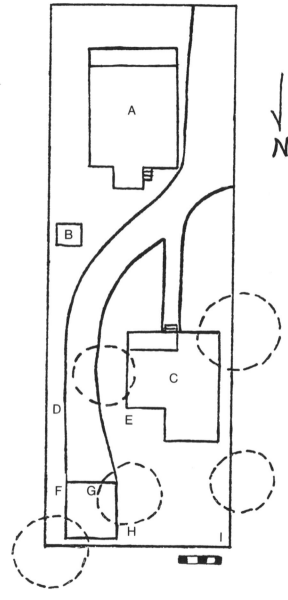

Figure 5.3. Plan of Simmons's Yard

Figure 5.4.   Simmons's Blacksmith Shop

windows; one on the east side and the other opposite it. The shop is fairly dark all the time, even on the brightest days, because of three shade
trees that provide a kind of canopy over the building. The darkness is compounded by the fact that there is no chimney to carry smoke from the
forge out of the shop. Consequently the ceiling and the walls are stained
black by the soot. The dark atmosphere is intentional since sunlight
disguises the color of hot metal.[20] The two most striking objects in the
shop are the forge and the anvil (fig. 5.6). The forge is one that Simmons
made himself. It consists of a sheet metal tub, twenty inches high and two
feet in diameter, lined with bricks and fire clay so that a small opening
remains in the center. An electrically driven fan forces air into the forge
from the bottom. Simmons has two anvils. One is used in the shop, while
a smaller one (which once belonged to Peter Simmons) is relegated to the
scrap yard and rarely used. The main anvil is attached to a chunk of tree
stump which in turn is mounted on two pieces of 6″ × 6″ post. This setup
is not as unstable as it would seem. The weight of the anvil is great enough
that any rocking motion is negligible. In fact, Simmons prefers that the
anvil not be firmly attached to the floor since he likes to move it around
according to the size of the piece of iron he is working.

A. work table
B. bench grinder
C. oxygen-acetylene torch
D. vise
E. work table
F. anvil
G. water bucket
H. fuel bucket
I. forge
J. box of anvil tools
K. storage cabinet
L. paint shelf
M. storage table
N. trailer with electric welder and
   oxygen-acetylene torch

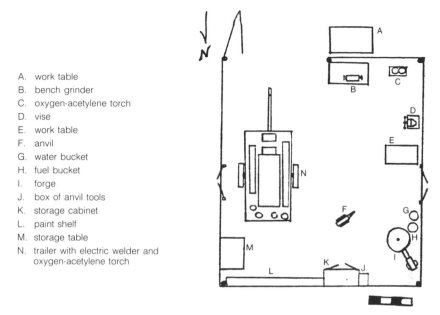

Figure 5.5. Floor Plan of the Blacksmith Shop

Simmons has many tools (see appendix A) but only a few are frequently used: a ball peen hammer, a chisel (used to cut iron bars), the welder, the oxygen-acetylene torch, a forge rake (used to keep clinkers from clogging the forge), and a blacksmith stand (used to hold extra long stock that projects over the edge of the forge). He has a set of tongs that was used by Peter Simmons but prefers to work the iron in long sections. This way he can hold onto the piece while beating it with the hammer. Hand-holding the iron gives him a better "feel" of the blows so he can determine if a piece needs to be re-heated. His hands are heavily calloused and hence much less sensitive to the burning heat. Sometimes he will gingerly reach into the forge and knock away chunks of molten slag with his bare hands, much to the fascination of onlooking visitors.

The Ironwork of Philip Simmons

An ironworker, like any craftsman, has criteria for making an object. The item must suit its purpose well—it must be functional—and it must look and "feel" right—it must have an aesthetic quality.[21] Sometimes it is the maker's intent that the object be used more than seen, that it be more prac-

Figure 5.6.   Anvil and Forge

tical than visually pleasing. Such is the case when a blacksmith makes a tool. But when pleasure is the goal, as in an ornamental gate or window grill, an aesthetic intent dominates and the item becomes art. However, a craftsman's work is never really art alone or craft alone; it is instead a subtle combination of both. Simmons can make tools that are simultaneously functional and fancy. His gates serve their purpose and yet are pleasing to the viewer. The functional and aesthetic realms of Simmons's creativity can be more clearly revealed by a close investigation of the making of a tool and an art work.[22]

A Traditional Fire Tool

Once when Simmons had just completed a banister for the interior of a house in Georgetown, South Carolina, I asked him if he could show me how he would have made a tool in the old-fashioned way. He answered me with a question: "Have you ever seen a log roller [a fire poker]?" When I replied that I hadn't, he drew pictures of three types (refer to fig. 5.7). They all had different kinds of handles. One had a brass handle (fig. 5.7A) while the other handles were fashioned from the end of the poker's shank.

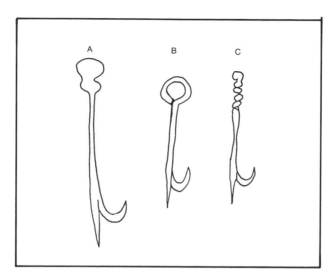

Figure 5.7.   Log Rollers as Drawn by Phillip Simmons

The simple ring was called a "poor man's handle" (fig. 5.7B). Simmons said that his grandfather had had one like that. The fancy spiral design was a "rich man's handle" (fig. 5.7C). Simmons decided to make the poker with the rich man's handle because that would show more of the "old time ways."

A good piece of wrought iron had to be selected first. Simmons wanted to use a piece of old Swedish iron because it could be worked more easily, it welded more efficiently, and it resisted corrosion better than American iron.[23] In the yard he picked out an old gate which had a network of ⅜" rods. He cut out a five-foot section and was ready to start (refer to fig. 5.8 in the following steps).[24]

1. A section of rod four inches from one end was heated in the forge until red.

2. Four inches of the rod were bent into a loop with hammer blows (A).

3. The place where the end of the loop touched the rod (circled in A) was heated until red.

4. A welding flux made of borax and sand was sprinkled on the area.[25]

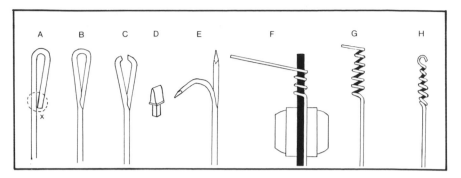

Figure 5.8.   Steps for Making a Log Roller with a "Rich Man's Handle"

5. When the area was white hot (melting temperature), the piece was removed from the forge and welded with hammer blows (B).

6. The loop was cut at the end (C) with hammer blows on a hardy, a cutting tool inserted into a slot in the anvil (D).

7. The two prongs were heated until red.

8. The poker was given its final shape. The welded prong was straightened and pointed with hammer blows. The continuous part of the rod was shaped into a hook by hammer blows over the horn of the anvil (E).

9. A three-inch portion of the rod two feet from the handle end of the poker was heated until red.

10. The rod was placed in the vise and bent 90° to form an "L" such that twenty-two inches were left to form the handle.

11. A ten-inch section of the bent portion nearest the angle was heated until red.

12. The poker was placed in the vise next to a 1″ diameter rod.

13. The handle was wrapped around the 1″ rod three times with hammer blows (F).

14. Ten inches of the unbent portion of the handle were heated until red.

15. The poker was placed in the vise next to a ¾″ diameter rod, which was inserted through the previously formed coils.

16. The ten-inch portion of rod was wrapped three times around the ¾″ rod with a small pair of tongs, yielding a handle represented in G.

17. The whole handle was heated until red.

18. The coils were compressed with hammer blows and spaced over the hardy until the handle became, in Simmons's terms, "egg-shaped."

19. The remaining bit of rod at the end was turned into a hook with hammer blows. The handle was then complete (H).

The entire process took about twenty minutes. When finished Simmons told me that the poker should be exactly thirty-six inches long. He had done all the work—except for cutting out the original piece of iron—without the benefit of measure. However, when he checked the finished product it was exactly as he had predicted, thirty-six inches. His uncanny accuracy in the perception of lengths was further emphasized as he then sketched out in chalk on the floor a full-size fire tool of a different type. I placed the tool he had just made on top of the drawing and found it to be a perfect match in length and the placement and curvature of the hook.

Simmons was happy with the finished tool. He said that he had not done a forge weld for a long time and was "rusty on his blacksmithing." But "rusty" or not, his final product was an example of traditional craftsmanship at its best, combining function and beauty to make a tool well-suited to its task. The hook, a gracefully curving prong, could easily get a secure "bite" on a burning log to pull it over efficiently. It was also flat enough so that if it turned up it could be used to push logs back into the fire. The handle, though it might seem designed for elegance (as suggested by the name "rich man's handle") also had utilitarian considerations. Its elliptical shape fits well into the hand. The hook in the end is a thoughtful convenience, as it allows the tool to be easily hung away on a peg or nail. The pragmatic and aesthetic are bound closely together in this object. However Simmons indicated that this piece was to be considered a tool and not an art work. He performed a brief pantomime to demonstrate the proper use of the poker. As he pulled and pushed at an imaginary fire he proved that this tool was indeed a log *roller.* It had been designed to do a specific job in a particular way; its function was primary.

Wrought Iron Art

I was also present when Simmons made a "divider," a partition screen between a kitchen and a dining room. It was composed of four sections: a doorway panel, a "pilaster post," a section that would rest on a counter top, and a panel surrounding a wall cabinet (fig. 5.9). Mrs. Mackey, the customer, was asked what kind of decoration she wanted and a sketch was made on the spot. Simmons later converted the sketch into a kind of plan. The area where the divider was to be installed had been thoroughly measured. These dimensions were carefully scaled out at $\frac{3}{4}''$ to a foot, but the scroll and leaf work was simply drawn according to what looked right. The drawing process was tedious. Decorations were continuously drawn, erased, and redrawn. The paper was almost worn through when the "plan" was finished (fig. 5.10). This drawing became a blueprint that Simmons constantly consulted as the work progressed. The crumpled and abused sketch was cast about the shop—hung on the wall, tossed on the floor— as the piece took shape. But it was never discarded; Simmons kept it close at hand. The drawing's importance was clearly demonstrated when it accidentally got left outside during a brief rain. Simmons hastily retrieved it but not before the sketch was thoroughly soaked. Although it looked like a lost cause, he carefully revived it. Delicately unfolding the paper, he laid it over some smoldering embers on the forge. When the drawing was dry and just about to burn, Simmons snatched it up and went back to work.

The following steps were accomplished over a two-day period. There were constant interruptions and delays ranging from a tornado that knocked out the electrical power (the forge fan is electric) to running errands to telephone calls. Some of the pieces were fabricated when I was not present. I did however see all of the parts assembled.

First a frame was made for the scroll work in the doorway panel and pilaster post (fig. 5.11).

1.   An $84\frac{3}{4}''$ section of a twenty-foot length of $\frac{1}{2}'' \times \frac{1}{2}''$ bar was marked off for the top of the divider frame.

2.   A wedge-shaped section was cut at that mark with the torch and the bar was bent 90°.

3.   The angle was checked with a square and welded.

4.   A three-foot length was measured off along the wall-side of the doorway panel and cut with a torch.

5.   The pilaster post was marked off on the top of the frame.

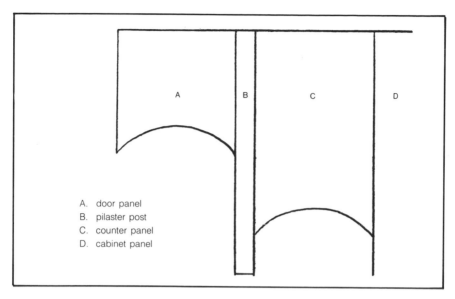

A. door panel
B. pilaster post
C. counter panel
D. cabinet panel

Figure 5.9. The Divider

6. Two six-foot lengths of ½″ × ½″ bar were cut with the torch.

7. The two lengths were welded in position five inches apart.

8. A 43½″ length of ½″ × ½″ bar was cut to form the arch at the bottom of the door panel.

9. The arch was shaped on the anvil. It was curved to fit into a space thirty-five inches wide.

10. The ends of the arch were cut with the torch so it would fit snugly against the vertical pieces (fig. 5.12).

11. The arch was welded in place.

12. A five-inch piece of ³⁄₁₆″ × ½″ flat stock was cut for the bottom of the pilaster post with a chisel and welded in place.

The frame was laid on the floor of the shop and the pilaster post decoration was shaped (fig. 5.13, *left*). This step involved forge work and bending an iron rod on the work table.

13. An 8′6″ length of ⅜″ diameter rod was cut for the pilaster post scroll.

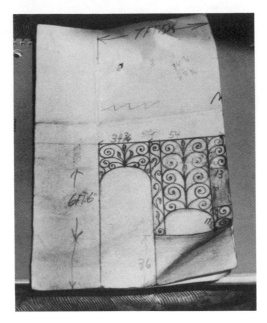

Figure 5.10. Simmons's Plan of the Divider

14. The end was heated until red in the forge.

15. The end was turned back and beaten into a 1″ diameter disk on the anvil.

16. Using notches on the side of the work table, Simmons bent the end into a half-circle.

17. The pilaster design was chalked out on the floor inside the frame.

18. Working from the top down, Simmons bent each curve and checked it against the drawing on the floor.

19. The last half-circle at the bottom of the post was measured and the last six inches of rod was cut off with a chisel.

20. The end was curled as in steps 15–17.

21. The whole piece was then welded to the frame. Simmons welded from the dining room side because the divider would be seen more from the kitchen.

The work then changed tempo as he began to make leaves. All the leaf decorations were made at one time. Two pieces of stock were worked

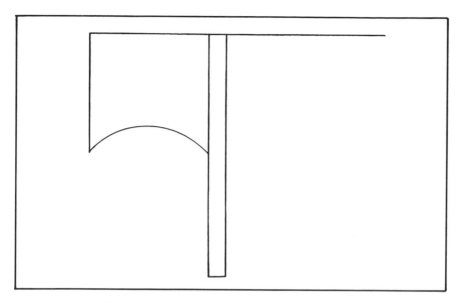

Figure 5.11. Frame for Door Panel and Pilaster Post

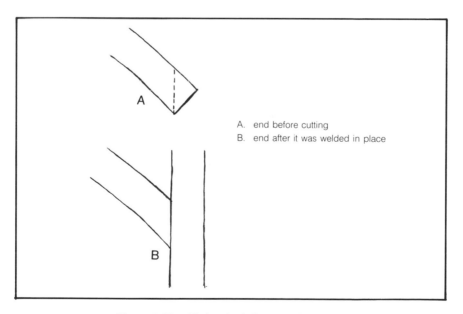

A. end before cutting
B. end after it was welded in place

Figure 5.12. Fitting Arch Piece to the Frame

Figure 5.13.   Scroll Decoration for Pilaster Post (*left*), Detail of Leaf (*right*)

simultaneously so that while one was being worked on the anvil the other could be heating on the forge. Simmons used a natural metaphor in his design (fig. 5.13, *right*). He explained that no two real leaves were the same. To illustrate his point he plucked two leaves from a nearby tree. He pointed out that one of them was slightly rounded while the other had a jagged point. "No two leaves are alike," he said, "and that's the way I make mine. I want them all different" (refer to fig. 5.14 for the following steps):

22.   The end of a ⅜″ diameter rod was heated until red and pointed with hammer blows (A).

23.   About four inches of rod was heated until red and turned back with hammer blows (B).

24.   The loop was then closed by welding. (The arc welder was used here instead of forge welding due to problems with dirty coal. It wouldn't burn hot enough to get the iron up to welding heat.)

25.   The whole loop was heated until red and then beaten on the anvil into leaf shape. The opening in the loop became a central spine on the leaf. The edge rather than the face of the hammer's striking surface was used to raise a number of ridges resembling leaf veins (C).

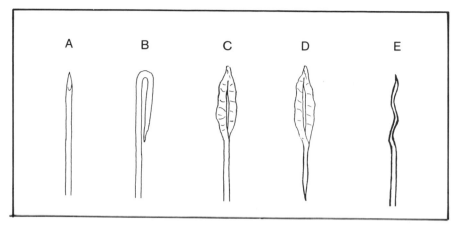

Figure 5.14   Steps for Making a Leaf (A–D) and Profile of a "Wiggletail"
Shape for Leaf (E)

26.   Steps 23–26 were repeated until twelve leaves were completed.
(Eventually all but one was used on the divider.)

27.   All the leaf stems were heated until red and pounded into a flat
point to provide a good welding surface (D).

Simmons does have a special kind of leaf that he calls the "sleeping leaf."
It has a 1″ diameter disk that hangs from a curled stem: "It's just like at
night and it's sleeping."

28.   A "sleeping leaf" was made following steps indicated in figure
5.15.

Next the scrolls for the doorway panel (fig. 5.16, *left*) were fashioned with
templates (see appendix B). Again Simmons worked from the top down.
All the scrolls were made from ³⁄₁₆″ × ½″ flat stock and worked cold.

29.   Half of the scrolls were chalked out on the floor.

30.   Sixty-three inches of stock were measured off for the first scroll.
(Lengths are determined by bending the tape measure over the
chalk lines.)

31.   The metal was tapered on one end and given a tight curl with
hammer blows. A special technique is used in tapering. The stock
is first narrowed widthwise so that as it is drawn out the metal
will spread back to its original width. If the metal were simply

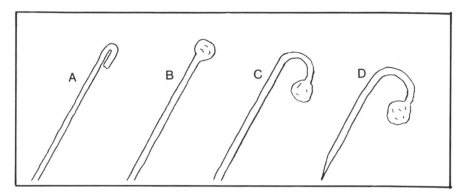

Figure 5.15.   Steps for Making a "Sleeping Leaf"
A. one inch turned back; B. loop flattened into disk;
C. disk turned into half-circle; D. stem cut and pointed

flattened, the scroll would have an uneven flare at the end (fig. 5.17).

32.   The piece was then curled around template #2 and then matched to the drawing on the floor. When that scroll was correctly shaped it was used as a "sample" for all others of that diameter.

33.   A companion was made for that scroll No. 1 following steps 30–32.

34.   A second set of scrolls was made using fifty-three inches of stock.

35.   A third set of scrolls was made employing template #6 but with the same procedures as with pieces twenty-four inches long.

36.   The last set was made from pieces nineteen inches long using template #8.

37.   All the scrolls and three leaves were arranged in the doorway panel. Leaves were set in the pilaster post.

38.   Leaf stems were bent on the anvil and the leaves were bent into what Simmons called a "wiggletail" (see fig. 5.14E).

39.   The shank on the center leaf of the doorway panel was extended. A length of ⅜" diameter rod was welded to the stem so that the leaf could fill an empty space between the top set of scrolls.

40.   All of the pieces were welded in place in the doorway panel and pilaster post (see fig. 5.16, *left*).

Figure 5.16.   Decoration in Door Panel and Pilaster Post (*left*), Counter
Panel (*center*), and Cabinet Panel (*right*)

Work on the divider stopped here for the day. It was 10:00 p.m. Simmons
had by then put in a seventeen-hour day. I returned the next morning at
9:00 a.m. to find that the rest of the frame had been completed.

41. A six-foot length of $\frac{1}{2}'' \times \frac{1}{2}''$ bar was welded to the top of the
    frame to separate the counter and cabinet panels.

42. $43\frac{1}{2}''$ of $\frac{1}{2}'' \times \frac{1}{2}''$ bar was shaped in an arch and welded to the
    bottom of the counter panel following steps 9–11.

The counter panel had ten scrolls. Four pairs were all the same (see fig.
5.16, *center*).

43. Intervals for the scrolls were marked off on the floor.

44. The first eight scrolls were shaped as in steps 32–33 using pieces
    sixty-two inches long.

45. The last set of scrolls was shaped using thirty-nine-inch lengths
    and template #4.

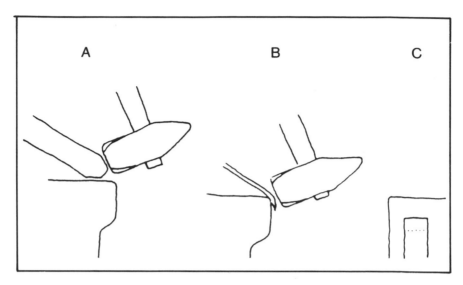

Figure 5.17.   Tapering Scroll Ends
A. narrowing the width; B. flattening to a taper; C. top view
of tapered piece showing uniform width

46.   Leaves were set out in a pattern similar to those in the doorway
panel.

47.   A long piece of ⅜″ diameter rod was attached to the stem of
the center leaf so that it could touch the top of the frame.

Finally the cabinet panel was formed (see fig. 5.16, *right*). Since the scrolls
in this section had to fit both against the wall and around a projecting
cabinet some tricky maneuvering was required. The scrolls were set up
with some "play" so they could be adjusted once the divider was in place.

48.   The cabinet profile was chalked out on the floor.

49.   Two scrolls were formed around template #3 from pieces fifty
inches long.

50.   One scroll was made from a nineteen-inch piece with template
#3.

51.   An S-scroll was made using two templates. One end of the sixty-
eight inch piece of stock was curled on template #1 and the other
end was curled in the opposite direction on template #5.

52.   The leaves for the counter and cabinet panels were modified as
in step 40.

Figure 5.18.   Welding Parts of the Divider

53.   All of the parts for the two panels were welded in place (fig.
      5.18). The divider was then essentially complete (fig. 5.19). All
      that remained were a few decorative and finishing touches. All
      the welds were ground smooth and sealed with a glazing putty
      which "fulled the cracks." Bits of slag were filed and wire
      brushed away. Finally the whole piece was given two coats of
      "antique gold" paint at the request of Mrs. Mackey.

The procedures for making the divider are complicated, but even more
complex is Simmons's mental visualization of the piece. The aesthetic decisions that convert craft into art are revealed in the processes of mind
previous to the physical composition of this piece. As stated above the
work is first charted out in a sketch. A great deal of trial and experimenta-
tion goes into that drawing, which eventually becomes the guiding plan.
However, this plan is still fairly arbitrary. For example, before the door
panel was laid out Simmons remarked that the scrolls would have to be
"humped up" more than was shown in the drawing. Furthermore, when
the scrolls for that panel were chalked on the floor they didn't seem right.
Simmons erased the lines several times before he was satisfied. Yet he then
went back to the plan to check the differences between it and his new
arrangement. His goal was to keep a balance between "openness" and

Figure 5.19.   Drawing of the Finished Divider

"closedness." It was as if the drawing was a pattern, the visualization of a structure, in which a number of substitutions could be made. The pattern showed him where the scrolls should touch the frame, but the curvature of each scroll was up to him. In the pilaster post he deviated markedly from his sketch. The scroll was reversed; Simmons faced it to the left instead of the right. Also he used four regular leaves whereas on the plan four sleeping leaves were indicated. Furthermore he changed the scroll arrangement over the cabinet. The plan called for three scrolls of the same size and two leaves. Simmons decided that there wasn't enough space for all that decoration, that area wouldn't have "openness." Thus he opted for a three-scroll pattern having two pieces with a smaller one between them.

The final composition of the leaf pattern in the counter panel demonstrates another expression of the Simmons sense of balance and shows that visual balance is to be distinguished from the symmetry of the design. Simmons didn't realize that there could be a repetition of leaf patterns in the doorway and counter panels until he reached the lay-out stage (steps 46–47). Both panels were the same width and both had the same arch at the bottom but the possibility of balancing decorative motifs only occurred to Simmons when he was actually composing the counter panel. His sketch shows two leaves lined up vertically. Experimenting with the layout Simmons saw not only that a cluster of three leaves would match the design over the door, but also that such a cluster would have to be modified. To make the counter design proportional, Simmons expanded it and stretched it out. The balancing then was consistent externally between panels and internally within the counter panel.

As Simmons progresses through the making of a piece of decorative iron his mental vision is constantly modified. As he changes design elements he says out loud "That's got it; that's the one; that's the one," encouraging himself that the particular alteration is a proper one and that his new mental template is workable. Working within a certain structure, the frame of the piece, he is able to experiment with various metal motifs: half C-scrolls, S-scrolls, leaves. The appearance of decorative components is only partially fixed by the structure. Many options can follow as the work is fashioned. Curves can be tight or open; they can be rounded or straightened. No leaf looks like another; each is a variation. The final product is drawn into order by Simmons's own sense of visual balance and the symmetry conventional to local Charleston ironwork. As pieces go together the template that was once only mental and then visual becomes a tactile reality. James "Sonny Ford" Thomas, a black sculptor from Mississippi, in referring to the way that he makes his pieces said: "If you ain't got it in your head, you can't do it in your hand. . . . If you can't hold it in your head, you can't shape it."[26] Like Thomas's clay skulls the concept of Mrs. Mackey's divider moved from Simmons's mind to paper to chalk lines on the floor to bits and pieces of metal; finally all those parts became a divider. In each of those moves there were options for change. Sometimes the concept was shuttled back and forth between stations before progressing along. Decisions at those points were made by experimenting, manipulating, improvising, and innovating with the structure or the components of the piece. In the end what began as a notion and a crumpled piece of paper had become an art work.

The distinction then between Philip Simmons's art and craft should be made on the basis of intention. In ornamental work he endures extensive anguish to "get it right." His repeated trials, tests, and debates are the overt expression of a struggle to mentally form a unique template for one particular art work. When he made the log roller, he worked quickly and assertively. There were no false starts, no dry runs. He simply selected a standard type and made the tool. The techniques of craft and art in ironwork are similar. Compare, for example, the first steps in making a leaf and fire poker. It is therefore the marshalling of mental energy to create a beautiful object rather than a practical one that makes Mrs. Mackey's divider an art work. That this effort of mind is unique to each art piece was clearly expressed by Simmons when he talked about a masterwork that he has yet to make. He said that he wanted to leave a contribution to Charleston, a gate that would be different from all others: "Most [gates] just borrow something from one and something from another. I don't want to take part from St. Andrew's and part from St. Philip's." *His* gate would somehow take up the theme of Charleston as a city between two rivers. The scheme or design wasn't yet clear to him but he knew it would be different. He was thinking about it.

Conclusion

It is important that we have worried so much about the way Simmons creates a piece in his mind because the mind is the locus of culture and tradition.[27] The techniques and procedures of Simmons's trade in Charleston are largely derived from Euro-American traditions. The artifacts he fashions conform to the models established by white iron workers. Africanisms do not overtly exist in Simmons's work; the snake that decorates the Gadsden gate (see p. 30) was used because in 1775 Christopher Gadsden designed the "Don't Tread on Me" flag, which featured a rattlesnake emblem.[28] However his aesthetic process, which is distinguished by a sense of innovation and improvisation, seems to relate him to a host of other Afro-American artists whose works are undeniably part of a black tradition.

Near Charleston on John's Island, Joe Hunter, a blues singer, uses a simple verse pattern while inserting the names of different members of his family and friends into his lyrics.[29] This is just a simple innovation. A Galveston street performer, "Bongo Joe," has an improvised line of patter that results from the commingling of his drumming and "rapping" talents. He uses jokes and rhymes as well as snatches of blues, jazz, and calypso songs in spontaneously composed routines.[30] Charles Keil, in discussing blues styles in general, comments on how the standard twelve-bar sequence may be contracted to eight bars or expanded to sixteen or twenty-four. Furthermore a vast array of tonal blends, twists, slides, and dips are employed to give standard songs a different feel and texture.[31] These features suggest that the musical form derives its vitality from the ability of the artist to continually change and innovate within the structure of performance. Certainly that is so among Bahamian tale-tellers. In their case the aesthetic of the folktale depends on how an "old-story" can be made new in each re-telling; familiar motifs are constantly arranged into different plots.[32] A similar pattern has been delineated in the rhetoric of black

Figure 5.20. Phillip Simmons at His Forge

preachers. Bruce A. Rosenberg has argued that the chanted sermon hinges upon the use of stock formulas around which a unique text is composed.[33] The same innovative character has been observed in the oral literature of black boys in Philadelphia: "Their active oral repertoire encompasses a range from neat repetition of quatrains, to improvisation with traditional components, to freewheeling creation out of experience and environment within thin traditional frames."[34] A striking example of a distinct Afro-American aesthetic is found in Sea Island quilt tops. Laid out asymmetrically in strips, they employ a random color sequence in contradistinction to Euro-American quilts, which have rigid and highly repetitious designs.[35] It would appear then that Simmons's works provide yet another example of the innovative and improvisational art style that is said to characterize Afro-American culture. Certainly the plausibility of innovation as a normative mode in Afro-American art is strengthened by its discovery in blacksmithing.

It is important that Simmons's aesthetic be linked to a black mode of creativity. Artifacts fashioned under the pattern of that approach represent the work of an Afro-American artisan. If such a connection could not be made, Philip Simmons could only rightfully be considered a technician, a skillful follower of white models. But since Simmons's art works are molded and shaped in a loose, open-ended, experimental way, they may be considered as the representation of an Afro-American tradition in blacksmithing.

First there is the flicker of flame in the splintered kindling. Then the bigger chunks catch fire. The fan is switched on and, in a great rush, tongues of fire dance over the damp fuel. As the coal turns to scorching, burning embers under billows of acrid gray smoke, an orange glow glides through the darkened corner of the shop. There, standing at the forge, ignoring the heat, is Philip Simmons. His dark skin takes on the orange glow just like the coal. He looks knowingly into the fire. It has been his life. It is his future. He is the blacksmith; he is the master now (fig. 5.20).

Notes

1. Three pieces of ornamental work ascribed to Peter Simmons are on display in the Old Slave Mart Museum in Charleston. For an illustration see Judith Wragg Chase, *Afro-American Art and Craft* (New York: Van Nostrand Reinhold Company, 1971), 71.

2. For further works on ornamental iron work in Charleston see: Elizabeth Gibbon Curtis, *Gateways and Doorways of Charleston, South Carolina in the Eighteenth and Nineteenth Centuries* (New York: Architectural Book Publishing Co., 1926); Alston Deas, *The Early Ironwork of Charleston* (Columbia, S.C.: Bostick and Thornly, 1941); C. Stuart Dawson, "Gateways of Old Charleston," *Country Life* 39 (1921):48–49; M. R. Dockstader, "Wrought Iron Gates of Charleston," *South Carolina Magazine* 34 (1939–40):32; and Henning Cohen, "The Wrought Iron Gates of Charleston," *American Antiques Journal* 2 (1947): 4–6.

3. The most extensive discussion of African ironwork is by Walter Cline, *African Mining and Metallurgy* (Menasha, Wis.: George Banta Publishing, 1936). African blacksmithing is further explored by Rene S. Wassing in *African Art: Its Backgrounds and Traditions* (New York: Harry N. Abrams, 1968), 52, 117, 196–97; and by Michael Leiris and Jacqueline Delange, *African Art* (London: Thames and Hudson, 1968), 99, 210. The making of utilitarian objects is illustrated by M. D. W. Jeffreys, "Some Notes on the Bikom Blacksmiths," *Man* 52 (1952):49–51 and William Fagg, "Ironworking with a Stone Hammer Among the Tula of Northern Nigeria," *Man* 52 (1952): 51–53.

4. For an interesting comparison see Robert Goldwater, *Bambara Sculpture from the Western Sudan* (New York: University Publishers, 1960), 52, plate 88.

5. Chase, *Afro-American Art and Craft,* 67–69.

6. Leonard Price Stavisky, "Negro Craftsmanship in Early America," *American Historical Review* 54 (1949): 315.

7. Carl Bridenbaugh, *The Colonial Craftsman* (New York: New York University Press, 1950), 10.

8. Ibid., 17–18.

9. W. E. Burghardt Du Bois and Augustus Granville Dill, eds., *The Negro American Artisan* (Atlanta: Atlanta University Press, 1912), 35.

10. Bridenbaugh, *The Colonial Craftsman,* 139–41.

11. J. Francis Brenner, "Master Ironworkers Come to Practice Art in City," *Charleston Courier,* 21 August 1932, n.p.

12. Mary Willis Shuey, "Charleston *Signed* Ironwork," *The Reading Puddle Ball* 4:1 (1935):5; Albert Simons and Samuel Lapham, Jr., *The Early Architecture of Charleston* (Columbia: University of South Carolina Press, 1970), 176.

13. Ulrich B. Phillips, "The Slave Labor Problem in the Charleston District," *Political Science Quarterly* 22 (1907): 435.

14. Chase, *Afro-American Art and Craft,* 74.

15. Marina Wikramanayake, *The Free Negro in Ante-Bellum South Carolina* (Ph.D. Dissertation, University of Wisconsin, 1966), 130–32.

16. Philip A. Bruce, *The Plantation Negro as a Freeman* (New York: G. P. Putnam's Sons, 1889), 231.

17. W. E. B. Du Bois, ed., *The Negro Artisan* (Atlanta: Atlanta University Press, 1902), 91, 114.

18. Du Bois and Dill, *The Negro American Artisan,* 47, 75.

19. Ibid., 76.

20. In *The Wheelwright's Shop* (1923, reprinted London: Cambridge University Press, 1963), 164, George Stuart described the darkness of Will Hammond's smithy: "The sunshine, he said, put his fire out; and very likely it did affect the look of the heat."

21. For a more detailed discussion of the dichotomous philosophy of craft and art distinctions see Henry Glassie, "Folk Art," in Richard M. Dorson, ed., *Folklore and Folklife: An Introduction* (Chicago: University of Chicago Press, 1972), 253–80.

22. J. Geraint Jenkins in *Traditional Country Craftsmen* (London: Routledge and Kegan Paul, 1965), 3, lists three characteristics of craftsmanship: that beauty is combined with

utility, that craftsmen don't depend on complex equipment, and that craftsmen expand upon the past. The second principle may not be widely applicable to blacksmithing. Simmons's electric welder and oxygen-acetylene torch are sophisticated pieces of machinery that many blacksmiths never used. It seems however that ironwork, requiring as it does massive physical exertion, has always been prone to labor-saving developments. The use of a water-powered trip hammer to forge tools and the development of the "Champion No. 400 Blacksmith Blower," which "revolutionized the world's hand blacksmith fires," are but two examples (Peter S. Vogt, "The Axe and Oakland, Maine," *Pioneer America* 1:2 [1969]: 1–6; H. R. Bradley Smith, *Blacksmiths' and Farriers' Tools at Shelburne Museum,* Museum Pamphlet Series, No. 7 [Shelburne, Vermont: The Shelburne Museum, 1966], 251). The fact that both the welder and the torch are essentially hand-tools allows them to be considered as a normal part of the inventory of a craftsman's shop.

23. The characteristics of wrought iron are explained in detail by James Aston and Edward B. Story, *Wrought Iron* (Pittsburgh: A. M. Byers Company, 1939), 59–69. See also Cyril Stanley Smith, "On the Nature of Iron," in *Made of Iron* (Houston: St. Thomas University Art Department, 1966), 29–42.

24. The following section has been substantially reprinted from my note "The Fabrication of a Traditional Fire Tool," *Journal of American Folklore* 86 (1973): 54–57.

25. Welding flux lowers the melting temperature of the scale that forms on the iron's surface while being heated. It thus can burn off as the iron reaches its melting stage at white heat. The iron is then clean and can be welded without defect-causing impurities. Simmons explains: "It's like putting in dirt to keep other dirt out."

26. William Ferris, Jr., " 'If You Ain't Got It In Your Head, You Can't Do It In Your Hand:' James Thomas, Mississippi Delta Folk Sculptor," in *Studies in the Literary Imagination* 3:1 (1970): 96.

27. For a more detailed discussion of this principle see Claude Lévi-Strauss, *The Savage Mind* (London: Weidengeld and Nicolson, 1966) and H. G. Barnett, *Innovation: The Basis of Cultural Change* (New York: McGraw-Hill, 1953).

28. Hon. Frederick Hicks, *The Flag of the United States* (Washington, D.C.: W. F. Roberts Co., 1926), 69.

29. Mary A. Twining and William C. Saunders, " 'One of These Days': The Function of Two Singers in the Sea Island Community," in *Studies in the Literary Imagination* 3:1 (1970): 66.

30. Patrick B. Mullen, "A Negro Street Performer: Tradition and Innovation," *Western Folklore* 29 (1970): 91–103.

31. Charles Keil, *Urban Blues* (Chicago: University of Chicago Press, 1969), 51, 53.

32. Daniel J. Crowley, *I Could Talk Old-Story Good: Creativity in Bahamian Folklore* (Berkeley: University of California Press, 1966), 40–41.

33. Bruce A. Rosenberg, *The Art of the American Folk Preacher* (New York: Oxford University Press, 1970), 100–102.

34. Henry Glassie, " 'Take That Night Train to Selma': An Excursion to the Outskirts of Scholarship," in *Folksongs and Their Makers* (Bowling Green, Oh.: Bowling Green University Popular Press, 1970), 44.

35. The quilts referred to were on display in the Indiana University Museum in an exhibit entitled "Afro-American Arts and Crafts of South Carolina" in 1973.

Tool Inventory for Philip Simmons's Blacksmith Shop*

2 anvils

2 bench vises
5 C-clamps

3 ball-peen hammers
1 eight-pound sledge hammer
1 four-pound sledge hammer

8 Tongs: 2 flat tongs
   3 pick up tongs
   1 hollow bit tongs
   1 pincer tongs
   1 oval iron tongs

1 clip puller

1 box of anvil tools (swages, hardies, fullers, etc.)
15 bending templates (see appendix B)

5 calipers
3 travellers
2 levels
2 squares
2 bevel squares
1 measuring tape

1 drawshave
1 wood saw
1 hack saw
1 hatchet
2 electric drills w/wood bits

1 pipe cutter
2 chain cutters
3 bolt threaders
2 oxygen-acetylene torches
12 chisels
2 punches

1 forge rake
1 blacksmith stand

2 shovels
1 post hole digger
2 pointed bars (5½')

1 bench grinder
1 portable grinder
1 file
1 rasp
2 wire brushes

1 arc welder
2 push brooms

---

*For analogs and sources for these tools see H. R. Bradley Smith, *Blacksmiths' and Farriers' Tools at Shelburne Museum—A History of their Development from Forge to Factory,* Museum Pamphlet Series, No. 7 (Shelburne, Vermont: The Shelburne Museum, 1966).

Appendix B

Templates for Bending Scrolls

Type	Length*	Turns	Diameter
1. Half C	68"	2	15"
2. Half C	43"	1½	12"
3. Half C	38"	1	11"
4. Half C	40"	2	9"
5. Half C	34"	1⅓	7½"
6. Half C	12"	1½	6"
7. Half C (oblong)	32"	1	6"
8. Half C	17"	1	4½"
9. Half C	30"	1½	4"
10. Half C	27"	1¼	4"
11. Half C	13"	¾	3"
12. C (symmetrical)	34"	1	3¾"
13. C (asymmetrical)	1. 16"	1. 1	1. 3½"
	2. 18"	2. 1	2. 4"
14. C (asymmetrical)	1. 11"	1. 1	1. 1½"
	2. 12"	2. 1	2. 2½"
15. S 1. oblong	1. 18½"	1. 1	1. 5"
2. round	2. 4"	2. 1	2. 2¼"

---

*Lengths for templates with two sizes of scrolls are measured from midpoint of template to end of curl.

6

"Us Quarters Fixed Fine": Finding Black Builders in Southern History

During the last two decades the interpretation of American history has experienced an important shift. No longer are scholars content with the old tales of great generals, great presidents, and great businessmen, and the familiar sagas of wars, elections, and economic adventures. They look instead for the smaller, more humane narrative of the soldier in the trenches, the man in the street, the worker on the line. What these folks have accomplished, endured, or felt has for too long gone unheeded or ignored. What was once presented as history is, in fact, a very myopic and biased account representative only of perhaps the least representative creators of the American experience. Whether motivated by a sense of fair play or by the realization that the most accurate account is the most inclusive one, scholars must admit all the makers of history into the history books.

Those who planned and constructed the buildings of the South are a case in point. Moreover, we must realize that many thousands of those builders were black, that many southern buildings (both great and plain) were the results of black effort and ingenuity. Until recently only buildings rendered in the metaphor of a classic fine art style were considered worthy of scholarly attention. The bulk of southern architecture was denigrated as "mere building."[1] But since common houses and structures provide space and shelter for the daily experiences of 90 percent of the population they cannot be dismissed as insignificant and neither can their builders.

Never have people such as Tom Chisolm from South Carolina, Berry Smith from Mississippi, or William Henry Towns from Alabama been recognized for their contribution to the southern landscape.[2] They are part of the unheralded populace that has lived on for years beneath the view of history (fig. 6.1). Perhaps their presence was recorded by a census taker, but a column of statistics is an inadequate measure for flesh and blood and

This article originally appeared in *Perspectives on the American South* 3 (1985): 101–18. Reprinted by permission of Gordon and Breach Science Publishers S.A.

Figure 6.1.   Haywood Dixon, ca. 1854
Daguerreotype. Dixon (1826–ca. 1889) was a slave carpenter
who worked in Greene County, North Carolina, and
is posed in this picture with a sign of his profession, the
carpenter's square. It is men like Dixon whose efforts have
generally gone unrecognized.
*(Courtesy of Catherine W. Bishir from the collection of
William L. Murphy, Jr.)*

spirit. Maybe some person will occasionally recall that a certain big plantation house, a set of fortifications, a system of roads and canals, or a row of cabins was built by slaves. Such collective credit, while deserved, submerges the vibrant personalities of individuals who poured their labor and often their intelligence into their tasks. The black worker in such recollections becomes an anonymous laborer whose achievement appears minor because no one seems truly responsible for it. Slave labor becomes invisible labor, and the credit for its products is assigned elsewhere, as Carl Anthony has noted of the forgotten black contribution to southern built forms: "it is not unreasonable to suppose that the millions of African slaves upon whom Europeans depended taught them more about tropical architecture than they later cared to remember."[3] Simply providing the names of those builders will not give them a place in history. Only people in action make history and consequently a history of Afro-American builders requires consideration of their tangible achievements as well as their personal identities.

Writing the history of so-called ordinary people's lives is often difficult because the data required are so diverse and are often uneven and spotty in coverage. Moreover, the subject matter usually touches upon topics that are commonplace and seemingly unremarkable and mundane. Yet such actions as hewing timbers, shingling roofs, daubing mud on chimneys, and the like were essential, and the modest structures that Blacks created stand as mute but reliable statements of ability and will. A silent building speaks volumes about daily lives as actually lived and allows the modern observer to replace imaginary average routines with the truth. The task of writing popular history, although arduous, is therefore worthwhile.

It is certainly not news that black people possessed a wide assortment of craft skills, but historians have rarely considered the impact and importance of those abilities. In times past Blacks were not considered worthy of the historian's attention, and more recently the product of their handiwork has seemed simple and rudimentary compared to the more grandiose buildings of professional architects. Consequently, a great amount of information has been swept under the rug. It is time to examine the lump under the rug of consensus history. That fancy carpet needs to be turned back so that one might see the floor beneath it. Whittington Bernard Johnson initiated such a move in his dissertation "Negro Laboring Classes in Early America, 1750–1820," in which he observes: "Due largely to prosperity, expansion, and population growth after 1763, carpentry eventually surpassed cooperage as the most commonly practiced trade among black artisans. In early America carpentry was in its glory for the carpenter started with natural resources in the raw and converted them into finished products ranging from crude barns to stately mansions."[4] Johnson indicates that Blacks were a major factor in the building trades, but he also shows us that their impact can be effectively assessed. His approach is the conventional procedure used by most historians: he went to the available documentary sources like diaries, letters, court records, newspapers, travel accounts, and personal reminiscences. These are the same kinds of resources that were used by earlier generations of historians to fashion accounts of southern life devoid of black achievement. These materials can be mined once again with a different outcome. Holding new expectations for old materials will yield new finds: black builders will at last be discovered.

Newspaper Accounts

Consider the following item from the April 16, 1767, edition of the *Virginia Gazette:*

> RUN AWAY from the subscriber near Williamsburg, last Saturday night, a Negro fellow named BOB about 5 feet 7 inches high, about 26 years of age, was burnt when young, by which he had a scar on the wrist of his right hand, the thumb of his left hand burnt off, and the hand turns in; had on a double breasted dark coloured frieze jacket, yellow cotton breeches. He was lately brought home from *Hartford* County in *North Carolina,* where he has been harboured for three years past by one *Van Pelt,* who lives on *Chinkopin* creek; he passed for a freeman, by the name of *Edward* or *Edmund Tamar,* and has a wife there. He is an extraordinary sawer, a tolerable carpenter and currier, pretends to makes shoes, and is a very good sailor.[5]

There is information in this runaway notice not only of a successful escape but of one of the shortcomings in the slavery system that allowed a man to avoid bondage. And the reader learns about a remarkably skilled craftsman with diverse talents that are all the more remarkable in light of his serious injury. Continuing to peruse the newspapers one finds that the occurrence of multiple skills among slaves was not all that rare. On March 7, 1771, the *Virginia Gazette* again gave notice of an escaped slave. Named Sam, his description notes that: "He was bred partly to the Plantation and Farming Business as he informed me [his owner, Stafford Lightburn Jr.], was employed as an Axe Man and Sawer, about Ship building."[6] The *South Carolina Gazette* proved to be an important source for Peter H. Wood who, in his book *Black Majority,* was able to describe in detail the contribution of Blacks to the development of Carolina during its colonial phase. He found one account describing a Charleston hatter who claimed to have four men who could "whet, set, and lay timbers."[7] In another case a slave was advertised on the basis of his potential as it was noted that he had "an extraordinary inclination to learn the carpenter's trade."[8]

A few decades later this same Charleston paper carried an advertisement that read in part:

> TO BE SOLD on Tuesday the 17th of April next, upon the spot, where PETER HALL, Cabinet maker, now lives, in Queen Street, At Public Outcry to the highest bidder, upon terms which shall be declared previous to the beginning of the said intended sale: Four very valuable NEGROES, two of them good workmen at the cabinet maker's business: one a good sawyer, and handles his tools so well in the coarser branches of that trade, as to be capable of making a tolerable country carpenter, and is very diligent and lively.[9]

The more one culls through the yellowed pages of old newspapers, the more one is sure to find. These findings are more than proof of existence of black workmen. The evaluative comments often included are important indicators of how black workers were once regarded (ironically they were more appreciated during slavery than now). Moreover, taken collectively, these brief statements reveal specific patterns of employment, the assignment of tasks, tools and techniques used, and achievements attained.

Private Letters

Personal letters held by families, donated to libraries, or stored in archives are another important source to be considered in creating a historical account of black builders. Despite the generally enforced rules that prohibited slaves from learning to read and write there were exceptions. In such cases these Blacks often had special skills, which they described in their correspondence. Letters to Thomas Jefferson written by John Hemings, the son of Jefferson's slave Elizabeth Hemings and a white carpenter named John Nelson, give precise details of nineteenth-century house repairs. On August 11, 1825, he described the progress of re-roofing a mansion damaged by fire. Hemings suggested to the designer of Monticello: "We shoul go about perparing the chines [Chinese] raling & Puting up the ornamentes of the hall marster F. Eppes was saying something abot tining the flat rouft [roof] over the hall you can deside it between you how it shal be don Sir plese to send the tin as soon as you can the flat rouft will take 3 boxis thats 7 in all."[10] The complexity of his reconstruction tasks was detailed in a letter written two months later on September 18 when he described the problems involved in installing the sash weights for five windows and hanging a set of folding doors.[11] Clearly Hemings was a finish carpenter, not a run-of-the-mill rough out man; he tended to such complex details as "Parlour cornices." He was well aware of the level of his skills, and we detect a note of self-confidence and his control over his circumstances when he informs Jefferson: "I hope by the nex to be able to Let you no when I shul finech and when to send for me."[12]

Another interesting set of letters found among the John Hartwell Cocke papers at the University of Virginia Library provide repeated mention of the role played by black builders and artisans in Greene County, Alabama, between 1847 and 1865. The black slave driver George Skipworth, while reporting on the 1847 spring activities of his charges, credits Leander Creacy and Archer Creacy with building a cotton press.[13] By the winter he reported that: "frank has put Brick chimneys to all the houses in the yard. he is now got a smal Job for mr. parker but he will finish it in a few days."[14] The next year the two Creacys were directed to move the slave quarters for hygenic reasons to a new site while continuing to build a mansion house: "Lea and Archa have got up the boddy of the house and boards for covuring they are now waiting for an oppertunity to get lumber from the Landing in the mean time they are getting timber in the woods of difernt lenths."[15] Later correspondence mentioned the construction of several corn cribs as well as carts for hauling produce. These letters reveal, then, the range of tasks for the carpenters at the Hopewell Plantation. They felled timber, made boards, and framed and finished buildings both domestic and agricultural for both Blacks and Whites, in addition to making whatever machinery could be fashioned from wood. Together with a local mason they created the architecture of the plantation. Such findings are highly significant but researchers should be warned that the letters of slave builders are often written in a hand that is difficult to decipher and use a vocabulary replete with personalized spellings. Care in analysis, however, may yield not only information on the work that slave builders completed but also the sounds of their dialect since the letters usually reflect an oral English not a received standard version of the language. The tangible document thus yields insight into intangible performances within black culture and takes the researcher a step closer to reaching his distant informants.

Official Documents

Legal documents such as court proceedings, tax records, estate inventories, and wills are often worked by historians for information on the textures of daily life. A life style that included slavery as a central institution will leave its mark in these documents. When tradesmen owned slaves they usually trained them in their particular occupations, making them very valuable human property; so valuable that craftsmen's wills often record their slaves' skills and monetary value as well as their identities. On this matter Kenneth M. Stampp was quite explicit: "Executors hired out slave property while estates were being settled. Sometimes lands and slaves together were rented to tenants. Heirs who inherited bondsmen for whom they had no employment put them up for hire. Many spinsters, widows, and orphans lived off the income of hired slaves who were handled for them by administrators. Masters often directed in their wills that slaves be hired out for the benefit of their heirs."[16] Studying the various papers drawn up to accompany such actions would doubtless carry one well into the work of black laborers. A white carpenter's or mason's will, while focused on his own family's concerns, may lead to the discovery of black builders and, further, it might include specific instructions for those enslaved artisans. Wood discovered in an eighteenth-century will from Charleston that "It was the last wish of Mary Mullins that future proceeds from the work of her 'two Negroe Bricklayers . . . employed about the Rebuilding of the Presbiterian Meeting House' be divided between the minister and the church."[17] The two slave masons, Tony and Primus, would later be reported in the local newspaper as secretly selling their services for their own profit. The will in this case states the owner's intention while the newspaper reveals the slaves' actions. The researcher should attempt to use such documents in a complementary manner with other materials so that their collective contents provide a more complete portrait of black employment.

Probate inventories, even though primarily intended to settle contested estates, can also yield information about slave builders. One often finds a number of woodworking tools listed as found in the slave quarters by the assessors who made a room-by-room, building-by-building inspection of the designated property. For example, in Prince George's County, Maryland, in 1726 a cabin that housed seven slaves also contained: "1 old x cutt saw," "1 old hand saw," "1 old frow," "2 old augers," "1 old draw knife," "1 set of wedges," and "1 broad axe."[18] There were, of course, other kinds of domestic equipment, like iron cooking pots and frying pans, in the quarters, but the assortment of cutting tools strongly implies that these slaves were, for the most part, employed as sawyers if not builders. The inventory made in 1779 of Landon Carter's Sabine Hall plantation in Virginia expressly mentioned a "set of carpenters tools" valued at twenty pounds.[19] This fact when coupled with the other descriptions of slave carpentry activities provided by Carter's letter and diaries indicates just who was using these tools and for what purposes.[20]

Ex-Slave Narratives

Historians tend to trust documentary sources like newspaper advertisements, day books, ledgers, and estate inventories more than personal narrative accounts. Such sources are thought to be factual and free from bias and are considered to be objective because they are so dispassionate.[21]

The keepers of such records seem to have had no particular axe to grind or special causes to tout, at least when they penciled figures in columns or made observations of the number of furrows hoed on a particular June day. The matter-of-fact nature and consequent trustworthiness of mundane documents has tempted historians to avoid those accounts taken directly from Blacks themselves. The numerous personal interviews recorded by Federal Writers Project (FWP) workers from ex-slaves in the late 1930s have been hailed as the authentic voice of the black past.[22] However, John W. Blassingame has pointed out their shortcomings, particularly the problems of black informants being frank and honest about slavery with white interviewers, the lack of verbatim recording, and the seventy-year time gap between the experience of slavery and the interviews. Summarizing the biases, distortions, editing problems, and the skewed distribution of the FWP interviews, Blassingame comments: "Most of the interviews are so limited in scope or are so short that it requires considerable skill to extract reliable information from them."[23]

The ex-slave narratives are, nevertheless, as even Blassingame admits, filled with specific information about black life in the nineteenth and early twentieth centuries. One needs to be aware of the flaws in these interviews, to account for their probable distortions, but a researcher can cull out the many facts they contain. C. Vann Woodward has noted: "Full of paradox and evasions, contrasts and contradictions, lies and exaggerations, pure truths and complete fabrication as they are, such sources still remain the daily bread on which historians feed."[24] Hence when approached with care and sophistication the ex-slave narratives can be expected to reveal a great deal about black building efforts.

The state of Texas was one of the better-covered areas in the slave narrative project; 306 interviews were conducted.[25] Included in this body of texts are fifty reports on slave housing or the skills of black carpenters and masons. In Texas and elsewhere slave labor was used to create the architecture for both Whites and Blacks, both the big house and the quarters. A. M. Moore recalled of his Harrison County plantation: "My mistress was Lucinda Sherrad and she had a world of children. They lived in a big log house but you wouldn't know it was a log house unless you went up in the attic where it wasn't ceiled. The slaves helped master build the house. The quarters looked like a little town with houses all in lines."[26] A similar continuity in the houses of Blacks and Whites was perceived by Harriet Barret: "Us have log quarters with stick posts for bed and deer skin stretch over it. . . . They [white people] live in big log house, four rooms in it and the great hall both ways though it."[27] In another instance cited by ex-slave Fred Dibble from Orange County the quarters and big house were both made of logs, except that his owner's house was two stories tall.[28] Plantation mythology is overturned by the observation that the master's house was in many cases no more than an impressive arrangement of slave quarter dwelling units, log pens stacked higher or strung out further than was normal in slave row.

The ex-slave narratives suggest that in Texas most Blacks lived in double-pen cabins, the most common house type in the South.[29] Ordinarily this kind of structure employed one room as a kitchen and the other room as a bedroom. These two-room cabins were commonly enlarged by the addition of a lean-to shed across the back which was used as a kitchen, with the two front rooms serving as bedrooms. On some plantations there was a modest variety in the quarters. James Jackson's recollection included mention of one-, two-, and three-room houses.[30] Knowing what kind of houses slaves lived in provides some insight into what black builders were doing, but one need not simply speculate on their activities, for some of the ex-slave narratives are clear on the ways in which black builders worked. Ellen Polk provided an extensive account of log construction by black Texans, describing the process for producing logs that were semilunate or half-round in cross section, a pattern still primarily associated with black sections of East Texas.[31] Although most log cabins were roughly finished structures they were not necessarily rude shelters. Ellen Polk's statement mentioned smooth boards and Mandy Morrow from Williamson County, Texas, noted that "Grandpappy am the carpenter and 'cause of that us quarters fixed fine and had regular windows and handmade chairs and a real wood floor."[32] Such recollections are important for they reveal that, despite the frustrations of bondage, slave craftsmen could give their best effort in order to make a comfortable environment for their families.

Black builders in Texas also worked with a variety of materials besides logs. A number of quarters were framed with planks, and at Double Bayou, according to Hiram Mayes, the slave cabins were made with bricks.[33] In other instances where limestone was used to build plantation houses, slave masons showed their skill in that medium.[34] The ex-slave narratives reveal that in West Texas Mazique Sanco built adobe and pecan pole structures and that in Medina County Monroe Brackins covered his roof with thatch.[35] Black builders generally did what they were directed to do and conformed to the southern norms for built form, but they were quite adaptable and ready to face the requirements of a range of environmental conditions.

The many volumes of the ex-slave narratives do much to reduce the anonymity of black builders in other states. Hundreds are named or were interviewed directly and many of the structures they erected are described and located. One of the more exceptional structures was the hide-out built by a runaway slave in the Dismal Swamp near the Virginia-North Carolina border. It was a shelter appropriate for so-called maroon communities, which provided havens for fugitive Blacks.[36] Ishreal Massie recalled it in some detail:

> We had one slave dat runned away an' he had a vault in th' woods fixed jes like dis room an' he had a wife an' two boys dat he raised under dar. Waal, you say, "Scribe"—ya mean tell how 'twas built? Dar wuz a hole cut in de groun'. I don' cut a many a one an' stole lumber at night to kiver hit over wid. Den dirt wuz piled on top of dis plank so dat hit won't rain in der. Den he has him some piping—trough—like—made of wood dat runned so many feet in de groun'. Dis carried smoke way away from dis cave. Fer fir[e] used oak bark 'cause hit didn't give much smoke. He had him a hole on lan'. Dar was sticks, pine board, and trash on top to kiver de hole. Ha, ha, ha. Yas could stan' right over dis hole an' wouldn't kno' hit.[37]

FWP interviewers working in Arkansas gathered the testimony of several ex-slaves who had either been carpenters or knew them intimately. Charles Dortch took affectionate pride in his father who had worked as carpenter, chair maker, basketmaker, and coffin maker. He capped his father's list of achievements by noting: "He could put a roof on a house beautifully and better than anyone I know. Nobody could beat him putting shingles on a house."[38] The same variety of skills was also remembered by J. H. Beckwith who stated that his father "could do blacksmithing, carpenter work, brick work, and shoe work." Beckwith himself was also successful in the building trades, as he recalled: "I used to be called the best negro journeyman carpenter between Monroe, Louisiana and Little Rock, Arkansas. I made quite a success in my trade. I have a couple of United States Patent Rights. One is a brick mold holding ten bricks and used to make bricks of concrete the other is a sliding door."[39] His ingenuity was at least partially inspired by his father's example. The multiple talents of the father, which surely must have stimulated the son's desire to excel, are the foundation of an Afro-American tradition in the building trades.

Ex-slave narratives collected closer to the period of slavery and recorded in diverse accounts also present in some detail the activities of black carpenters. One of the more noteworthy accounts was collected by W. D. Goodman in 1879 and illustrates how building skills gave one slave a means to attain his freedom. The narrative reads in part:

> Rev. Emperor Williams was born a slave in 1826, in the family of General Gaines, Nashville, Tenn. He went to Louisiana in 1839, and in 1840 was sold for six hundred dollars to a Negro who treated him badly. He was sold in 1841 to James McIntosh, a builder. Williams was a master mason, and from 1846 to 1858 was the trusted foreman of his owner. He joined the [Methodist Episcopal] Church in 1845. He had been promised his freedom for years, but that soon came in 1858 under peculiar circumstances. His master had a difficult piece of cornice work on the corner of Perdido and Carondelet Streets. None of the white men could put it up. Williams said he could, and his master replied that if he did, he should have his freedom. He took the plans of the difficult

piece of work, laid them on the floor of his cabin, and studied them all night until he got every part perfectly in his mind. The next day he took his gang of men and accomplished his difficult work. The promise was redeemed, and our friend was a free man.[40]

Narrative accounts constitute an indispensable base upon which to construct a history of Afro-American architecture. Taken individually they can provide the rich texture and feeling of specific events, particularly when they are as detailed and intriguing as the Emperor Williams tale. Taken collectively they can be used to uncover broader patterns. One gains some measure of understanding of what was typical, common, and representative, when finding repeated references to a particular craft or type of building. Thus even if the narrative accounts are minimal, with enough of them to review, they will still prove useful. The thousands of FWP ex-slave narratives and other kinds of reminiscence, flawed as they might be with personal bias, should therefore be thoroughly analyzed for their architectural references.

Oral History

If oral histories were a good idea in the 1930s, they remain an important way to capture important details concerning black builders' current attitudes and actions.[41] Written testimony can be supplemented with current oral testimony to test whether earlier skills are still in use or whether older traditions have passed into oblivion. Contemporary conditions for black workers in the building trades constitute elements of the most recent chapter in the history of Afro-American architecture and should not be overlooked. What workers can say about their current jobs may reflect the evolution of a new cultural pattern, a new tradition, if indeed the past has no relevance for them. Because skills were passed from generation to generation, just like stories and memories, current craftsmen often owe their livelihood to their forebears. Ace Jackson, a seventy-year-old mason from Mobile, recently said of the generations of builders that preceded him: "They came up through slavery times. They was masters of it all. The white man didn't do any of that work in those days—it was too heavy, too hard. He didn't like those trades. They made unions. Unions were segregated all but for the bricklayers, the masons, and the plasterers. The carpenters wouldn't take any colored, and even today the plumbers and electricians don't. We were the only one."[42] The absence of segregation in the Plasterers and Cement Masons Local no doubt channeled many Blacks into that particular trade. But this social condition also built upon an earlier traditional competence among enslaved Blacks who were frequently employed as masons. The men in Ace Jackson's family had always been masons: "I was raised into the trade. My mother's father was a brick mason. My father's father was a full-blooded African, and he was a brick mason."[43] His choice of occupation, it would seem, is as much a statement of traditional preference as a condition of social limitation. Such statements, when added to testimony like the FWP ex-slave narratives help establish themes of continuity that can unify the history of black builders so that it may read as a sensible saga and not as a string of isolated facts.

Contemporary masons can develop a deserved feeling of confidence with the knowledge that they were preceded by men like Jack Smith of Jacksonville, Florida, who "was regarded as a fairly good carpenter, mason, and bricklayer; at times his master would let him do small jobs of repairing of building[s] for neighboring planters," or George Harris of Raleigh, North Carolina, who was a brick maker, or Simon Walker of Birmingham, Alabama, who was a hod carrier from 1888 to 1913.[44] It is important, then, that oral history recording be conducted with an awareness of earlier documentation and that tape-recorded interviews not be thought of as a complete and closed account. Current memories probably go back to the early twentieth century; beyond that point one must use the evidence hidden away in the ex-slave narratives and other documentary sources. Contemporary black builders can bring us up to date on the history of Afro-American construction confirming or challenging the patterns that seem to emerge from piecing together the parts of the past.

Buildings and Building Sites

Finally we can turn to the buildings constructed by black craftsmen for information on their work. The wood, stone, and brick can be made to speak when studied closely, and to speak eloquently since the surviving buildings are the direct product of the history we are seeking. Let us consider just one kind of slave-crafted building. The timbers of a log cabin resonate with implications about the technology employed. Felling axes were used to chop down the trees and trim away the branches. Teams of horses rigged with harnesses and collars next snaked the logs to the building site. After being positioned with peavys and cant hooks the logs were marked with chalklines and secured with hewing dogs. After a series of deep V cuts at intervals of six inches all along the length of the log had been chopped with a felling axe, a special broad axe with a beveled blade and handle curved to the left or right (depending on whether the axeman was left-or right-handed) was employed to square up the log. A foot adze might have been brought out to smooth the rough spots, but by now the log was converted into a timber that would go into the wall of the house. Squares and scribes and saws were then used to align, mark, and cut the notches at the ends of the timbers that held the logs in place when all the timbers (usually more than forty) were stacked up to form a log pen. Other timber was sawn into rafters for the roof and studs for the gables and still other timbers were sawn or riven into planks that would cover the gables. Shingles would have to be split from sections of logs, and holes for doors, windows, and fireplace mouth cut into the pen of logs and finished off with board frames. Each of these processes described here employed different tools: special saws, wedges, mauls, froes, shaves, planes, chisels, mallets, and hammers. Finally a fireplace and chimney would be built with brick, stone, or logs and sticks plastered with mud. Leaving the problem of design aside, just the basic means and techniques alone that were required to build a log house could be quite involved. Warren E. Roberts has recently shown that as many as seventy-six tools might be required in the construction of a log cabin.[45] A log house can thus tell a tale of complicated carpentry and reveal to us the competence of a black carpenter in a forthright and direct way.

Most people would be incapable of hanging a door and could not even consider building a house from standing trees, yet log buildings are considered crude structures, mere shelter. While any act can be done poorly, all log cabins were not badly constructed. The inspection of surviving slave quarters shows the quality of slave work by the very fact that these structures still stand after so many years, and the details of construction reveal that oversimplified perceptions of slave skills have prevented credit from being given where due.

Houses built in the medium of hewn logs illustrate the Afro-American adoption of a new technology, one with European origins.[46] Indeed, the adoption of new cultural traits is an important aspect of the black experience in America. But the technology of built form used by Blacks in the South also shows the occasional survival of African traits and consequently some resistance to change. Consider the following statement by Ben Sullivan of St. Simons Island, Georgia: "Ole man Okra he say he want a place like he have in Africa so he built him a hut. I remember it well. It was about twelve by fourteen feet and it have dirt floor and he built the side like basket weave with clay plaster on it. It have a flat roof what he made from bush and palmetto and have one door and no windows. But Massa make him pull it down. He say he ain't want no African hut on he place."[47] Here we have testimony to the continued use in the United States of the wattle-and-daub construction and the thatch roofing common to tropical Africa and the Caribbean. Ex-slave narratives from South Carolina refer to a plantation in Lynchburg that had three buildings called "clay houses," which possibly had walls made of courses of solid mud after the example of the Yoruba, Fon, and Edo of West Africa.[48] In Texas there were memories in the 1930s of thatched roofs on slave quarters in Halletsville made with corn shucks and grass.[49] Just at the start of the twentieth century near Edgefield, South Carolina, a one-room thatched house built by Tahro, a former slave from western Zaire, was still standing and was photographed by anthropologist Charles Montgomery.[50] All of these examples suggest that an alternative building tradition was present within the minds of black laborers while they acquired new skills. But how can one learn to appreciate the earlier African skills of black builders? Mud and thatch were perishable and did not stand up to the elements. Time has claimed those buildings and erased their presence from the landscape—or has it? Current research in historic archaeology has recovered significant aspects of collapsed structures built by Blacks. One of the most interesting was located in Plymouth, Massachusetts, an area of the United States not particularly known for its black population.[51] Plantation archaeology has greatly improved understanding of the domestic life of enslaved Afro-Americans.[52] Along the way the archaeologists have given insight into domestic building practices revealing not only floor plans and specialized uses of space but something about the technology employed. Recent excavations of the Curiboo Plantation in Berkeley County, South Carolina, turned up a number of structures (several of which were identified as slave quarters) built with trench wall techniques.[53] The foundations of these buildings had so disturbed the ground that many years after the structures had collapsed they could still be located. Inspection of the sites of black building activity, whether the structures are still standing or have been destroyed, will prove valuable. What is required to gain insight is a predisposition to treat whatever is encountered as serious and important. What people did with their lives was important to them. What they left behind, no matter how meager, provides a way to grasp the importance of their experiences.

Conclusion

The three general resources for the study of black builders—written documents, personal histories (both written and verbal), and buildings and building sites—are not a novel triad; historical archaeologists have for sometime recognized the usefulness of this variety of data.[54] The main virtue of this multiplicity of sources is that, while there may be some redundancy in the information they provide, a researcher gains some means to assess the validity of a tentative oral statement or to amplify the significance of a dry statistic or to situate specifically a commonplace occurrence. A surplus of information in one area fills the void in another. Scholars in various disciplines such as history, sociology, folklore, American Studies, architectural history, art history, and cultural geography might attempt to study the role of Blacks as builders of the South. Each discipline would probably claim its own "turf," its own data, as a basis for study and research. What, however, may be more rewarding is an approach such as has been outlined here where all scholars avail themselves of all the kinds of information they can find. This may require an expansion of one's perspective and a retooling and fine tuning of research skills, but only if researchers get better at the business of scholarship will their findings improve. Only then will a holistic history of southern life, one filled with the voices of all its participants, be written.[55] Attempts to find out about black builders will simultaneously shed new light on hundreds of questions relating to work, social class, ethnicity, tradition, the economy, social history, and so on. Scholars at last might learn who actually built what plantation, courthouse, or railroad station. Beyond such basic questions of fact lies the connection between slave skills and their access to freedom either by escape or manumission. Or the researcher might be able to relate moments of economic expansion to the availability of black labor. Further one might ask whether leadership in the trades led to leadership in other social spheres such as business or politics. One might also ask what importance a legacy of skill might have for the current generation of Blacks who are about to enter the marketplace. The history of black builders presents an exciting challenge with many potential benefits to be realized. Some of these benefits might be quite tangible, such as the compilation of archival documentation or the creation of museum exhibits. Other less-immediate benefits would include the sense of well-being that comes from knowing specifically what one's ancestors did, and where, when, and how they did it. Whether they are concrete or spiritual in nature, the advantages of new information cannot be doubted. Such information can lead to the reexamination of past motives and values, an important step in the process of turning knowledge into wisdom.

Notes

1. Wayne Andrews, *Social History of Southern Architecture,* quoted in *Southern Exposure* 8 (1980):69.

2. George P. Rawick, *The American Slave: A Composite Autobiography* (Westport, Conn.: Greenwood Press, 1972), Vol. 2, 1, 290; Vol. 7, 130; Vol. 6, 392.

3. "The Big House and the Slave Quarters, pt. II," *Landscape* 21 (1976):13.

4. Ph.D. dissertation, University of Georgia, Department of History (1970), 95.

5. Quoted in Michael Mullin, ed., *American Negro Slavery: A Documentary History* (Columbia, S.C.: University of South Carolina Press, 1976), 111–12.

6. Quoted in Ibid., 113.

7. *Black Majority: Negroes in Colonial South Carolina from 1760 through the Stono Rebellion* (New York: W. W. Norton, 1974), 206–7.

8. Ibid., 197.

9. *South Carolina Gazette,* 9 March 1767, 3 from the craftsmen files of the Museum of Early Southern Decorative Arts in Winston-Salem, North Carolina.

10. "Letters to the Jefferson Family" in John W. Blassingame, *Slave Testimony: Two Centuries of Letters, Speeches, Interviews and Autobiographies* (Baton Rouge: Louisiana State University Press, 1977) 16.

11. Ibid., 17.

12. Ibid.

13. Randall M. Miller, *"Dear Master": Letters from a Slave Family* (Ithaca: Cornell University Press, 1978), 153.

14. Ibid., 166.

15. Ibid., 168, 169.

16. *The Peculiar Institution: Slavery in the Ante-Bellum South* (New York: Vintage Books, 1956), 69.

17. *Black Majority,* 207.

18. *Inventories,* GS – 2, 258, Maryland Hall of Records.

19. *Inventory of the Estate of Landon Carter, 1779,* manuscript, Alderman Library, University of Virginia.

20. *The Diary of Colonel Landon Carter of Sabine Hall, 1752–1778,* ed. by Jack P. Greene (Charlottesville: University Press of Virginia, 1966), Vol. 1, 369; Vol. 2, 735, 855–56.

21. Mullin, *American Negro Slavery,* 27.

22. Norman Yetman, *Life Under the "Peculiar Institution": Selections from the Slave Narrative Collection* (New York: Holt, Rinehart and Winston, 1970), 1.

23. "Introduction," *Slave Testimony,* 11; see Paul D. Escott, *Slavery Remembered: A Record of Twentieth-Century Slave Narratives* (Chapel Hill: University of North Carolina Press, 1979) for an analysis of the ex-slave narratives that partially responds to Blassingame's demands for careful study.

24. "History from Slave Sources: A Review Article," *American Historical Review* 79 (1974):475.

25. See Rawick, *The American Slave,* vols. 4, 5. Since this article was written Rawick located and published nine supplemental volumes of slave testimony from Texas. Their content considerably expands my findings regarding black builders in this state.

26. Ibid., vol. 5, pt. 3, 118.

27. Ibid., vol. 4, pt. 1, 49.

28. Ibid., vol. 4, pt. 1, 18.

29. Henry Glassie, *Pattern in the Material Folk Culture of the Eastern United States* (Philadelphia: University of Pennsylvania Press, 1968), 101–6.

30. Rawick, *The American Slave,* vol. 4, pt. 1, 55; vol. 5, pt. 3, 253.

31. Ibid., vol. 5, pt. 3, 189.

32. Ibid., vol. 5, pt. 3, 139.

33. Ibid., vol. 4, pt. 1, 45; vol. 5, pt. 3, 73.

34. See the Friday Mountain home of Thomas Johnson built in 1852 in Hays County, Texas, for an example. The house is described in Willie Kemp, "Bear Creek and Friday Mountain," *Frontier Times* (Dec.–Feb. 1970):34–35.

35. Rawick, *The American Slave,* vol. 4, pt. 1, 124; vol. 4, pt. 1, 267.

36. See George A. Davis and O. Fred Donaldson, *Blacks in the United States: A Geographical Perspective* (Boston: Houghton Mifflin, 1975), 25–26, esp. fig. 2.4 for locations of maroon communities in the United States.

37. Charles L. Perdue, Jr., Thomas E. Barden, and Robert K. Philips, eds., *Weevils in the Wheat: Interviews with Virginia Ex-Slaves* (Charlottesville: University Press of Virginia, 1976), 209–10.

38. Rawick, *The American Slave,* vol. 8, pt. 2, 170.

39. Ibid., vol. 8, pt. 1, 132–33.

40. From *Gilbert Academy and Agricultural College: Sketches and Incidents* (1893) quoted in Blassingame, *Slave Testimony,* 621.

41. On the value of contemporary oral history see David F. Kyvig and Myron A. Marty, *Nearby History: Exploring the Past around You* (Nashville: American Association for the Study of State and Local History, 1982), 110–25.

42. Ben Fewel, "Ace Jackson," *Southern Exposure* 8 (1980):11.

43. Ibid.

44. Rawick, *The American Slave,* vol. 17, 22; vol. 14, 373; vol. 6, 406.

45. "The Tools Used in Building Log Houses in Indiana," *Pioneer America* 9 (1977):32–61.

46. For a history of American log architecture consult Fred Kniffen and Henry Glassie, "Building in Wood in the Eastern United States: A Time-Place Perspective," *Geographical Review* 56 (1966):40–66.

47. Georgia Writer's Project, *Drums and Shadows* (1940) (rpt. Garden City, N.Y.: Doubleday, 1972), 171–72.

48. Rawick, *The American Slave,* vol. 3, pt. 3, 158; John Michael Vlach, "Sources of the Shotgun House: African and Caribbean Antecedents for Afro-American Architecture," Ph.D. dissertation, Indiana University (1975), 145, see esp. fig. 30.

49. Rawick, *The American Slave,* vol. 4, pt. 2, 267.

50. "Survivors of the Slave Yacht *Wanderer,*" *American Anthropologist* 10 (1908):611–23.

51. James Deetz, *In Small Things Forgotten* (Garden City, N.Y.: Anchor Press, 1977), chap. 7, "Parting Ways."

52. For a review of the growing literature on archaeological studies of plantations, see Geoffrey M. Gyrisco and Bert Salwen, "Archaeology of Black American Cultures: An Annotated Bibliography" in Robert L. Schuyler, ed., *Archaeological Perspectives on Ethnicity in America* (Farmingdale, N.Y.: Baywood Publishing, 1980), 76–85.

53. "Cooper River Rediversion Canal Project," *Newsletter of the Society for Historical Archaeology* 13 (1980):22.

54. See Robert L. Schuyler, "The Spoken Word, the Written Word, Observed Behavior and Preserved Behavior: The Contexts Available to the Archaeologist" in Robert L. Schuyler, ed., *Historical Archaeology: A Guide to Substantive Theoretical Contributions* (Farmingdale, N.Y.: Baywood Publishing, 1978), 268–77.

55. See George W. McDaniel, *Hearth and Home: Preserving a People's Culture* (Philadelphia: Temple University Press, 1982) for a recent example of an inclusive grass roots social history written from an architectural perspective.

Part Three

Black Buildings

Introduction to Part Three

The two articles included in this section treat very different aspects of Afro-American folk architecture: the first examines the origins of a specific building type, the second evaluates the black contribution to a regional landscape. In the essay on the shotgun house, the development of a distinct house type is chronicled by searching back through time and across space to discern how this alternative building form came into the United States. What is crucial in this saga is that its designers and builders in New Orleans, the point where the house type enters North America, were the *hommes de couleur libres,* or the "free men of color." There were enough of these free Blacks working as contractors and carpenters that they left a durable architectural imprint on the city. The shotgun house was later to become ubiquitous as it was used all over the South when and wherever there was a need to house either black or short-term workers. The conditions examined in the article on slave housing in Virginia were quite different. Those houses did not stand out boldly as signs of an alternative culture; the cabins of Virginia slaves looked just like the houses of poor, and sometimes middle-class, Whites. Nevertheless, an argument is made that some aspects of those houses can be profitably understood as African qualities, particularly for the earlier decades of the eighteenth century. Surprisingly, it was in the invisible part of a house, in its contained space, that a distinctive ethnic quality may have been expressed. Because those cabins were possibly a familiar size to their African occupants, they may have felt right to them, while to their masters they looked like the appropriate sort of shelter in which to house slaves. Moreover, the fact that slaves were not always policed with great diligence led to a certain opportunism on the slaves' part so that within the plantation regime there arose a black orientation that was at cross purposes to the white order.

The important point that should not be missed is that built form, even when it is technologically simple, is much more than meets the eye. In the case of free black American builders, when they had full control of the design process, they could produce structures that were formally distinct. But when choices were severely crimped by the institution of slavery, buildings constructed by Blacks manifested only a slight degree of difference from the dominant cultural norm. However, even when a cultural trait is only subtly manifested, it is no less significant. Indeed, slaves in Virginia were able, with the minimal means available to them, to create a residential and working landscape no less meaningful than that developed by the free men of color in New Orleans.

Few scholars have yet taken up the challenge of Afro-American vernacular architecture. Still there are some significant books and articles that should be mentioned. Slave housing in the Chesapeake region is treated extensively by George McDaniel in his *Hearth and Home: Preserving a People's Culture* (Philadelphia: Temple University Press, 1982), and specific sets of quarters are interpreted by Bernard Herman in "Slave Quarters in Virginia: The Persona behind Historic Artifacts," in David G. Orr and Daniel G. Crozier, eds., *The Scope of Historical Archaeology: Essays in Honor of John L. Cotter,* Occasional Publication of the Department of Anthropology, Temple University (Philadelphia: Laboratory of Anthropology, 1984), 253–83. For more background on New Orleans's black architecture one should consult Sally Kittridge Evans, "Free Persons of Color," in Roulhac Toledano, Sally Kittredge Evans, and Mary Louise Christovich, *New Orleans Architecture. Volume 4: The Creole Faubourgs* (New Orleans: Pelican Publishing, 1974), 25–36. The most extensive recent treatment of the subject of traditional black architecture in New Orleans is Naohito Okude's "Architectural Design Among New Orleans Free Persons of Color, 1820–1880: Application of Linguistic Concepts to the Study of Vernacular Architecture," Ph.D. dissertation, The George Washington University, 1986. An overview calling for more study on all fronts was authored by Steven L. Jones, entitled "The African-American Tradition in Vernacular Architecture," in Theresa A. Singleton, ed. *The Archaeology of Slavery and Plantation Life* (Orlando, Fla.: Academic Press, 1985), 195–213.

While archaeologists are concerned with more than the architectural features of the sites they excavate, the recent work at plantation sites has yielded useful information about the houses built and occupied by slaves. The anthology by Theresa Singleton just mentioned provides a convenient survey of much of what has been discovered over the past decade and a half. Two book-length studies that provide substantive treatments of slave housing from an archaeological perspective are: John Otto, *Cannon's Point Plantation 1784–1860: Living Conditions and Status Patterns in the Old South* (New York: Academic Press, 1984), and William M. Kelso, *Kingsmill Plantations 1619–1800: The Archeology of Country Life in Colonial Virginia* (New York: Academic Press, 1984). At this point, it can be safely stated that the archaeologists are leading the way in the study of Afro-

American vernacular buildings even though their evidence is largely confined to foundations and marks in the ground.

Two social historical assessments of eighteenth-century Virginia that pay close attention to material culture evidence are by Rhys Isaac, *The Transformation of Virginia 1740–1790* (Chapel Hill: University of North Carolina Press, 1982), and Mechal Sobel, *The World They Made Together: Black and White Values in Eighteenth-Century Virginia* (Princeton, N.J.: Princeton University Press, 1988). These two books are complemented and extended by the recent investigations of two historians of vernacular architecture: Dell Upton, "White and Black Landscapes in Eighteenth-Century Virginia," *Places* 2, no. 2 (1985), 59–72; and Camille Wells, "The Eighteenth-Century Landscape of Virginia's Northern Neck," *Northern Neck of Virginia Historical Magazine* 38 (1987), 4217–55. These studies present a fusion of fieldwork with conventional historical research and suggest a productive method for future investigation.

Today museums are playing an important role in the study of early Afro-American architecture. At the Smithsonian Institution a good share of exhibit space is given to the subject. In two current exhibitions at the National Museum of American History, After the Revolution: Everyday Life in the Eighteenth Century and From Field to Factory, commonplace black buildings are prominently featured. At Colonial Williamsburg slave quarters are being painstakingly recreated at Carter's Grove. This reconstruction project is utilizing all that is known about such structures from the evidence of archaeological investigation, the study of historical documents, and the inspection of standing structures of a similar type.

It should be clear from this short list of books, articles, and museum exhibits that the study of black folk and vernacular housing is being pursued most energetically along the eastern seaboard, in those areas where large plantations were once common. While such studies are valuable and necessary, a much broader net needs to be cast. Afro-American vernacular architecture involves more than slave cabins and certainly more slave cabins than just those built on major estates. There is much to be done not only on the housing of the slaves but on all the buildings in which the institution of slavery was experienced. Further, urban black housing, particularly buildings designed and constructed by free Blacks, remains a topic for further research although the subject is touched upon by Richard Wade in his *Slavery in the Cities: The South 1820–1860* (New York: Oxford University Press, 1964), and again in Marie Tyler-McGraw and Gregg D. Kimball, *In Bondage and Freedom: Antebellum Black Life in Richmond, Virginia* (Richmond: The Valentine Museum, 1988).

7

The Shotgun House:
An African Architectural Legacy

One of the little understood dimensions of American culture has been the material contribution of Afro-Americans. The material achievements of Blacks are generally assumed to have been negligible, if not nonexistent. Yet, now and again, diligent scholarship brings to light an Afro-American tradition in basketry, ironwork, pottery, and other crafts.[1] The continued study of Afro-American artifacts will presumably heighten awareness of both black creativity and the existence of Afro-American material culture. Some African artifacts survived the period of slavery because of their similarity to items employed by Whites. The mortar and pestle, two African tools, were used for winnowing rice among Blacks from the Sea Islands largely because the same implements were also found to be useful to members of the dominant white culture.[2] While the black artifactual repertoire has never dominated the material culture of the United States, it has in some cases provided a central influence in the creation of significant items. Notably, the dugout canoes of the Chesapeake region and the banjo are thought to have benefited from Afro-American influence.[3] There has been a constant interaction of black and white material repertoires leading not only to the sharing of items, but to the borrowing of them as well. It is here argued that in the development of the shotgun house we find an Afro-American artifact that has been adopted by Whites and effectively incorporated into popular building practices. The significance of this postulated cultural borrowing cannot be overlooked, for it represents an important contribution of Afro-Americans to the cultural landscape. The shotgun house is, moreover, a central building type in the development of an Afro-American architecture.

The assertion that the humble shotgun, the narrow frame shack of cotton fields and mill towns, is an African-derived house will no doubt

This article originally appeared in *Pioneer America* 8 (1976): 47–80. Reprinted by permission of the Pioneer America Society.

raise some eyebrows. It is my intention to trace the history of the shotgun house and indicate how it is associated ultimately with an African architectural heritage. The links to Africa are not simple and direct. The story behind the shotgun involves long migrations, the conduct of the Atlantic slave trade, the rise of free black communities, the development of vernacular and popular traditions in architecture, and the growth of American industrial needs. The history of the shotgun extends back at least to the sixteenth century and is too intricate to be traced exhaustively here.[4]

Students of folk architecture have been aware of shotgun houses at least since 1936 when Fred B. Kniffen published his landmark paper "Louisiana House Types."[5] The shotgun house type was one of several building forms that Kniffen found useful as an index for cultural regions. He defined the type as "one room in width and from one to three or more rooms deep, with frontward-facing gable."[6] Since the number of rooms was highly variable and the plan of a minimal shotgun closely resembled trapper and oysterman house types, he might have suggested a historical sequence. But Kniffen was concerned primarily with the interpretation of spatial diffusion so that chronology did not enter directly into his study. He did note that the shotgun was "strikingly" associated with Louisiana's waterways, but again he chose not to comment on the historical significance of this geographical distribution. Twenty years later his student, William B. Knipmeyer, felt confident enough to assert that the shotgun had evolved from Indian dwellings and was itself the evolutionary precursor of the bungalow house.[7] It is probably because Kniffen so stressed the regional affiliation of the shotgun that Knipmeyer constructed a thesis of native origins. Accompanying this theory was the suggestion of recent development; he claimed that shotguns were built only after 1880 when inexpensive lumber was readily available.[8] Yvonne Phillips supported the idea that the shotgun was a late nineteenth-century or early twentieth-century creation by emphasizing the dominance of timber-framed examples.[9] The modernity of the house type was also accepted by John Burkhardt Rehder who, in his analysis of Louisiana's sugar plantations, relied heavily on Knipmeyer's view of the shotgun house.[10] These studies, when taken together, portray this house form as a regional peculiarity, created solely from the idiosyncratic factors of southern Louisiana's cultural and ecological resources, and commonplace only in the twentieth century. It is true that many of the current Louisiana shotguns can be found along the bayous and that most are examples of 1920s and 1930s frame construction (fig. 7.1). But this viewpoint ignores a major aspect of the building's development. No consideration is given to the matter of origins.

The origins of the house type remain murky and difficult to comprehend. Yet, it is a history with more antiquity than most have allowed.

Geographer Milton B. Newton, Jr., has suggested that the shotgun is an old house form; but he does not state just how old.[11] Architectural historians, while ignoring the rural versions of the type, have shown that the shotgun became common in New Orleans well before the onset of the 1890s lumbering boom.[12]

Three elaborately decorated shotgun houses were illustrated in the 1880 catalog of Roberts and Company, a New Orleans firm that specialized in decorative house trimmings. The sophistication of these examples suggests that the urban shotgun had undergone a much longer period of development than its country cousin (fig. 7.2). At the very least, the house type must have been around long enough to require updating of its architectural details. With a new set of cornices or balasters, an old-fashioned house could appear appropriately stylish. The Roberts company apparently provided the means to keep shotgun houses in step with the flamboyance of changing styles.[13] It would then seem that the shotgun is an older house form and that the search for its origins must involve urban as well as rural versions.

New Orleans should be considered the specific center of shotgun development. This city is the cultural focus of southeastern Louisiana, the region definable by the presence of the shotgun house. The house probably radiated out across the countryside from New Orleans rather than climbing the folk-urban continuum that is assumed to exist in folk architecture. The presence of several subtypes bespeaks the long acquaintance of New Orleans with the shotgun. In addition to the basic single shotgun, there are double shotguns, "camelback" houses, and North Shore houses (fig. 7.3). The double shotgun, as the name suggests, consists of two single houses built side by side under one roof. Such houses were double-occupancy units that helped to maximize the use of expensive city land. Camelback houses, also referred to as "hump-backs," are single and double shotguns that have two-story rear sections. Since most of the house remains only one story high, these last rooms do resemble "humps." The vertical expansion of these houses is clearly a response to urban crowding. The Louisiana North Shore type, consisting of a single shotgun surrounded on three sides by wide verandas, illustrates how additive secondary features, like porches, can be manipulated to create a regional personality for the standard house type. This subtype occurs frequently across from New Orleans along the north shore of Lake Pontchartrain. What is most significant about the formation of subtypes is that time is required for such variations to develop and become standardized. Folk houses are affected slowly by cultural processes; their basic plans remain relatively fixed and are changed only with cautious innovation. Subtypes arise from experimental attempts to solve problems not initially anticipated when a house form

Figure 7.1. Rural Shotgun Houses
a. (*above*) frame shotgun near Fairview, Chicot County, Arkansas; b. (*opposite, top left*) plan of a shotgun south of Schriever, Terrebonne Parish, Louisiana; c. (*opposite, top right*) plan of a shotgun south of Theriot, Terrebonne Parish, Louisiana; d.(*opposite, bottom*) plan of a shotgun north of Theriot, Terrebonne Parish, Louisiana
(*All of these illustrations are from fieldwork by the author in August 1973*)

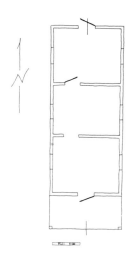

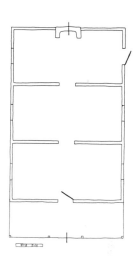

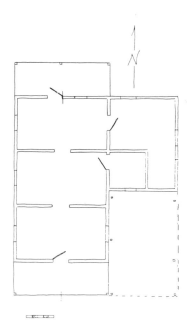

444

Figure 7.2. Extremely Ornate Shotgun House Illustrated in the Catalog of
Roberts and Company in 1880
(From Illustrated Catalogue of Moulding, Architectural and
Ornamental Woodwork, *compiled by William Bell, Louisiana
Steam Sash, Blind, and Door Factory [New Orleans, M. F.
Dunn Bro., 1880], p. 81)*

is first used. The proliferation of shotgun subtypes in and around New Orleans would then, in theory, indicate that the house type has long been known in that city.

But the antiquity of the shotgun need not rest on informed speculation alone. There are a few documents that can be used to verify early urban origins. The Notarial Archives of New Orleans maintains a large collection of old posters advertising the sale of property. The posters usually contain a map of the general location of the property, a detailed map of the exact lots, which sometimes include measured floor plans, elevations of the fronts of any buildings, and occasionally a perspective view of the property. All of this information is extremely valuable for deciphering the history of old buildings. These records, however, were only kept intermittently for the earlier years of New Orleans history and thus require interpretive analysis. For example, if a house was sold in 1840, it would not be unreasonable to suspect that it existed as much as ten or fifteen years earlier. If a building is a particular subtype of the basic form, it may be further safely assumed that buildings closer to the essential type would have been older.

The oldest shotgun house appearing in these records was located on Bourbon Street near St. Philip in the French Quarter and was sold in November 1833.[14] It is a prototypical shotgun, one room wide and several deep, with its gable facing the street. The roof was, however, hipped only in the front. Thus, even this early example was already modified by the local roof style, which suggests that this house was patterned on yet older examples. Dimensions for buildings in early contract records suggest that shotguns were being built. A house of three rooms in 1835 was twenty-two feet by fifty-eight feet, including the gallery on the side and rear. Another building constructed in 1837 was sixteen feet across the front and forty feet deep.[15]

A more elaborate variation of the shotgun was built in the lower Garden District. Four identical houses were built in 1837 at Constance and Euterpe Streets, which were three-room shotguns with two-room additions along the side.[16] A porch surrounded each building on three sides in the manner of a North Shore subtype. These city houses are probably antecedents for the shotguns built in Mandeville and Abita Springs forty years later. This set of shotguns is significant because they are a subtype. Given the time that is required for the development of house variations, early origins for the basic New Orleans shotgun can be posited. The sale of a double shotgun in 1854 in like manner suggests antiquity for the single shotgun house.[17]

These records, though sketchy for the early years of the nineteenth century, show that the shotgun had taken root as a local type. It has been

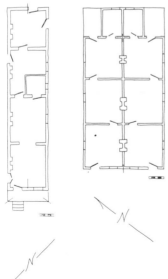

Figure 7.3.

New Orleans Shotgun Types
a. (*opposite, top left*) single
shotgun, Burgundy Street;
b. (*opposite, top right*) double
shotgun, Bourbon Street;
c. (*opposite, bottom*) camelback
shotgun, Dumaine Street;
d. (*top*) North Shore shotgun,
Abita Springs, St. Tammany
Parish, Louisiana; e. (*bottom,
far left*) plan of a single
shotgun, Chartres Street;
f. (*bottom, left*) plan of a double
shotgun, Eighth Street.
*(Photographs, August 1973;
plans, June 1974)*

in New Orleans certainly since the first quarter of the nineteenth century. It is this early origin that allows the shotgun to be associated with Afro-American architectural traditions.

New Orleans had a community of free Blacks from its earliest days. They are mentioned in legal records in 1722.[18] Their members grew steadily: 98 in 1764, 353 in 1778, 1,355 in 1803.[19] By the nineteenth century free Negroes, including many mulattoes, constituted one-ninth of the population of New Orleans. The most significant increase in the black community occurred in 1809 with a massive influx of free Negroes from Santo Domingo. After the revolt led by Toussaint l'Ouverture in 1791, a few black immigrants came to New Orleans and were easily assimilated.[20] But by the time the Louisiana territory was acquired by the United States, Haitian Negroes were considered undesirable. It was thought that they would incite local slaves to rebellion and consequently in 1806 legislation was passed prohibiting the immigration of free Blacks from Haiti.[21] But between May 10 and August 19, 1809, some fifty ships brought to New Orleans 1,887 whites, 2,113 slaves, and 2,060 free people of color fleeing conditions in Haiti—6,060 in all.[22] The dimensions of this migration were overwhelming for the local authorities. What was most disrupting about this immigration of Haitian refugees was the change it caused in the racial balance of the city. In 1810 New Orleans had 12,223 people: 4,507 whites, 4,386 slaves, and 3,332 free people of color. The 7,718 Negroes were almost twice the number of Whites.[23] The influx of Haitian immigrants made New Orleans a truly black city.

The newly enlarged black community apparently attained both economic success and social recognition.[24] Free Blacks were also active in the building trades. By 1850 there were 355 free Negro carpenters and 325 masons.[25] While these figures only represent conditions in the later history of the black community, the large number of Negro craftsmen clearly implies that there were free black house builders from the start of the nineteenth century. The massive increase in the population of New Orleans in 1809 created a severe shortage of housing. Free Blacks were in a position to both buy and build houses of their own choosing. They controlled enough financial resources and physical skills to develop their own architectural environment.

Documents in support of this claim are rare but they do exist. In 1787, a free mulatto named Charles was contracted to build a plantation house.[26] Bazile Dede, a free Negro mason, is mentioned in building contracts in 1810 and 1811.[27] James Jolles, an *homme de couleur libre,* in 1835 built a house for Uranie Marsenat Chapieaux that was fifteen feet across the front and forty-five feet long. This house may have been a shotgun and the dwelling that he built next year for Ursin Drouet, described as a one-story frame house, may also have been a shotgun.[28] In 1837, J. B. Joublanc, a free Negro builder, constructed a "typical cottage" for J. B. Massicot.[29]

Of special interest to my thesis are references to the building practices of Haiti, the previous home of many free Blacks. In 1839, François Ducoing requested that Laurent Cordier build a *maison basse*.[30] This term is used in Haiti for buildings of the shotgun type. This house was built on Elysian Fields, a major street in the Third Municipality, which was at that time a black Creole neighborhood.[31] The connection between Haiti and New Orleans is more pronounced in the case of Martial Le Boeuf who, in 1840, stated in a contract that his house was to be built after the example of buildings in Santo Domingo.[32] Even viewing these records critically, it must be granted that free Blacks were building houses that were sometimes not conventional Creole house types, and that those houses were partially affected by Haitian building traditions.

Kniffen, in wondering where the shotgun could have originated, suggested that either Indians or Haitian slaves were responsible.[33] It would appear, however, that free Haitians built the first shotgun houses. Slave cabins in 1805 were square houses about twelve feet on a side. Although they were constructed with wattle-and-daub like rural Haitian buildings, there is no clear connection between these dwellings and the shotguns that may have been built in New Orleans at the same time.[34] The shotgun house developed in New Orleans about the same time that there was a massive infusion of free Blacks from Haiti. The circumstance suggests that the origins of the shotgun are not to be found in the swamps and bayous of Louisiana but in Haiti.

In the towns of southern Haiti there are some houses that are very similar to the shotgun houses of Louisiana. These dwellings (fig. 7.4), like the shotgun, are one room wide and one story high, and have their gable and front entrance facing the road. There is almost always a front porch formed by the forward projection of the gable. Even the same set of shotgun subtypes may be identified in Port-au-Prince. The single camelback occurs with some frequency as well as the double shotgun. Secondary features are also manipulated in the construction of Haitian houses so that some have elaborate verandas resembling those of the North Shore house. On formal grounds these Haitian dwellings must be placed in the shotgun category. The occurrence of the same house types in both Haiti and Louisiana can be explained by the historical links between them via a similar exposure to French culture, trade and commerce, and finally the migration of Haitian Creoles to Louisiana. The shotgun house is perhaps the best document of those ties since the shotguns of Port-au-Prince and New Orleans are similar not only in type but also in specific detail.

The precise size of the floor plans of some Louisiana and Haitian shotgun houses is in some cases almost identical. I found one Port-au-Prince house that measured 13′ × 65′, while two New Orleans shotguns were 13′ × 64′ and 14′ × 64′. The room shapes of New Orleans shotguns are generally squarish, averaging 12′ × 14′. The same rule or proportion holds for Haitian houses. Even though room units are usually smaller in Port-au-Prince, commonly about 12′ × 12′, there is often an exact agreement with the measurements of rooms in new Orleans houses.

The ceiling heights of shotguns are also comparable. Haitian houses are distinctively tall with steeply pitched roofs. They sometimes have the look of small two-story houses. Floor-to-ceiling dimensions are consistently near twelve feet. This height, when accompanied by full-length, louvered shutters, facilitates the ventilation necessary for comfort in the tropics. Older New Orleans shotguns may have twelve-foot ceilings either because of local architectural fashion or because southern Louisiana also has a tropical climate. But since tall ceilings were established in Port-au-Prince as a constant feature, the high ceilings of some New Orleans houses may have been copied as much as an aspect of form rather than function alone.

It certainly seems that formal considerations govern the arrangement of the facades of New Orleans shotguns. A pattern of two frontal openings occurs in most urban Haitian shotguns. The double front "door" pattern occurs repeatedly in New Orleans shotguns. As in Port-au-Prince, the two openings are full-length and shielded by louvered shutters. Even when glass panes are installed, the pattern of two tall, evenly spaced apertures cannot be missed. This type of facade seems to have been copied from the Haitian shotgun. The double-opening pattern was so basic to the early shotgun that it was maintained even when the house plan was significantly altered in the late nineteenth century. At that time it became common for shotguns to have a hallway running the length of one side of the house. However, the door that opened onto the hall was often placed out of rhythm with the other openings. Squeezed against the side of the house, the door could easily be visualized as a part of the addition to the house rather than its entrance.[35] Since the facade pattern endured despite the important modification of the house plan, it must have been a feature firmly

---

Figure 7.4.   (*Opposite*) Urban Haitian Shotguns
a. (*top left*) frame shotgun, Avenue Magloire Amboise, Port-au-Prince;
b. (*top right*) half-timbered shotgun, Rue St. Honoré, Port-au-Prince;
c. (*bottom left*) plan of frame shotgun, above; d. (*bottom right*) plan of half-timbered shotgun, Avenue Magloire Amboise, Port-au-Prince. This house has a screen of open lattice work between the first and second rooms and thus has a spatial organization similar to the house shown in figure 7.3e.
(*All of these illustrations are from fieldwork by the author in October and November 1973*)

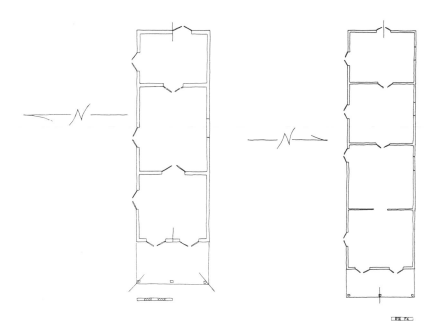

established by a traditional precedent. Undoubtedly the houses of Haiti provided a model to be copied and thus served as a basis for the form.

Similarities in internal partitioning of Haitian and Louisiana shotguns is also evident. In the more elaborate shotguns of Port-au-Prince, the first and second rooms are barely divided at all. Instead there is a large opening without doors; sometimes almost ten feet wide. Several houses had screens of lattice work that separated the *salle* from the *salon*. Since these "walls' are not solid partitions, they are essentially decorative rather than functional. Although New Orleans shotguns do not have this type of screen, they do occasionally have wide openings between the first and second rooms. These openings can usually be closed by sliding doors that recede into the side partitions when not in use. Thus, the rooms may be sealed off, although normal use habits require that they be left apart. If the doors are left open, a spatial pattern similar to the Haitian shotgun is created. This aspect is not essential to the shotgun form and only occurs in elaborate versions of the house, but it may be related to the social behaviors of the class of elites who required a *salon* for conversation. Since it was the upper-class Black who migrated to Louisiana, this feature may underline the social as well as the historical circumstances in which the shotgun was introduced into New Orleans.

Haitian shotguns are built with an open-bay framing technique. A strong timber frame is built with a minimum of structural pieces, either $4'' \times 4''$ or $3'' \times 4''$ timbers. Sills are laid on the foundation and vertical posts installed only at the corners or next to openings in the walls (fig. 7.5). The walls are braced with diagonals in either a regular or random pattern and capped with plates. All pieces are fitted together with a mortice-and-tenon system of joints. The walls are completed by either covering the frame with siding or filling the spaces with brick and mortar. This building technique, sometimes called half-timbering or *briquette entre poteaux,* is well known throughout Europe and in early America. The technique was introduced into both Haiti and Louisiana by French colonists.[36] Since half-timbering is known in these two areas, a continuity in shotgun construction methods may be suggested, although no half-timber shotguns are known to still exist in New Orleans.

The half-timbering technique may be used to achieve an artistic effect by painting the structural and fill units in contrasting colors. However, this potential is only utilized on the fronts of Haitian shotguns. The X braces that occur on the gable ends are highlighted for decorative reasons. Structural and aesthetic intentions were thus complementary (fig. 7.6). Yet, it was more common to cover the front with clapboards, which were seven to ten inches wide with a decorative bead at the edge or center. This siding was then painted and thus distinguished the front of the house from its

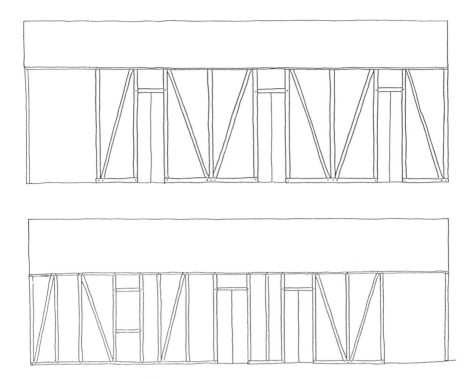

Figure 7.5.   Haitian Half-Timbering Patterns (side views)
(*Upper*) symmetrical framing for a shotgun house, Rue Mgr.
Guilloux, Port-au-Prince; (*lower*) asymmetrical framing for a
shotgun house, Avenue Magloire Amboise, Port-au-Prince.
*(From fieldwork by the author in October and November
1973)*

sides by both color and medium. The custom of giving special attention
to the front of shotguns is also practiced in New Orleans. The side of a
house may be unpainted, but the front might be given a veneer of brick
or painted, or the clapboards on the front will be wider than those on
the sides. In rural shotguns one finds instances where only the front of
the house will be whitewashed. Creole house types are also treated in the
same way, but not so much for decorative reasons. Kniffen explains that
the "practice harkens back to the days when Creole half-timber houses
were weather boarded with unpainted cypress, except for the front which,
protected by the porch overhang, was merely plastered and whitewashed."[37] But in the case of the Haitian shotgun, where only the front
of the half-timbered house is clapboarded and that part is always protected

Figure 7.6.   Decorative Framing on Haitian House Facades
              (*Left*) front of house shown in figure 7.5a; (*right*) front of
              house, Rue St. Honoré, Port-au-Prince.
              *(From fieldwork by the author in October and November
              1973)*

by a porch, the custom has specific aesthetic intent. The embellishment of the front of shotguns would seem to be a Haitian custom that continued to be associated with specifically Haitian houses even when they were built in Louisiana.[38]

The architectural links between Port-au-Prince and New Orleans cannot be denied. All the nonessential details that are associated with the shotgun in Haiti are also associated with the shotgun in Louisiana, although not always to the same degree. It is evident that the concept of the shotgun house was imported from Haiti, and with the idea of that form came a host of practices that Haitians considered appropriate and fitting for the type. The continuation of these secondary features in Louisiana clearly shows that Haiti provided the basic model for New Orleans's own shotgun culture.

Having linked the New Orleans shotgun to Haiti clearly establishes the involvement of Afro-Americans with the house. The origins of the shotgun, however, lie further back than the late eighteenth century. The urban Haitian shotgun is the end product of a series of transformations and changes. These city dwellings were simply more elaborate versions of a type of plantation house. The largest of these rural houses is almost the same size as the smallest urban examples. The development of the Port-au-Prince shotgun occurs simultaneously on spatial, material, and social levels. The house was expanded from a small two-room dwelling to a sizeable building with as many as four rooms. Sophisticated French half-timbering techniques were used in place of the ordinary wattle-and-daub and thatch. Finally the house became the residence for a freedman as well as a slave. The shotgun had been an element of the slave experience and became an architectural expression with a distinct mulatto identity. The house was a signal of difference and perhaps independence. It has been referred to as an "architecture of defiance."[39]

The prototype for the half-timbered urban shotgun can be found among the small rectangular wattle and thatch huts of rural Haiti.[40] One type is clearly a shotgun house. It is composed of two small rooms oriented perpendicularly to the road (fig. 7.7). Its front entrance is in the gable wall and is shaded by a porch. Occasionally extra rooms are incorporated into the house at the rear or to the side. The dimensions of these houses are remarkably consistent; measurements rarely stray more than two feet from a 10' × 21' average.[41] Rooms are usually ten feet wide and eight feet deep. A space of about four feet is then left for a front porch. Melville J. Herskovits noted that "no house lacks its veranda, however small."[42] The volumetric stability of the rural shotgun indicates that it is a standardized house type constituting a basic pattern for country dwellings. This pattern was established during the plantation era. Pierre de Vaissiere described Haitian slave cabins as "20 to 24 feet long by 12 feet wide and 15 feet high and each of them is divided by partitions into two or three rooms."[43] These dimensions are very close to the measurements of current dwellings and point up the long affiliation of the shotgun house with the history of the New World Negro.

But the shotgun is not simply an Afro-American house even though it has been used repeatedly by New World Blacks. The relationship between the Haitian shotgun and black architectural traditions is complicated by the occurrence of a similar house among the Arawak Indians. These indigenous peoples had a house type, called a *bohio* by the Spanish, that is very similar to a shotgun type (fig. 7.8). It consisted of one rectangular room with a frontward-facing gable and even had a small front porch. While the mode of construction for the Arawak house is only slightly similar to the Haitian country shotgun, in form it is almost identical.

Early French settlers lived in what amounted to an imitation of this Indian dwelling. Pere Labat, an early traveler to Haiti, built such a house in 1698:

> J'avois envoye nettoyer un place dans le bois, au bord de notre rivière, environ à quinze cens pas de la Maison, ou j'avois fait faire un grand ajoupa, c'est-a-dire, une grande case à la legere & covert de feuilles de balifer & de cachibou, pour s'y retirer en case de pluye.[44]

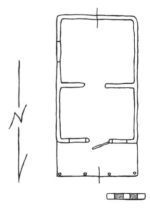

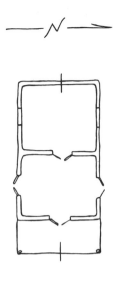

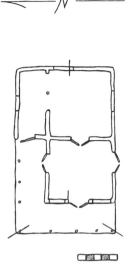

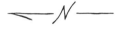

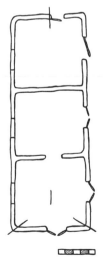

Figure 7.7.

Rural Haitian Shotguns
a. (*opposite, top*) wattle-and-daub shotgun,
Chancerelles, one-half mile north of Port-au-
Prince; b. (*opposite, bottom left*) wattle-and-
daub shotgun, Cazeau; c. (*opposite, bottom
right*) plan of wattle-and-daub shotgun,
Cazeau; d. (*above left*) plan of a wattle-and-
daub shotgun, Cazeau; e. (*above right*) plan
of a wattle-and-daub shotgun, Chancerelles
(this small addition to the side of the second
room is a bed outshot); f. (*left*) plan of a
wattle-and-daub shotgun, Chancerelles (this
three-room house is a developmental link
leading to larger urban shotgun houses).
*(All of these illustrations are from fieldwork
by the author in October 1973)*

Figure 7.8.   Engraving of an Arawak Bohio, Sixteenth Century
(From Gonzalo Fernandez de Oviedo y Valdes, Historia
General y Natural de las Indias, Islas y Tierra Firma del Mar
Oceane [1535; reprint, Madrid: Imprenta de la Real Academia
de la Historia, 1851], plate 2)

(I have tried to clear a place in the woods, at the edge of our river, about 1500 feet
from the big house, where I have had built a big ajupa, that is to say, a big thatch house
covered with the branches of balifer and cachibou, so one can find shelter in case of rain.)

Even though his description concentrates on the materials used for the
construction of the dwelling, the use of an Indian term suggests that the
house form might also have been derived from the Indians. A vague engraving showing early French houses presents a structure that is, at least, not
contradictory to the design of an Arawak house (fig. 7.9). Labat notes that
it was only in 1705 that half-timbered Creole houses became the preferred
type.[45] The French by then had been in Haiti for almost eighty years and
during that time they established the *ajupa* or *bohio* as a legitimate, familiar
house form. When a profitable plantation economy began to develop in

Figure 7.9. Engraving Showing the Houses of the French
Boucaniers, Seventeenth Century
(From Maurice Besson, The Scourge of the
Indies *[London: George Routledge and Sons,
1929], p. 2)*

the eighteenth century, they shunned their thatched huts for a building type common to Normandy.

The shotgun was not simply borrowed by African slaves from the Arawak via the sugar plantations. Even if Europeans copied Indian houses to use as slave cabins, those dwellings were satisfactory because of similarities to houses that the African slave preferred. A tight syncretic process links the buildings constructed by the Arawaks, the French, and Africans. Rectangular house forms as well as wattling and thatching techniques are certainly to be found in Europe and West Africa. The Haitian shotgun house was affected by an aboriginal population, European settlers, and unwilling African migrants. In the commingling of peoples each saw in the *bohio* its own type of dwelling. It then is important to look to African house forms in order to understand how and why Haitian Blacks adopted the shotgun house type as one of their common houses. The long and intimate association of Blacks with the building form suggests that the New World house may significantly reflect the influences of African architectural traditions. It was after all the memory of Africa that guided Blacks' first perception of the slave experience.

Philip D. Curtin has noted that the slave trade in the Bight of Benin area of West Africa reaches a peak in the 1780s and suggests that military raids by the Yoruba were responsible for the increase.[46] It was in the decade 1780–90 that French slaving reached its greatest extent when 26,100 slaves were imported annually.[47] Most of the recorded 117 Guinea Coast cargoes for that period were loaded in the Bight of Benin. There is then a significant correspondence in trade patterns. At a time when the Yoruba controlled a large part of the Bight of Benin slave trade, the French were also carrying their greatest number of slaves to Haiti. It seems probable that a large portion of those slaves were Yoruba. They had been brought to Haiti in the beginning of the active slaving period and counted as *Nagos* until 1791. Many were disguised under other names. But what is most important is the pattern of cultural emphasis encouraged by the historical turns of the slave trade. Yoruba and Yoruba-related peoples were brought to Haiti in the first days of slavery in sufficient numbers to preserve many traits of their African culture. The trade then shifted gradually to include more peoples from Central Africa, but toward the end most West African slaves were still Yoruba. The common memory of Africa in 1791, when Haiti became an independent nation, was very likely a reminiscence of the region known now as Nigeria. The dominant Yoruba elements in Haitian life were reinforced by the newer arrivals. Since they were among the last Africans brought to Haiti, they served as a major link to Mother Africa.

My fieldwork shows that the basic Yoruba house form is a 10' × 20' two-room building and is used by both the Yoruba and their Edo neighbors to the southeast. The first room encountered upon entering the house is always a kitchen/parlor, while the second room (without an exterior doorway) serves as bedroom. This double unit constitutes a basic module for the development of other building types (fig. 7.10). It may be reduced to one room to provide a storehouse for cocoa or if more space is required for a special purpose, a single volume can be added to the basic house. The two-room module may also be modified by the omission of the partition wall to create a large room that still has the same overall 10′ × 20′ dimensions. The basic unit can also be multiplied; very often a house will consist of two or more two-room units strung out end to end. Even the impluvial compound house contains two-room units.

There are several correspondences between the houses of rural Haiti and western Africa that became clear in my field research. The most striking shared feature is the reliance on the rectangular two-room module. The Yoruba 10′ × 20′ unit coincides closely with the 10′ × 21′ rural shotgun of Haiti. Vertical dimensions are also similar so that wall heights commonly range between six and eight feet in both Haitian and African houses. The Yoruba house thus contains the spatial features of the shotgun. While the aspect of orientation is variable in Yoruba architecture, it does happen that the two-room house will have its gable facing the front like Haitian shotgun houses. In such cases all that is required to convert the Yoruba hut into a morphologically completed shotgun is a shift of the doorway. In the Yoruba house, as in the shotgun, one passes first through a parlor before entering the bedroom; room functions did not need to be shifted. Since the two-room house is a working unit in Yoruba architecture that is intended to be elongated, compressed, and reordered into different building types, the movement of a doorway or the shift from a parallel to a perpendicular alignment is an expected kind of change. Such modifications occasionally occur in the African context and thus the Haitian shotgun may be considered a product of a continuing process of African architectural modification. Haitian houses certainly include in their design the same spatial preferences that are found in West Africa. The rural shotgun thus retained a core of African expectation while satisfying the plantation owners' needs for slave quarters and so there was a meeting of priority and preference.

The form of the shotgun develops essentially from the retention of a version of a Yoruba two-room house, a building form about which several African architectural traditions could cluster. The basic 10′ × 20′ module was first oriented with its gable to the front, and then modified by the shift of the front door to the gable and subsequent incorporation of the gable porch. These latter features were probably copied from the Arawak *bohio*. The new form was often close to 10′ × 21′ with rooms averaging 10′ × 8′ The depth of the rooms was apparently shortened so that the

Figure 7.10.   The Yoruba Two-Room House and Related Building Types
a. (*above*) two-room house, Ilefunfun, Nigeria; b. (*opposite, top left*) plan of a two-room house, Aroko, Nigeria; c. (*opposite, bottom left*) plan of a house composed of three two-room units, Atiba, Nigeria; d. (*opposite, top right*) plan of two adjacent compounds in Aroko, Nigeria (the three buildings to the left belong to an Edo family, the remaining two form the household of a Yoruba family—note the use of two-room modules and the alternative orientations of gable ends with the road); e. (*opposite, bottom right*) plan of an impluvial compound house, Ile Ife, Nigeria (room volumes here are similar to those used in rural linear houses. Two-room modules are also employed in the urban compound. All of these houses have solid mud walls laid in courses of between 1½ and 2 feet in height and 1 foot thick).
(All of these illustrations are from fieldwork by the author in February and March 1974)

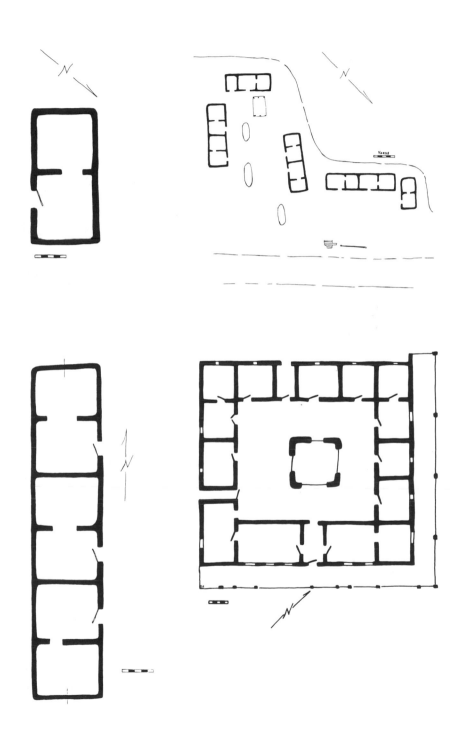

house could include the porch without severely altering the overall dimensions of the Yoruba module. Since the mud wall construction technique used in Nigeria necessitates very thick walls the interior volumes of Yoruba houses are only 9′ × 9′. When compared in terms of square feet, Haitian and Yoruba rooms differ by only one square foot. This similarity suggests a cultural connection between the two house forms. The construction of the shotgun, however, was derived from the French. The roof framing has a system of principal and common rafters that is typical of Norman roof trusses.[48] While the wattle-and-daub method is used in Africa, the technique of making individual panels between posts used in Haiti is more reminiscent of European half-timbering than African modes of construction.[49] Shotgun houses, then, represent an innovative solution to the problem of shelter. African slaves maintained their own house form by making one morphological change (shifting a doorway), adapting one secondary feature (a front porch), and learning a new technology.

The architectural response to slavery presented here suggests that a people's reaction to adversity can be tenaciously conservative. Africans in Haiti did not drift aimlessly in a sea of alien experiences. Their response was to make sense of their new environment by transforming it so that it resembled a familiar pattern. Cultural contact did not necessitate an overwhelming change in architecture; what was needed was rather an intelligent modification of culture. The shotgun house form is the result of this kind of mental transposition.

The history of the shotgun that has been traced here has accounted both for the physical development of the type and for some of the cultural motivation behind that development. The Yoruba solution to the problem of plantation shelter was enough like other African house forms that non-Yorubas could also be satisfied with the house in their own terms. The African contribution to the Haitian shotgun thus involves both a form and philosophy of architecture. Because both aspects were part of the design process, the shotgun form achieved stability and became deeply imbedded within Haitian culture so that mulattoes used this form while trying to establish their identity as free men. They later carried the idea of the shotgun house to Louisiana. The shotgun of Port-au-Prince then became, quite directly, the shotgun of New Orleans. The shotgun house form has thus been associated with a black population since its first appearance in the United States and it remains largely so today. It can be found in the black sections of almost every southern town. The frequent association of the house with Blacks led Glassie to suspect that the origins of the house might be connected to African or West Indian building traditions.[50] Reaching back into the history of the house we have found that the American shotgun is connected directly to Haiti and consequently represents the final product of a set of developments that are ultimately derived from African architecture. Thus by association with black populations and by virtue of African and Caribbean antecedents, the shotgun house is an example of Afro-American architecture.

Notes

1. See Robert Farris Thompson, "African Influence on the Art of the United States," in *Black Studies in the University,* ed. Armstead L. Robinson, et al. (New Haven: Yale University Press, 1969), 128–77.

2. Henry Glassie, *Pattern in the Material Folk Culture of the Eastern United States* (Philadelphia: University of Pennsylvania Press, 1968), 116–17.

3. Henry Glassie, "The Nature of the New World Artifact: The Instance of the Dugout Canoe," in *Festschrift für Robert Wildhaber,* ed. Walter Escher, et al. (Basel: G. Krebs, 1972), 153–70; Gene Bluestein, "America's Folk Instrument: Notes on the Five String Banjo," *Western Folklore* 23, no. 4 (October 1964): 241–48.

4. See John Michael Vlach, "Sources of the Shotgun House: African and Caribbean Antecedents for Afro-American Architecture," Ph.D. diss., Indiana University, March 1975.

5. *Annals of the Association of American Geographers* 26 (1936): 179–93, reprinted in Philip L. Wagner and Marvin W. Mikesell, eds., *Readings in Cultural Geography* (Chicago: University of Chicago Press, 1962), 157–69.

6. Ibid., 165.

7. "Settlement Succession in Eastern French Louisiana," Ph.D. diss., Louisiana State University, 1956, 68–71, 87.

8. Ibid., 177.

9. "The Shotgun House," *Louisiana Studies* 2, no. 3 (Summer 1963): 178–79.

10. "Sugar Plantation Settlements of Southern Louisiana: A Cultural Geography," Ph.D. diss., Louisiana State University, 1971, 174–76.

11. *Louisiana House Types: A Field Guide,* Melanges, no. 2 (Baton Rouge: Museum of Geoscience, Louisiana State University, 1971), 6.

12. Bureau of Governmental Research, *Plan and Program for the Preservation of the Vieux Carré: Historic District Demonstration Project,* 1968, 33.

13. For a more detailed statement of the activities of the Roberts company see Samuel Wilson, Jr., "New Orleans Prefab, 1867," *Journal of the Society of Architectural Historians* 22, no. 1 (March 1963): 38–39.

14. Plan Book 15, folio 33, New Orleans Notarial Archives.

15. "Collection of Building Contracts and Excerpts, 1800–1900," compiled by Samuel Wilson, Jr. (New Orleans: Tulane University Library, Special Collections Division). All contracts are abstracted on cards and filed chronologically without any reference numbers or other designation.

16. Samuel Wilson, Jr., and Bernard Lemann, *New Orleans Architecture,* vol. 1, *The Lower Garden District* (Gretna, La.: Friends of the Cabildo and Pelican Publishing, 1971), 94.

17. Plan Book 87, folio 87, New Orleans Notarial Archives, reprinted in Wilson and Lemann, *The Lower Garden District,* 85.

18. Donald R. Everett, "Free Persons of Color in Colonial Louisiana," *Louisiana History,* no. 7 (Winter 1966): 26–27.

19. Edwin Adams Davis, *Louisiana: A Narrative History* (Baton Rouge: Louisiana State University Press, 1971), 131–32.

20. H. F. Sterkx, *The Free Negro in Ante-Bellum Louisiana* (Rutherford, N.J.: Fairleigh Dickinson University Press, 1964), 84.

21. Robert C. McConnell, *Negro Troops of Antebellum Louisiana: A History of the Free Men of Color,* Louisiana State University Studies: Social Sciences, no. 13 (Baton Rouge: Louisiana State University Press, 1968), 46.

22. Ibid., 47.

23. Ibid., 48.

24. Charles Barthelemy Rousseve, *The Negro in Louisiana: Aspects of His History and His Literature* (New Orleans: Xavier University Press, 1937), 24.

25. Robert C. Reinders, "The Free Negro in the New Orleans Economy, 1850–1860," *Louisiana History,* no. 6 (Summer 1965): 275–79, 281.

26. "Collection of Building Contracts and Excerpts, 1800–1900," comp. Wilson.

27. Ibid.

28. Ibid.

29. Ibid.

30. Ibid.

31. Leonard V. Huber, *New Orleans: A Pictorial History* (New York: Crown Publishers, 1971), 52.

32. "Collection of Building Contracts and Excerpts, 1800–1900," comp. Wilson.

33. Fred B. Kniffen, "The Physiognomy of Rural Louisiana," *Louisiana History,* no. 4 (Fall 1963): 293.

34. C. C. Robin, *Voyage to Louisiana, 1803–1805,* abridged, trans. Stuart O. Landry, Jr. (1807; reprint, New Orleans: Pelican Publishing, 1966), 122–23, 237.

35. For illustrations of this aspect of shotgun facades see Wilson and Lemann, *The Lower Garden District,* 98; and Joseph Judge, "New Orleans and Her River," *National Geographic* 139, no. 2 (February 1971): 173.

36. See Fred B. Kniffen and Henry Glassie, "Building in Wood in the Eastern United States: A Time-Place Perspective," *Geographical Review* 56, no. 1 (January 1966): 40–66, for examples of half-timbering.

37. Kniffen, "The Physiognomy of Rural Louisiana," 297.

38. Roger D. Abrahams, "Worlds of Action and Order: The Crossroad and the Yard," unpublished manuscript, notes that on St. Vincents there are a whole series of behaviors associated with the facade of a house.

39. Sibyl Moholy-Nagy, *Native Genius in Anonymous Architecture* (New York: Horizon Press, 1957), 120.

40. See Alfred Metraux, "L'habitation paysanne en Haiti," *Bulletin de la societé neuchateloise de géographie 5* (1949): 3–14, for a survey of Haitian house types.

41. These figures are derived from personal fieldwork but also compare closely with the findings of John M. Street, who notes that the average Haitian house was 3.6 m × 7.2 m or $10\frac{1}{2}'$ × $21\frac{1}{2}'$. See his "A Historical and Economic Geography of the Southwest Peninsula of Haiti," Ph.D. diss., University of California, 1960, 419.

42. Melville J. Herskovits, *Life in a Haitian Valley* (1937; reprint, Garden City, N.J.: Doubleday, 1971), 8.

43. Pierre de Vaissiere, *Sainte-Dominique (1692–1789). La societé et la vie creoles sous l'ancien regime,* quoted in Street, "Historical and Economic Geography of . . . Haiti," 134.

44. R. P. Labat, *Nouveau voyage au Isles de L'Amerique,* vol. 6 (Paris: Jean de Nully, 1742), 9.

45. Ibid., vol. 9, 210; see Glassie, *Pattern in the Material Folk Culture,* 120–21, for plans of Creole houses.

45. Philip D. Curtin, *The Atlantic Slave Trade: A Census* (Madison: University of Wisconsin Press, 1969), 178, 225.

47. Ibid., 79.

48. See G. Jeanton, *L'habitation paysanne en Bresse* (Paris: Librairie E. Droz, 1935), 74, figs. 1–2, for the French mode of roof framing. Compare with Metraux, "L'habitation paysanne en Haiti," 9.

49. See Jeanton, *L'habitation paysanne en Bresse,* plates 6, 48, for illustrations of wattle-and-daub filling in half-timbered buildings in rural France.

50. Glassie, *Pattern in the Material Folk Culture,* 221.

8

Afro-American Housing in Virginia's Landscape of Slavery

The artifacts of everyday life used by Afro-Virginians in the eighteenth century reveal that Blacks were held at the bottom of the social scale. While such a statement does not present a particularly novel insight, an analysis of the material record can reveal some of the ways that this status was signaled and enforced. The hierarchical system of rank in eighteenth-century Virginia society was most graphically portrayed in the built environment. The most elaborate statement in the architectural vocabulary of the period was the wealthy planter's great house or mansion seated prominently with a view of a river.[1] Churches rivaled the houses of the planters in size and in the elaborateness of their decoration, but still they came off in second place.[2] Civic rituals of public importance occurred in a courthouse that was significantly smaller and plainer than a church. Divine law was thus architecturally asserted to be more significant than the laws of the state.[3] Most Virginia farmers, at this time, lived in two-room framed dwellings, unpretentious houses measuring in the neighborhood of sixteen by twenty-four feet.[4] The slaves' cabin was often built to the same dimensions but with materials that were discernibly more crude. Rough log walls generally contrasted with the yeoman planter's riven clapboards. Harry Toulmin observed near Norfolk in 1793: "Adjoining the house of the master was a hut for his blacks, formed of small pine trees laid upon another and fastened at the end by a notch; but they were not plastered, either on the inside or outside."[5] The basic message to be read from the architectural system of Virginia could not be missed. Slave habitation was the smallest, most primitive element in the colony (fig. 8.1). While slave houses were not so very different from the cabins in which many white Virginians lived for some time, they were very different from the great houses of the "great men" who owned both the largest tracts of land and the largest numbers of slaves.

Landon Carter's Sabine Hall was one of the most prominent estates on Virginia's Northern Neck. True to the pattern of Virginia, his slave hous-

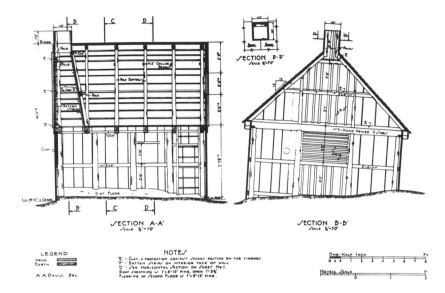

Figure 8.1.   Kitchen, New Kent County, Virginia
Although built in the nineteenth century, this kitchen
illustrates the impermanent mode of the construction now
known to be most representative of vernacular structures in
Virginia during the early colonial period. This small building
had its posts sunk directly into the ground, an expedient
technique that cost much less than a more durable carpentered
frame built on a raised foundation. The lath and plaster
chimney hood indicated in section A-A′ is likewise an archaic
feature. Essentially a one-room square cabin measuring approximately 14′ x 14′, this structure closely resembles the
quarters in which planters of eighteenth-century Virginia
housed their slaves.

ing was so humble that it rarely attracted any comment. This scarcity of
commentary is very telling because Carter wrote extensively about the conduct of his slaves. In his lengthy diaries there are copious comments regarding his slaves' behavior, but only rarely does he mention slave dwellings.
He did note, however, on September 3, 1774: "This morning I proposed
to the man, John Bethel by name [a prospective overseer] who I saw to
be an honest man . . . that he should this fall take 4 to 6 hands, one half
women, and as soon as he could knock up a set of log houses . . . as I
found he behaved I would continue him to seat more quarters on my
backlands."[6] We might surmise that these were probably not very large
structures since earlier he had ordered his slave carpenters to build a house

Figure 8.2.   Row of Single-Pen Slave Cabins, Roseberry Plantation,
Dinwiddie County, Virginia
This configuration strongly conveys the sense of power,
regimentation, and order that could be indicated by archi-
tectural means.
*(From the Historic American Buildings Survey, Library of
Congress)*

for two slaves that was to be only twelve feet on a side.[7] On another occasion Carter ordered that the house of a slave named Juggs be moved
to a new location.[8] This building could not have been very large if it could
be placed wherever the master desired. From these few passing references
to slave houses we learn that, while they were not very often on Carter's
mind, he firmly believed his human property to be well within his control. Kept in small, boxy cabins, his slaves could be placed and moved as
it suited him (fig. 8.2).

There were, however, slave houses at Sabine Hall plantation of a more
durable sort. The nature of these buildings is inferred from Carter's description of the cellar holes that they had dug out of their floors.[9] Such buildings
were probably not dragged from site to site. If built with timber frames,
these houses would have been identical to those lived in by middle-class
Virginians.[10]

Many plantations in the region used two kinds of slave quarters. As Gerald W. Mullin has noted, slaves who acquired some of the skills of Anglo-European culture, namely the ability to speak intelligible English, were given a "privileged" status that was manifested in part by providing them more substantial quarters. Trusted slaves were trained in technically complex trades like blacksmithing or carpentry, or they became house servants. Robert Wormley Carter wrote in his diary on December 1, 1774: "Sent my boy Billy to work under Guthrie for one year, he is constantly to keep him at his trade and particularly to learn him to make wheels, I am to cloath him, he is 16 years of age last month."[11] A slave like Billy would be obviously of great value once trained. He, and others like him, could not only perform important tasks on their plantations, but also could be hired out at a fee to other planters who did not have skilled hands on their estates. Because slaves like Billy would augment the profits of their owners, it was not uncommon for them to be housed in better quarters than other lesser-skilled slaves. Such a manifestation of generosity on the part of the planter may have resulted from humane concern, but it is not too difficult to see that in such a case fair treatment only made good economic sense. Prized assets like skilled craftsmen were abused only by the imprudent manager.

The social hierarchy within a slave community was marked architecturally in manner not unlike the rest of Virginia—the better-off, black or white, had better houses. Consider the case of Aron Jameson, slave of Joseph Ball owner of Morattico plantation in Lancaster County. Ball, writing from London on April 23, 1754, to his overseer Joseph Chinn, gave specific orders that Jameson was to have a solidly built house:

> As soon as can be I would have a framed house twelve foot long and ten foot wide built for him and the end sill where the fire is to be must be at least three foot above the upper side of the other sill and it must be made up from the ground to that with clay, and then from that [sill] quite up to the top lathed and filled, and the whole house must be lathed and filled, and the lock I have sent with him put upon the door. . . . I wanted [to] have the house no more than seven foot pitch from the upper side of the sill to the lower side of the plate and I would have the loft with inch plank, of which there must be left of the old house that may be blown down and I would have it under pinned with brick some five inches above the ground if it can be reasonably done. Also I would have sills of locust, cedar, or mulberry or other lasting wood lain part in the ground and five inches above, and the other sills lain upon them; and the house must be jutted four inches; and it must be very well and tight covered and I would have the floor raised within two inches of the upper side of the sill.[12]

From this description, it is easy to imagine a tiny cottage that was not only substantially built with superior materials but finished to such a degree with lath and plaster that it would have rivaled most planters' parlors. Why

Jameson was so architecturally favored is never indicated in Ball's letter, but the fact that he was marked for privilege is very clear.

Aron Jameson's cabin illustrates the upper range of slave housing and suggests the condition of some of the cabins on plantations where large numbers of slaves were held. When Landon Carter died, the inventory of his estate, drawn up in 1779, listed 181 slaves in Richmond County.[13] While he had his share of skilled slaves including carpenters, coopers, blacksmiths, wheelwrights, and tailors, most of his slaves were field hands. This may in part be due to the fact that a nearby plantation, Mount Airy, owned by John Tayloe, had an unusually large number of slave artisans who were regularly employed off the plantation estate. Tayloe's corps of skilled Blacks in 1807 included thirty-three men and fourteen women, twelve percent of his slaves.[14] Because of this local pool of skilled labor, Landon Carter needed relatively fewer trained slaves. Consequently he would not have had many substantial slave dwellings of the sort constructed for Aron Jameson at Morattico. Four plantation quarters surrounded Landon Carter's "home fields," the cultivated acreage near his mansion. The bulk of his slaves were set up at quarters on the "backlands," where they lived in rough log buildings.

A quarter was an assemblage of structures and spaces including, potentially, an overseer's house, slave dwellings, barns, pens, planted fields, pastures, woodlots, slave gardens, and other work spaces like saw pits or clothes lines. The quarter can be productively understood then as a farm within a larger farm. Observers in both Virginia and southern Maryland saw plantation quarters in pretty much the same way. Travelling through Maryland in the early 1740s, Edward Kimber recorded in a footnote to his "itinerant jottings": "A Negro Quarter is a Number of Huts or Hovels, built some Distance from the Mansion-House; where the Negroes reside with their wives and Families and cultivate at vacant times little Spots allow'd them. They are indeed true pictures of Slavery, which begets Indolence and Nastiness."[15] Some forty years later a German doctor made a similar assessment in northern Virginia.

> A plantation in Virginia . . . has often the appearance of a small village, by reason of the many separate small buildings which taken all together would at times hardly go to make a single roomy and commodious house. . . . [Slave dwellings are] commonly so many small, separate, badly kept cabins of wood, without glass in the windows, of the structure and solidity of a house of cards. . . . Thus are built gradually a good many small houses and cabins, commonly without the assistance of carpenters, patched together by the people themselves and their negroes.[16]

Many of the slaves kept at plantation quarters no doubt shared the experience described above. They were sent in groups to the woods to clear the land and bring it under cultivation. There they lived under the not-too-watchful eyes of overseers who were considered by the planters to have questionable competence as agricultural foremen. On one occasion Joseph Ball labeled all overseers "a parcel of slubbering sons of bitches" and warned that a particular construction project that he ordered his overseers to supervise would have to be closely monitored or "it won't be worth a farthing when it is done."[17] In a similar vein Landon Carter recorded in his diary on May 23, 1766, that the overseer of the "Fork Quarter" had left without notice and that the slaves residing there had done little work for an undetermined period of time.[18] We see here conditions of inefficient management under which some slaves found a degree of autonomy. Given the lax supervision that they might encounter at a particular plantation quarter, the focus of daily life could shift from work in the master's fields to the tending of their own gardens.

Carter, in fact, encouraged his slaves to keep gardens and thus to work for themselves even while they were theoretically to accede completely to his wishes. He even found in slave gardens an economic advantage. "My people," he bragged in 1770, "always made and raised things to sell and I oblige them [to] buy linnen to make their other shirt instead of buying liquor with their fowls."[19] His statement draws attention not only to a private economy within the slave quarters but to alternative slave tastes that favored the purchase of liquor over clothing. Seven years later Carter's slaves were still spending some of their time doing their own work when he wrote: "My poor slaves raise fowls and eggs in order to exchange with their Master now and then."[20] Carter's attitude towards independent slave enterprise compares well with the opinion of other plantation owners. At Jones's Plantation near Charlottesville significant savings were realized when slaves were allowed to raise their own livestock and plant their own crops. Thomas Anburey, who was held prisoner there during the Revolutionary War, wrote: "The man at this plantation in lieu of these [supplies], grants his negroes an acre of ground, and all Saturday afternoon to raise grain and poultry for themselves."[21] Given the number of slaves held on the largest plantations, the number of acres given over to slave gardens had to be substantial. This land constituted a separate sphere of agricultural activity on the plantation, a sphere specifically under slave control. Moreover, it is particularly interesting to note that at times the slaves' gardening activities were at cross purposes with the goals of the planter. If, for example, slaves traded their vegetables for rum, they were likely to get drunk and not show up for work the next day.[22] While creating circumstances for slave initiative did prove to be problematic, the custom of allowing slaves ground of their own was not abandoned. We come then to see a plantation as gardens within farms within a yet larger farm. Just as there was a hierarchy of buildings, so too was there a hierarchy of soil.

Slave dwellings were only rarely substantially built. This is not an indictment against the skills of slave carpenters, who apparently built dwellings for their fellow slaves, but a statement of the economic conditions of Virginia during the eighteenth century. Few men could afford to build impressively and well. And when they could, their main instinct was to hoard their resources in order to set up lavish entertainments. The common pattern was to have a modest house and to dine on an extravagant scale that featured a diverse and lengthy menu.[23] In such a context the housing of one's slaves is not the highest priority. Further, if a slave owner's house was relatively plain, the condition of his slaves' houses could not be anything other than minimal shelter.

Many Anglo-Virginians in the eighteenth century lived in houses that were described in terms also used for slave cabins. From the following passage one might assume that Johann Schoepf was lost among a string of slave houses: "We had not gone many miles through the woods, had seen only a few wretched cabins, and arrived finally at a house that been indicated to us, which appeared not greatly different from the rest, not whole pane in the windows, neither rum, nor whiskey, nor bread to be had, a draughty empty place."[24] He was at the time seeking lodging at the home of a yeoman farmer. Slave houses generally had fireplaces and chimneys constructed of sticks that were then plastered with mud. This was a common method used both in England and colonial Virginia. Anburey noted that the finer Virginia houses had chimneys that were "often of brick, but the generality of them are wood, coated in the inside with clay."[25] The distinction between the architecture of free Whites and enslaved Blacks was then a blurred one and the differences could be collapsed altogether when slave carpenters were ordered to build the same houses for both classes of people. Such was the case at Robert Wormley Carter's plantation when, on February 1, 1768, he recorded: "Guy & Jimmy [two slaves] returned this day from Ring's Neck [a plantation quarter] where they have been building two Negroes quarters 20 by 16 and an Overseer's house 20 x 16."[26] An even more vivid instance of the lack of differentiation is found in J. F. D. Smyth's encounter with a backwoods quarter:

> That miserable shell, a poor apology for a house, consisted but of one small room, which served for the accomodation of the overseer and six negroes; it was not lathed or plaistered, neither ceiled nor lifted above, and only very thin boards for its covering; it had a door in each side, and one window but no glass in it; it had not even a brick chimney, and as it stood on blocks about a foot above the ground, the hogs lay constantly under the floor which made it swarm with flies.[27]

In this case, and probably quite a few others, Blacks and Whites shared what amounted to a context, if not a culture, of poverty. The main distinction between these two groups was that the Whites had some prospects for escape from their low status while the slaves, except in a few rare cases, did not.

The context of black life in eighteenth-century Virginia was marked by specific building forms and a distinctive spatial position in the overall layout of the rural landscape (fig. 8.3). Dell Upton, in his analysis of the black and white worlds of Virginia, identifies for the planters an "articulated, processional landscape." At the great Virginian estates owners not only carefully planned the location of their buildings, particularly of their mansion houses, but also carefully set up the pathways along which one approached and ultimately entered the mansion. They manipulated the way one moved across their land in order to make the best possible impression; essentially they made themselves appear important and their visitors small and insignificant.

To reach John Tayloe's mansion, for example, one first followed a road with several sharp turns that afforded different views of the property. At the end of the road one still had to move up over two terraces, through a forecourt, up a flight of stairs, across a loggia, and finally into a central, but still public, hall. The more intimate spaces were shielded by yet more doors and stairs. Upton summarizes the experience: "If one came to visit the Tayloes, one would pass through a series of seven barriers before reaching the goal, which might be the dining room table, the ritual center of Virginia hospitality. Each barrier served to reinforce the impression of John Tayloe's centrality, and each affirmed the visitor's status as he passed or she passed through it."[28]

The social control intended via this very formal program of architectural and spatial manipulations primarily affected the white community. Slaves did not move through the plantation in the same way as whites, nor were they expected to. Understood to be a servant people, their place was defined as both away from and outside of the obedient procession to the front door. They moved across the plantation in their own way, short-cutting and frustrating the formality that planters had so carefully laid out. Slaves were, by and large, located at the margins of authority whence they attended their masters at the big house or toiled in the fields. They were under control but they were not totally coerced by that control because, while they were being held down, they were also being held out and away from the center of authority (fig. 8.4). The distances involved in the definition of their spatial confines at a plantation like Sabine Hall or Mount Airy prevented their dwelling and work spaces from becoming an absolute maximum-security prison.

Slaves were generally out in the open and often out of the sight of their owners. Indeed, because slaves were permanent workers, the whole of a plantation, except for the mansion house, was seen as the appropriate

Figure 8.3.   Buildings at Effingham Plantation, Prince William
County, Virginia
This illustration defines a slave yard adjacent to the planter's
"Big House." At the far left is a kitchen, perhaps a kitchen-
quarter. In a line perpendicular to the kitchen are three slave
quarters, each one a slight variation of a two-unit house. The
repeated building forms arranged around the edges of fenced
space left no doubt in the minds of all visitors that the area
was the domain of the plantation's enslaved residents.
*(From the Historic American Buildings Survey, Library of
Congress)*

domain for slaves. Ironically, within a plantation, Blacks had more freedom
of movement than white visitors did. Moreover, many slaves had a personal stake in the quarter since some of their work time, mainly on Sundays,
contributed directly to their self-sufficiency and provided them a consequent measure of autonomy. The slaves at Nomini Hall were so embolden-
ed that they even claimed the master's barns, shops, and outbuildings as
their own. Philip Fithian, tutor to the master's children, reported that slaves
held cock fights for their own entertainment in the stable yard and that
he once had to pay a fine of seven and one-half pence to a slave baker
for trespassing in his kitchen.

     The clustering of Blacks on quarters resembling small villages also pro-
moted a racial solidarity that complemented whatever degree of autonomy

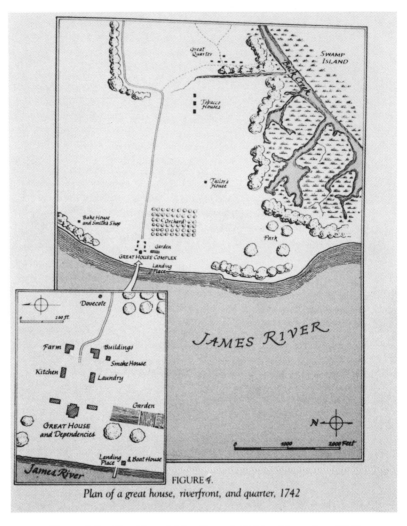

FIGURE 4.

Plan of a great house, riverfront, and quarter, 1742

Figure 8.4.   Site Plan of John Carter's Shirley Plantation, 1742
Note that the main house was prominently
located at the river's edge while one of the main
slave quarters sat almost a mile away and was
screened from view by an orchard and a tree line
beyond the tobacco barns. Discrete black and
white domains are thus clearly evident on this map.
(From The Transformation of Virginia, 1740–1790, *by*
Rhys Isaac. © *1982 The University of North Carolina*
Press. Published for the Institute of Early American
History and Culture. Reprinted with permission.)

they may have sensed. Gerald W. Mullin suggests that "from the slave's point of view, life on the quarter was perhaps preferable to daily contact with his captors [in the main house], because it allowed him to preserve some of his ways."[29] Among those ways were certain architectural traditions that might have been read by the slaves as African practices, particularly by those whose parents or grandparents were African-born.

Among the housing traits that might have evoked an African past was the general design of the dwellings. The square and rectangular components used were certainly commonplace aspects of English vernacular architecture, but they were equally African as well.[30] A key difference between Virginian and West African houses was the size of the rooms; the slave dwellings were considerably larger with room components frequently averaging sixteen by sixteen feet, a standard English unit. However, the earliest slave cabins were built to a different sense of measure. Upton determined, after surveying numerous historical descriptions of slave houses built in Virginia between 1650 and 1860, that before 1750 slave houses were commonly twelve by twelve feet or slightly smaller.[31] The use of a consistently smaller room unit matches up well with what is known of the usual spatial patterns for proxemic codes of West and Central Africa, where the common room dimension averages around ten by ten feet.[32] Thus the small rooms of the early slave cabins could have been understood by the slaves as African, while European and American commentators saw them as merely small. That the smaller dimensioned cabins were built chiefly before 1750 is significant because between 1690 and 1740 Virginia imported more slaves directly from Africa than at any other time in its history.[33] Thus in the first half of the eighteenth century, when the slave population of Virginia had a decidedly African focus, slave housing also manifested what can be considered an African proxemic quality.

Memories of Africa might also have been inspired by the construction methods of some Virginia slave houses. The older slaves, for example, would have seen in the thatched roofs that covered several of the barns and outbuildings at Sabine Hall an aspect of African architectural practice. The practice of using vegetal materials for roof covering was, of course, also known in Europe, but such precedents mainly suggest why the planters sanctioned the use of thatch, not what the slaves may have thought of it. At least one of the slave houses at Sabine Hall, the cabin belonging to Positillion Tom, was thatch-covered and hence it is likely that at least a few others were roofed in the same manner.[34] While slave cabins, like most buildings in Virginia, were built of wood, either in log or frame construction, there were at least two plantations along the James River where mud-walled slave houses were still standing into the twentieth century. The technology for one of these houses built in 1820 at Bremo Bluff in Fluvanna County is labeled *pisé,* earth rammed between removable forms (fig. 8.5).

Figure 8.5.   One of the Surviving Mud-Walled Houses Built at Bremo Bluff
Plantation, Fluvanna County, Virginia, by the Slaves of John Cocke.
*(From the Historic American Buildings Survey, Library of
Congress)*

The practice is considered to be an innovation recommended by Thomas
Jefferson based on mud-walled buildings he had seen in France.[35] Nevertheless, the net effect of using red Virginia clay to build a house yields
a structure highly evocative of any number of West African housing traditions. That African know-how in building mud houses may have been
deliberately sought by Virginia planters is confirmed in a letter by Robert
"Councillor" Carter of Nomini Hall plantation to John Ballendine, a slave
dealer, in which he asks for a Negro who "underst[ands] building mud
walls," a man who was "an Artist, not a Common Labourer."[36] If it happened that on some plantations small rectangular houses were built with
mud walls and thatched roofs, those buildings would have been identical
to African dwellings in every major way. Today we can only conjecture
whether such structures were ever built, but it is apparent that the essential components of form and construction technique were present in the
Virginia countryside.

The order that masters imposed on their slaves in Virginia unwitting-
ly provided those slaves with the chance to impose their own vision on

the landscape. If they so chose, they could silently claim a piece of Virginia for themselves. Certainly their territorial claims would not be as overt as those of the master class. Yet, as we have seen, there was within the cultural landscape of eighteenth-century Virginia not merely space allowed to the slaves but a terrain created by them. The material culture of slavery helps us to understand the complex cultural scenarios in which Afro-Virginians negotiated an identity both among themselves and between themselves and the Whites with whom they lived.[37] Most of the artifacts they used were probably seen ambiguously. Sometimes they cursed their fate and broke their hoes and harrows in gestures of frustration, rage, and despair. But the same slave saboteur might on another day take up his hoe, go to his garden, and raise a crop of African gourds. Later he might select one to become the base for a banjo or a drum and thereby he might recover a sense of well-being. Housing, too, provided a therapeutic benefit by serving as the context in which families were nurtured and where the wider black community began to take shape. By our standards, even by the standards of the day, slave housing appears merely to be part of the punishment for falling into the slavers' nets. Yet for those who built the houses and lived in them, there were other ways to regard those cabins. Often they were hardly different from the houses occupied by Whites. Consequently, slaves may have seen themselves as potential black yeomen if they could only find some way to obtain their freedom. Some of the slave quarters, as we have seen, by virtue of their design, spatial proportions, or materials, could have recalled African practices and thus may have comforted the mind if not the body. In the landscape of slavery we find evidence of slave endurance as well as evidence of Afro-American creativity; both are heroic achievements.

Notes

1. See Thomas Tileston Waterman, *The Mansions of Virginia, 1706–1776* (Chapel Hill: University of North Carolina Press, 1946).

2. See Dell Upton, *Holy Things and Profane: Anglican Parish Churches in Colonial Virginia* (Cambridge, Mass.: MIT Press, 1986), especially 214.

3. See Carl R. Lounsbury, "'An Elegant and Commodious Building': William Buckland and the Design of the Prince William County Courthouse," *Journal of the Society of Architectural Historians* 46 (1987): 228–40 for the most detailed analysis of a Virginia courthouse.

4. Dell Upton, "Vernacular Domestic Architecture in Eighteenth-Century Virginia," in Dell Upton and John Michael Vlach, *Common Places: Readings in American Vernacular Architecture* (Athens: University of Georgia Press, 1986), 317; Henry Glassie, *Pattern in the Material Folk Culture of the Eastern United States* (Philadelphia: University of Pennsylvania Press, 1968), 80–81.

5. *The Western Country in 1793,* ed. by Marion Tinling and Godfrey Davies (San Marino, Calif.: Huntington Library, 1948), 17.

6. *The Diary of Colonel Landon Carter of Sabine Hall, 1752–1778,* ed. by Jack P. Greene (Charlottesville: University Press of Virginia, 1966), Vol. 2, 855–56.

7. Ibid., Vol. 1, 509.

8. Ibid., Vol. 1, 523.

9. Ivor Noel-Hume, *Martin's Hundred* (New York: Knopf, 1982), 12, figs. 1–7; William M. Kelso, *Kingsmill Plantations, 1619–1800: Archaeology of Country Life in Colonial Virginia* (New York: Academic Press, 1984), 102–28.

10. See Cary Carson, Norman F. Barka, William M. Kelso, Gary Wheeler Stone, and Dell Upton, "Impermanent Architecture in the Southern American Colonies," *Winterthur Portfolio* 16 (1981), 135–96.

11. *Robert Wormley Carter Diary,* Colonial Williamsburg microfilm.

12. *Joseph Ball Letterbook,* Library of Congress microfilm, April 23, 1754.

13. *Inventory of the Estate of Landon Carter, February, 1779,* manuscript, Alderman Library, University of Virginia.

14. Richard S. Dunn, "A Tale of Two Plantations: Slave Life at Mesopotamia in Jamaica and Mount Airy in Virginia, 1799–1828," *William and Mary Quarterly* 3rd Series, 34 (1977): 52.

15. Cited in Alan Kulikoff, "The Origins of Afro-American Society in Tidewater Maryland and Virginia, 1700–1790," *William and Mary Quarterly* 3rd Series, 35 (1978): 247.

16. Johann David Schoepf, *Travels in the Confederation (1783–1784),* trans. by Alfred J. Morrison (New York: Bergman Publishers, 1968), 32–33.

17. *Joseph Ball Letterbook,* letter to Joseph Chinn, July 17, 1745.

18. *The Diary of Colonel Landon Carter,* Vol. 1, 301.

19. Ibid., Vol. 1, 484.

20. Ibid., Vol. 2, 1095.

21. *Travels through the Interior Parts of America* (London: Wilane, 1789), Vol. 2, 381–82.

22. Rhys Isaac, *The Transformation of Virginia, 1740–1790* (Chapel Hill: University of North Carolina Press, 1982), 345.

23. Ibid., 133.

24. *Travels in the Confederation,* 33.

25. *Travels through the Interior Parts of America,* Vol. 2, 323; see also Nathaniel Lloyd, *A History of the English House* (London: The Architectural Press, 1931), 347 for British examples of clay chimneys.

26. *Robert Wormley Carter Diary.*

27. "White and Black Landscapes in Eighteenth-Century Virginia," *Places* 2, no. 2 (1985): 66.

28. Cited in ibid., 70.

29. Gerald W. Mullin, *Flight and Rebellion: Slave Resistance in Eighteenth-Century Virginia* (New York: Oxford University Press, 1972), 62.

30. For examples see John Michael Vlach, "Affecting Architecture of the Yoruba," *African Arts* 10, no. 1 (1976): 48–43; also consult Susan Denyer, *African Traditional Architecture* (New York: Africana Publishing Company, 1978).

31. Dell Upton, "Slave Housing in Eighteenth-Century Virginia," A Report to the Department of Social and Cultural History, National Museum of American History, Smithsonian Institution, Contract No. SF20409440000, July 31, 1982; see in particular appendix 1, Comparison of Existing and Documented Quarters, 1650–1860, 68–72.

32. John Michael Vlach, "Sources of the Shotgun House: African and Caribbean Antecedents for Afro-American Architecture," Ph.D. dissertation, Indiana University (1975), 147–54.

33. Kulikoff, "Origins of Afro-American Society," 229–30; see also Mullin, *Flight and Rebellion,* 15–16.

34. *The Diary of Colonel Landon Carter,* Vol. 2, 630, 734–35, 920; see also George McDaniel, *Hearth and Home: Preserving a People's Culture* (Philadelphia: Temple University Press, 1982), 85–90.

35. John W. Cocke, "Remarks on Hedges, Bene Plants, and Pise Buildings," *American Farmer* 3, no. 20 (August 10, 1821): 157; also see the file on Bremo Bluff in the Virginia Landmarks Commission, Richmond, Virginia.

36. Mullin, *Flight and Rebellion,* 86.

37. Mechal Sobel, *The World They Made Together: Black and White Values in Eighteenth-Century Virginia* (Princeton, N.J.: Princeton University Press, 1988), discusses the mutual effort between racial groups in the formation of Virginia.

Select Bibliography on Afro-American Folklife

Abrahams, Roger D., and John F. Szwed, eds. *After Africa*. New Haven: Yale University Press, 1983.

Adler, Thomas. "The Physical Development of the Banjo." *New York Folklore Quarterly* 28 (1972): 187–208.

Anthony, Carl. "The Big House and the Slave Quarters." Pt. 1, *Landscape* 20, no. 3 (1976): 8–19; Pt. 2, *Landscape* 21, no. 1 (1976): 9–15.

Armstrong, Robert Plant. *Wellspring: On the Myth and Source of Culture*. Berkeley: University of California Press, 1975.

Barfield, Rodney. *Thomas Day, Cabinetmaker*. Raleigh: North Carolina Museum of History, 1975.

Barr, Alwyn. *Black Texans: A History of Negroes in Texas, 1528–1971*. Austin: Jenkins, 1973.

Bastide, Roger. *African Civilisations in the New World*, 1967. Translation, New York: Harper and Row, 1971.

Berlin, Ira. *Slaves without Masters: The Free Negro in the Antebellum South*. New York: Pantheon Books, 1974.

Bishir, Catherine W. "Black Builders in Antebellum North Carolina." *The North Carolina Historical Review* 49 (1984): 423–61.

Black, Patti C. *Made by Hand: Mississippi Folk Art*. Jackson: Mississippi Department of Archives and History, 1980.

Blassingame, John W. *The Slave Community: Plantation Life in the Antebellum South*. New York: Oxford University Press, 1972.

———, ed. *Slave Testimony: Two Centuries of Letters, Speeches, Interviews, and Autobiographies*. Baton Rouge: Louisiana State University Press, 1977.

Boles, John B. *Black Southerners, 1619–1869*. Lexington: University Press of Kentucky, 1984.

Bolton, H. Carrington. "Decoration of Negro Graves in South Carolina." *Journal of American Folklore* 4 (1891): 214.

Bonner, James C. "Plantation Architecture of the Lower South on the Eve of the Civil War." *Journal of Southern History* 11 (1945): 370–80.

Botkin, B. A. *Lay My Burden Down: A Folk History of Slavery*, 1945; rptd. Chicago: University of Chicago Press, 1969.

Bridenbaugh, Carl. *The Colonial Craftsman*. New York: New York University Press, 1950.

Burrison, John A. "Afro-American Folk Pottery in the South." *Southern Folklore Quarterly* 42 (1978): 175–99.

———. "Alkaline-Glazed Stoneware: A Deep South Pottery Tradition." *Southern Folklore Quarterly* 39 (1975): 377–403.

Burton, Orville Vernon. *In My Father's House Are Many Mansions: Family and Community in Edgefield, South Carolina*. Chapel Hill: University of North Carolina Press, 1985.

Cate, Margaret Davis. *Early Days of Coastal Georgia.* St. Simmons Island, Ga.: Fort Frederica Association, 1955.

Chase, Judith Wragg. *Afro-American Art and Craft.* New York: Van Nostrand Reinhold, 1971.

Christian, Marcus. *Negro Ironworkers of Louisiana, 1718–1900.* Gretna, La.: Pelican Publishing, 1972.

Combes, John D. "Ethnography, Archaeology, and Burial Practices among Coastal South Carolina Blacks." *Conference on Historic Site Archaeology Papers,* Vol. 7, 52–61. Columbia, S.C.: Institute of Archaeology and Anthropology, 1972.

Courlander, Harold. *Negro Folk Music: U.S.A.* New York: Columbia University Press, 1963.

Crum, Mason. *Gullah: Negro Life in the Carolina Sea Islands.* Durham, N.C.: Duke University Press, 1940.

Curtin, Philip D. *The Atlantic Slave Trade: A Census.* Madison: University of Wisconsin Press, 1969.

Dabbs, Edith M. *Face of an Island: Leigh Richmond Miner's Photographs of Saint Helena Island.* New York: Grossman, 1971.

David, Paul A., Herbert G. Gutman, Richard Sutch, Peter Temin, and Gavin Wright. *Reckoning with Slavery: A Critical Study in the Quantitative History of American Negro Slavery.* New York: Oxford University Press, 1976.

Davis, George A., and O. Fred Donaldson. *Blacks in the United States: A Geographic Perspective.* Boston: Houghton Mifflin, 1975.

Davis, Gerald L. "Afro-American Coil Basketry in Charleston County, South Carolina: Affective Characteristics of an Artistic Craft in Social Context." In Don Yoder, ed., *American Folklife,* 151–84. Austin: University of Texas Press, 1976.

Deetz, James., *In Small Things Forgotten: The Archaeology of Early American Life.* Garden City, N.Y.: Anchor Press, 1977.

Dover, Cedric. *American Negro Art.* New York: New York Graphic Society, 1960.

Driskell, David C. *Two Centuries of Black American Art.* New York: Alfred A. Knopf, 1976.

Du Bois, W. E. B. *The Negro Artisan.* Atlanta: Atlanta University Press, 1902.

———. *The Souls of Black Folk,* 1903; rpt., New York: Fawcett, 1961.

Du Bois, W. E. B., and Augustus Granville Dill. *The Negro American Artisan.* Atlanta: Atlanta University Press, 1912.

Epstein, Dena J. "The Folk Banjo: A Documentary History." *Ethnomusicology* 20 (1976): 347–71.

Escott, Paul D. *Slavery Remembered: A Record of Twentieth-Century Slave Narratives.* Chapel Hill: University of North Carolina Press, 1979.

Evans, David. "Afro-American One-Stringed Instruments." *Western Folklore* 29 (1970): 229–45.

Ferrell, Stephen T., and T. M. Ferrell. *The Early Decorated Stoneware of the Edgefield District, South Carolina.* Greenville, S.C.: Greenville County Museum of Art, 1976.

Ferris, William R. " 'If You Ain't Got It in Your Head, You Can't Do It in Your Hand': James Thomas, Mississippi Delta Folk Sculptor." *Studies in the Literary Imagination* 3, no. 1 (1970): 89–107.

———. *Local Color: Folk Arts and Crafts.* New York: McGraw-Hill, 1983.

———, ed. *Afro-American Folk Art and Crafts.* Boston: G. K. Hall, 1983.

Fine, Elsa Honig. *The Afro-American Artist.* New York: Holt, Rinehart, and Winston, 1973.

Fox-Genovese, Elizabeth. *Within the Plantation Household: Black and White Women of the Old South.* Chapel Hill: University of North Carolina Press, 1988.

Freeman, Roland. *Something to Keep You Warm: The Roland Freeman Collection of Black American Quilts from the Mississippi Heartland.* Jackson: Mississippi Department of Archives and History, 1981.

Fry, Gladys-Marie. "Harriet Powers: Portrait of a Black Quilter." In Anna Wadsworth, ed., *Missing Pieces: Georgia Folk Art, 1770–1976,* 16–23. Atlanta: Georgia Council for the Arts and Humanities, 1976.

Fuller, Edmund L. *Visions in Stone: The Sculpture of William Edmondson.* Pittsburgh: University of Pittsburgh Press, 1973.

Genovese, Eugene D. *Roll, Jordan, Roll: The World the Slaves Made.* New York: Pantheon, 1972.

Georgia Writers' Project. *Drums and Shadows: Survival Studies among Georgia Coastal Negroes.* Athens: University of Georgia Press, 1940.

Glassie, Henry. *Pattern in the Material Folk Culture of the Eastern United States.* Philadelphia: University of Pennsylvania Press, 1968.

Gutman, Herbert G. *The Black Family in Slavery and Freedom, 1750#1925.* New York: Pantheon, 1976.

Haley, Alex. *Roots: The Saga of an American Family.* New York: Dell Publishing, 1974.

Herman, Bernard. "Slave Quarters in Virginia: The Persona behind Historic Artifacts." In David G. Orr and Daniel G. Crozier, eds., *The Scope of Historical Archaeology,* 253–83. Philadelphia: Temple University Laboratory of Anthropology, 1984.

Herskovits, Melville J. *The Myth of the Negro Past,* 1941. Rpt., Boston: Beacon Press, 1958.

_____. *The New World Negro: Selected Papers in Afroamerican Studies.* Ed. by Frances S. Herskovits. Bloomington: Indiana University Press, 1966.

Ingersoll, Ernest. "The Decoration of Negro Graves." *Journal of American Folklore* 5 (1892): 68–69.

Isaac, Rhys. *The Transformation of Virginia, 1740–1790.* Chapel Hill: University of North Carolina Press, 1982.

Johnson, Jr., LeRoy, ed. *Texana II: Cultural Heritage of the Plantation South.* Austin: Texas Historical Commission, 1982.

Jones-Jackson, Patricia. *When Roots Die: Endangered Traditions on the Sea Islands.* Athens: University of Georgia Press, 1987.

Joyner, Charles. *Down by the Riverside: A South Carolina Slave Community.* Urbana: University of Illinois Press, 1984.

Kan, Michael. "American Folk Sculpture: Some Considerations of Its Ethnic Heritage." In Herbert Hemphill, ed., *Folk Sculpture USA* 55–71. Brooklyn: Brooklyn Museum, 1976.

Kelso, William M. *Kingsmill Plantations, 1619–1800: The Archaeology of Country Life in Colonial Virginia.* New York: Academic Press, 1984.

Kilson, Martin L., and Robert I. Rotberg, eds. *The African Diaspora: Interpretive Essays.* Cambridge, Mass.: Harvard University Press, 1976.

Lamb, Venice. *West African Weaving.* London: Duckworth, 1975.

Latrobe, Benjamin H. B. *Impressions Respecting New Orleans.* Ed. by Samuel Wilson, Jr. New York: Columbia University Press, 1951.

Leon, Eli. *Who'd A Thought It: Improvisation in African-American Quiltmaking.* San Francisco: Craft and Folk Art Museum, 1987.

Levine, Lawrence W. *Black Culture and Black Consciousness: Afro-American Folk Thought from Slavery to Freedom.* New York: Oxford University Press, 1977.

Lewis, Ronald. *Coal, Iron, and Slaves: Industrial Slavery in Maryland and Virginia, 1715–1865.* Westport, Conn.: Greenwood Press, 1979.

Littlefield, Daniel C. *Rice and Slaves: Ethnicity and the Slave Trade in Colonial South Carolina.* Baton Rouge: Louisiana State University Press, 1981.

McDaniel, George W. *Hearth and Home: Preserving a People's Culture.* Philadelphia: Temple University Press, 1982.

Meier, August, and Elliott Rudwick. *From Plantation to Ghetto.* New York: Hill and Wang, 1970.

Metcalf, Jr., Eugene W. "Black Art, Folk Art, and Social Control." *Winterthur Portfolio* 18 (1984): 271–89.

Mintz, Sidney W., and Richard Price. *An Anthropological Approach to the Afro-American Past: A Caribbean Perspective.* Philadelphia: Institute for the Study of Human Issues, 1976.

Montgomery, Charles J. "Survivors from the Cargo of the Slave Yacht *Wanderer.*" *American Anthropologist* 10 (1892): 611–23.

Mullin, Gerald W. *Flight and Rebellion: Slave Resistance in Eighteenth-Century Virginia.* New York: Oxford University Press, 1972.

Newman, Thelma R. *Contemporary African Arts and Crafts: On-Site Working with Art Forms and Processes.* New York: Crown Publishers, 1974.

Newton, James E., and Ronald L. Lewis, eds. *The Other Slaves: Mechanics, Artisans, and Craftsmen.* Boston: G. K. Hall, 1978.

Odell, Scott. "Folk Instruments." *Arts in Virginia* 12, no. 1 (1971): 32–35.

Orser, Jr., Charles E. *The Material Basis of the Postbellum Tenant Plantation: Historical Archaeology in the South Carolina Piedmont.* Athens: University of Georgia Press, 1988.

Otto, John. *Cannon's Point Plantation, 1784–1860: Living Conditions and Status Patterns in the Old South.* New York: Academic Press, 1984.

Peek, Phil. "Afro-American Material Culture and the Afro-American Craftsman." *Southern Folklore Quarterly* 42 (1978): 109–34.

Phillips, Ulrich Bonnell. *American Negro Slavery: A Survey of the Supply, Employment, and Control of Negro Labor as Determined by the Plantation Regime,* 1918. Baton Rouge: Louisiana State University Press, 1966.

———. *Life and Labor in the Old South.* Boston: Little, Brown, and Company, 1929.

Porter, James. "Four Problems in the History of Negro Art." *Journal of Negro History* 27 (1942): 9–36.

Price, Sally, and Richard Price. *Afro-American Arts of the Suriname Rain Forest.* Berkeley: University of California Press, 1980.

Puckett, Newbell Niles. *The Magic and Folk Beliefs of the Southern Negro,* 1926. Rpt. New York: Dover, 1969.

Rawick, George P., ed. *The American Slave: A Composite Autobiography.* Westport, Conn.: Greenwood Press, 1972.

Rosengarten, Dale. *Row upon Row: Sea Grass Baskets of the South Carolina Lowcountry.* Columbia, S.C.: McKissick Museum, 1986.

Rosengarten, Theodore. *All God's Dangers: The Life of Nate Shaw.* New York: Random House, 1974.

Shapiro, Linn, ed. *Black People and Their Culture: Selected Writings from the African Diaspora.* Washington: Smithsonian Institution, 1976.

Sieber, Roy. *African Furniture and Household Objects.* Bloomington: Indiana University Press, 1980.

———. *African Textiles and Decorative Arts.* New York: Museum of Modern Art, 1972.

Singleton, Theresa A. "An Archaeological Framework for Slavery and Emancipation, 1740–1880." In Mark Leone and Parker B. Potter, Jr., eds., *The Recovery of Meaning: Historical Archaeology in the Eastern United Sates,* 345–70. Washington: Smithsonian Institution Press, 1988.

———, ed. *The Archaeology of Slavery and Plantation Life.* Orlando, Fla.: Academic Press, 1985.

Smith, Julia Floyd. *Slavery and Rice Culture in Low Country Georgia, 1750–1860.* Knoxville: University of Tennessee Press, 1985.

Sobel, Mechal. *The World They Made Together: Black and White Values in Eighteenth-Century Virginia.* Princeton, N.J.: Princeton University Press, 1988.

Southern, Eileen. *The Music of Black Americans.* New York: W. W. Norton, 1971.

Stamp, Kenneth M. *The Peculiar Institution: Slavery in the Ante-Bellum South.* New York: Vintage Books, 1956.

Starobin, Robert S. *Industrial Slavery in the Old South.* New York: Oxford University Press, 1970.

Stavisky, Leonard Price. "Negro Craftsmanship in Early America." *American Historical Review* 54 (1949): 315–25.

Teilhet, Jehanne. *Dimensions in Black.* La Jolla, Ca.: La Jolla Museum of Art, 1970.

Terry, George D., and Lynn Robertson Meyers, eds. *Carolina Folk: The Cradle of a Southern Tradition.* Columbia, S.C.: McKissick Museum, 1985.

Thompson, Robert Farris. "African Influence on the Art of the United States." In Armstead L. Robinson, Craig C. Foster, and Donald H. Ogilvie, eds., *Black Studies in the University,* 128–77. New Haven: Yale University Press, 1969.

_____. *Flash of the Spirit: African and Afro-American Art and Philosophy.* New York: Random House, 1983.

_____. "From Africa," *Yale Alumni Magazine* 34, no. 2 (1970): 16–21.

Thompson, Robert Farris, and Joseph Cornet. *The Four Moments of the Sun: Kongo Art in Two Worlds.* Washington, D.C.: National Gallery of Art, 1981.

Toledano, Roulhac, Sally Kittredge Evans, and Mary Louise Christovich. *New Orleans Architecture, Vol. 4: The Creole Faubourgs.* Gretna, La.: Pelican Publishing, 1974.

Twining, Mary. "Harvesting and Heritage: A Comparison of Afro-American and African Basketry." *Southern Folklore Quarterly* 42 (1978): 159–74.

Tyler-McGraw, Marie, and George D. Kimball. *In Bondage and Freedom: Antebellum Black Life in Richmond, Virginia.* Richmond: The Valentine Museum, 1988.

Upton, Dell. "White and Black Landscapes in Eighteenth-Century Virginia." *Places* 2, no. 2 (1985): 59–72.

Vlach, John Michael. "Affecting Architecture of the Yoruba." *African Arts* 10, no. 1 (1976): 48–53.

_____. *The Afro-American Tradition in Decorative Arts.* Cleveland: Cleveland Museum of Art, 1978.

_____. *Charleston Blacksmith: The Work of Philip Simmons.* Athens: University of Georgia Press, 1981.

_____. "Slave Potters," *Ceramics Monthly* 26 (Sept. 1978): 66–69.

Wade, Richard. *Slavery in the Cities: The South, 1820–1860.* New York: Oxford University Press, 1964.

Webb, Robert Lloyd. *"Ring the Banjar!": The Banjo in America from Folklore to Factory.* Cambridge, Mass.: MIT Museum, 1984.

Wood, Peter H. *Black Majority: Negroes in Colonial South Carolina from 1670 through the Stono Rebellion.* New York: W. W. Norton, 1974.

_____. "'It Was a Negro Taught Them': A New Look at Labor in Early South Carolina." *Journal of Asian and African Studies* 9 (1974): 159–79.

Woofter, Thomas J. *Black Yeomanry: Life on St. Helena Island.* New York: Henry Holt, 1930.

Yetman, Norman. *Life under the "Peculiar Institution": Selections from the Slave Narrative Collection.* New York: Holt, Rinehart, and Winston, 1970.

Index